THE UNITED NATIONS,
INTERNATIONAL LAW,
AND
THE RHODESIAN
INDEPENDENCE CRISIS

THE UNITED NATIONS, INTERNATIONAL LAW, AND THE RHODESIAN INDEPENDENCE CRISIS

JERICHO NKALA

CLARENDON PRESS · OXFORD
1985

Oxford University Press, Walton Street, Oxford OX2 6DP

London New York Toronto
Delhi Bombay Calcutta Madras Karachi
Kuala Lumpur Singapore Hong Kong Tokyo
Nairobi Dar es Salaam Cape Town
Melbourne Auckland

and associated companies in
Beirut Berlin Ibadan Mexico City Nicosia

Oxford is a trade mark of Oxford University Press

Published in the United States
by Oxford University Press, New York

© Jericho Nkala 1985

British Library Cataloguing in Publication Data
Nkala, Jericho C.
The United Nations, international law, and the
Rhodesian independence crisis.
1. Zimbabwe—Politics and government—1965–1979
I. Title
341.26   JQ2923.5.U5
ISBN 0-19-825394-X

Library of Congress Cataloging in Publication Data
Nkala, Jericho.
The United Nations, international law and the
Rhodesian independence crisis.
Bibliography: p.
Includes index.
1. Zimbabwe—International status. 2. United Nations—Zimbabwe.
3. Recognition (International law)
4. Zimbabwe—Politics and government 1965–1979.
I. Title.
JX4084.R5N54   1985   341.2 '9'096891   84–18943
ISBN 0-19-825394-X

Set by Hope Services, Abingdon
Printed in Great Britain
at the University Press, Oxford
by David Stanford
Printer to the University

Foreword

J. C. NKALA was born in Southern Rhodesia (as it was then called) in 1938. He worked as a school teacher for many years in Southern Rhodesia and Zambia before coming to England to study law. In 1975 he received his LLB degree from the University of Leeds. During the next three years he worked as a research student under my supervision at the University of Keele.

The present book is a rewritten and updated version of the thesis for which he received a richly deserved degree of Ph.D. from the University of Keele 'in 1978. Although Dr Nkala is himself a Zimbabwean, and therefore emotionally involved in the subject-matter of this book, readers will not fail to be impressed by the judicious, fair-minded, and balanced way in which he treats his subject-matter.

Southern Rhodesia suffered many tribulations during the 1960s and 1970s before it eventually became the independent Republic of Zimbabwe in 1980. The story of those tribulations forms a major chapter in the history of decolonization. But the story is not only of historical interest. It raises many problems about the concept of statehood in international law, about the legal status of the principle of self-determination, and about the interpretation and effectiveness of the United Nations Charter. These problems will continue to be of interest to international lawyers, and to students of politics and international relations, for many years to come. Dr Nkala's book makes a major contribution to our understanding of these problems.

DR MICHAEL AKEHURST
Reader in Law at the University of Keele

Preface

IN *The United Nations, International Law, and the Rhodesian Independence Crisis*, I have tried to consider and analyse a large number of legal questions which were raised by the Unilateral Declaration of Independence (UDI) by the Rhodesian Government on 11 November 1965 and the consequent imposition of the United Nations enforcement action under Chapter VII of the Charter of the United Nations. Among others the book discusses the following questions: Was UDI illegal in international law? What was the legal basis of the United Nations intervention in the Rhodesian independence crisis? Was the Rhodesian situation really a threat to the peace? Has the Security Council unlimited discretion to declare a situation a threat to the peace? What legal effect did abstentions by some permanent members of the Security Council have on the Security Council resolutions concerned? What effect did Security Council resolutions have on non-members of the United Nations? Were the Security Council's general powers embodied in Article 24 of the Charter relevant to the Rhodesian problem? Furthermore, the book discusses the problems of international recognition and those of the use of military force in relation to Rhodesia. Finally, a question is posed as to the future of the United Nations non-military enforcement action in the light of the United Nations involvement in the Rhodesian independence crisis.

I wish to thank Dr Michael B. Akehurst, Reader in Law at the University of Keele, who originally supervised my Ph.D. thesis from which this book has emerged and who kindly read the manuscript and offered invaluable comments and criticisms. I am, however, solely responsible for whatever faults and weakness appear in the book.

My gratitude also goes to the University of Sokoto, which financed my research to update my manuscript following the termination of the United Nations enforcement action against the Smith regime.

I also wish to thank Mr Samuel Ezugwu, Secretary to the Dean in the Faculty of Law, University of Sokoto, Nigeria, who typed the draft of the manuscript, and Miss Rosemary Moyo, typist, Department of Law, University of Zimbabwe, who typed the final version of the manuscript.

J. C. NKALA

Contents

Abbreviations

ABA	*American Bar Association Journal*
AC	Appeal Cases
AJIL	*American Journal of International Law*
Alberta LJ	*Alberta Law Journal*
ANC	African National Congress/Council
ATU	African Telecommunications Union
Australian YBIL	*Australian Year Book of International Law*
BYBIL	*British Year Book of International Law*
California LR	*California Law Review*
Cambridge LJ	*Cambridge Law Journal*
CJEPS	*Canadian Journal of Economic and Political Science*
Canadian YIL	*Canadian Yearbook of International Law*
Columbia LR	*Columbia Law Review*
Crim. L.R.	*Criminal Law Review*
Doc.	Document
FROLIZI	Front for the Liberation of Zimbabwe
GA	General Assembly
GATT	General Agreement on Tariffs and Trade
Har. L.R.	*Harvard Law Review*
ICJ	International Court of Justice
I.C.J. Rep.	*International Court of Justice Reports*
ICL	International Law Commission
ICLQ	*International and Comparative Law Quarterly*
Illinois LR	*Illinois Law Review*
ILM	*International Legal Materials*
IMF	International Monetary Fund
Iowa LR	*Iowa Law Review*
ITU	International Telecommunications Union
JPR	*Journal of Peace Research*
MLR	*Modern Law Review*
Mtg.	Meeting
NDP	National Democratic Party
NATO	North Atlantic Treaty Organization
NYUJIL	*New York University Journal of International Law*
OAU	Organization of African Unity
ONUC	United Nations Operations in the Congo
Para.	Paragraph
PF	Patriotic Front
PCIJ	Permanent Court of International Justice
Proceedings: ASIL	*Proceedings: American Society of International Law*

Res.	Resolution
SAL	*South African Law Journal*
Suppl.	Supplement
Sydney LR	*Sydney Law Review*
UANC	United African National Council
UDI	Unilateral Declaration of Independence
UN	United Nations
UNCIO	United Nations Conference on International Organizations
UNEF	United Nations Emergency Force
UNFCYP	United Nations Force in Cyprus
UNGAOR	*United Nations General Assembly Official Records*
UNSCOR	*United Nations Security Council Official Records*
UPU	Universal Postal Union
Va. J.I.L.	*Virginia Journal of International Law*
WLR	Weekly Law Reports
WMO	World Meteorological Organization
YBUN	*Year Book of the United Nations*
YBWA	*Year Book of World Affairs*
YLJ	*Yale Law Journal*
ZANU	Zimbabwe African National Union
ZAPU	Zimbabwe African People's Union

I

Introduction

On 11 November 1965 the Rhodesian Government led by
Mr Ian D. Smith unilaterally declared Rhodesia independent
in defiance of British authority in the territory. That unilateral declaration of independence was a culmination of a
disagreement between the British Government which attempted to modify and liberalize the franchise that was in force in
the territory to enable more Africans to qualify to vote, and
the Rhodesian Government which aimed at achieving independence for the territory on the basis of the Constitution
then in force since 1961. To a certain extent one could argue
that the unilateral declaration of independence (UDI) was a
natural consequence of the Rhodesian historical development
which had resulted from an unprecedented autonomy of a
colonial territory.

Rhodesia came into being when on 12 September 1890 the
first white settlers hoisted the Union Jack on a small hill called
Harare, which was subsequently renamed Salisbury. These
'pioneers', as they were called, had been sponsored by Cecil
John Rhodes who had obtained a Royal Charter from Queen
Victoria in 1889 to enable the British South Africa Company
which he had formed to administer the 'region of South Africa
lying immediately to the north of British Bechuanaland, and
the north and west of the South African Republic, and west
of the Portuguese Dominions'.[1] The new territory was named
Southern Rhodesia[2] in the Order in Council of 1898.[3] The
same Order in Council also stated that the British South Africa
Company 'shall have and may exercise the general administration of affairs within the limits of this Order, in accordance
with the Charter . . .'.

The British South Africa Company administered Rhodesia
until 1923 when the territory achieved a limited form of

---

[1] Art. 1 of the Charter of 1889.
[2] The territory will be referred to throughout as Rhodesia.
[3] Art. 4.

responsible Government. The Order in Council, however, created a Legislative Council composed of the Administrator, the Resident Commissioner, and fourteen other members, seven of whom were nominated by the Company, with seven others elected by registered voters among the settlers.[4] By 1907 the settlers had practical majority in the Legislative Council by the courtesy of the directors of the Company who decided not to use two of their votes in the Council unless a financial question was in issue.

The significance of the Company rule for the purpose of this discussion is that during that period the British Government had no physical control of the territory, a point which was emphasized many times to good advantage by the British Government after UDI. It should be observed, however, that Britain did have powers to control legislative activities of the Company. Palley points out that during the period 1899–1909 these Imperial controls were strictly enforced. However, the most momentous decisions in the historical and political development of Rhodesia took place as a result of the pressure generated not by the Company, but by the settlers. In 1911 the elected members (settlers) formed a clear majority in the Legislative Council, and this majority was further increased between 1913 and 1914. The ascendancy of the elected members in the Council represented the growing strength of the settler community and a corresponding decline of that of the Company.

The relationship between the Company and the settlers was an unhappy one. The settlers were concerned about two issues. Firstly, they suspected the Company of being interested in short-term profits it could make out of Rhodesia rather than long-term developmental needs of the territory. Secondly, they questioned the Company's claim over the ownership of the unalienated land. As their strength increased, the settlers began to push for responsible government in Rhodesia. Britain took a decision in 1915 to grant the settlers a responsible government if by a clear majority they passed a resolution in the Legislative Assembly requesting that status.[5] Although the

---

[4] Art. 17 of the Charter; C. Palley, *The Constitutional Law and History of Southern Rhodesia* (Oxford, 1966), 196.

[5] Supplementary Charter of 13 Mar. 1916, Art. 2, Cd. 7970.

Legislative Assembly did pass such a resolution and presented it to the British Government, the settlers had to vote in a referendum to decide whether Rhodesia should be granted responsible government or be annexed by South Africa. On 27 October 1922 the vote was overwhelmingly in favour of responsible government. As Bowman points out, this choice represented a defeat for South Africa, Britain, and the Company, all of whom wanted Rhodesia to join South Africa.[6] One could go further and argue that this was the first major demonstration by the settlers of their strong will for autonomy and possibly independence too.

By Letters Patent of 1 September 1923, Rhodesia achieved responsible government subject to certain limitations. From 1923 the history of Rhodesia is dominated by the way in which the white settlers of that territory consolidated their power and ensured that the African majority in the territory remained for all time subservient to the interests of the white minority. Although under the 1923 Rhodesian Constitution Britain retained some controls over legislation which affected Africans, these controls were seldom used, if at all. As a matter of fact, there developed in Rhodesia over the years a body of laws which not only protected white interests but generally inhibited Africans from developing their skills or demonstrating their capabilities, and throughout the entire period Britain never exercised her legislative veto.[7] Nevertheless, the foundation of discriminatory legislation was laid during the Company rule. For example, the 1898 Order in Council, which introduced more explicitly the British supervisory powers over the British South Africa Company legislation, also 'contained all the pass laws, labour control measures, urban controls and land legislation' that had been implemented by the Company in 1890.[8] Similarly, the 1898 Southern Rhodesia Native Regulations established the structure for African administration which lasted throughout the colonial period.[9] The settler Government was therefore only

---

[6] L. Bowman, *Politics in Rhodesia: White Power in an African State* (Harvard Univeristy Press, 1973) 7.

[7] R. Good, *UDI: The International Politics of the Rhodesian Rebellion* (Faber and Faber, 1973), 33.   [8] Bowman, 10–11.

[9] Ibid.

following an established pattern when it passed the Native Affairs Act, 1927 which consolidated all the previous rules and regulations governing African administration.[10] The Native Registration Act, 1936 and the Native (Urban Areas) Accommodation and Registration Act, 1946 were also passed to consolidate previous regulations and augment the methods of urban controls of Africans.

Land was divided between African reserves, which were generally poor in fertility and had lower rainfall, and white-controlled land with the best agricultural potential. This was formalized by the Land Apportionment Act, 1930 which remained the cornerstone of Rhodesian racial discrimination until the enactment of the Land Tenure Act, 1969 which served the same purpose.[11] Skilled jobs were reserved for whites under the Industrial Conciliation Act, 1934 which defined employee so as to include all white workers and exclude blacks. The Act was stengthened by numerous regulations which ensured an inferior status for the African worker as compared with his white counterpart.

Generally, in all aspects of Rhodesian life the African had the worst deal of all the four races (African, European, Asian, and Coloured) in the country. As Barber, writing in 1967, stated:

After more than seventy years of European rule the outstanding feature of Rhodesian society today is the division between the races . . . which largely dictates the range of jobs open to a man, the education his children will receive, what wages he is paid, where he can live, and how he behaves to his fellows and to men of another race . . .[12]

Half-hearted attempts were made by the white rulers of central Africa comprising Southern Rhodesia, Northern Rhodesia, and Nyasaland, to moderate this racism which dominated the politics of the region when the three territories were joined in a federation. This completed an ambition for some form of association between the two Rhodesias which had taken root in the middle of the 1920s when white settlers sought amalgamation of the two territories. The whites in Southern Rhodesia coveted Northern Rhodesia's copper which

[10] R. Good, 33.   [11] Bowman, 12.
[12] J. Barber, *Rhodesia: The Road to Rebellion* (Oxford, 1967), 1.

had been discovered in 1924, while Northern Rhodesian whites admired Southern Rhodesia's racial policies. Naturally these aspirations were not shared by Africans, especially in the North. When Federation came in 1953 there was opposition also from some white settlers in Southern Rhodesia who feared that this association could delay that territory's march to independence. In fact the coming of the Federation did complicate Rhodesian politics because the Federal Government took over most governmental responsibilities. Responsibility for African affairs was, however, left under the territorial governments.[13] This ensured the continuance of the racialist policies in Southern Rhodesia notwithstanding the introduction of non-racial policies at the Federal level.

By 1957, however, the Africans were ready to challenge the order of things throughout the Federation. In Southern Rhodesia in that year the Africans formed their first truly mass nationalist movement in the territory, the African National Congress (ANC). The party was 'dedicated to a political programme, economic and educational advancement, social service and personal standards. Its aim is the national unity of all inhabitants of the country in true partnership regardless of race, colour and creed . . .'.[14] This was a very moderate and modest objective, but it was enough to frighten the authorities, especially as the movement decided to champion the grievances of the rural communities over the Land Husbandry Act, 1951 which restricted the number of animals the peasants could keep. In February 1959 the ANC was banned and most of its leaders were politically restricted or were detained.

On 1 January 1960 the African nationalists formed the National Democractic Party (NDP). The new party had strong urban orientation, utilizing the grievances of the urban workers to mobilize the masses. The objectives of the movement were stated in broad terms in the party's organ, *The Democratic Voice*,[15] which declared *inter alia*:

What the normal and true African wants today is bread not crumbs, and he wants to eat it at the table not under the table. In other words, nothing short of sitting in Parliament and passing laws to govern the

[13] Bowman, 22.   [14] Quoted in Bowman, *Politics in Rhodesia*, 51.
[15] Vol. 1, No. 5 of 18 Sept. 1960.

people of the country both European and African . . . The Government is what matters.[16]

The first President of the Party, Mr Michael Mawema, stated the position in these words:

We believe in a democratic Southern Rhodesia and to that end we are committed to achieve it within as short a time as possible. We believe in one man one vote. We repudiate the evils of prejudice.[17]

As a result of the agitation organized under the auspices of the NDP, the workers became extremely militant and vocal. This led to frequent strikes, boycotts, and even riots. Between July and October 1960 in particular, fierce rioting broke out in the main urban centres leading to many arrests of activists and shootings in which no less than eighteen Africans were killed by police bullets.[18]

Although the Government always got on top of these disturbances, the fact that they occurred at all demonstrated the need for constitutional change. Sir Edgar Whitehead, the Rhodesian Prime Minister, wanted to get rid of Britain's reserved powers over Rhodesian legislation. For instance he once told a questioner in 1961 that with the speed that Africa was moving, it was exceedingly dangerous to leave those reserved powers for another two years. He added, 'I want to see them removed this year.'[19] He lamented that over the previous twenty years, and even before the Second World War, the British Government had 'largely left us alone. We were not in the world's eye. But recently the Ministers of the United Kingdom have been entertaining members of the opposition groups. This is a new development — and the reserved legislation and the power of veto have become increasingly dangerous.'[20] The NDP on its part wanted a constitutional conference to deal with the unfolding political crisis.

In April 1960 the NDP sent a delegation to London to press Lord Home, the Commonwealth Secretary, for such a conference. The Rhodesian Government had hitherto refused to attend any constitutional conference, insisting on the

---

[16] Quoted in Barber, 59.   [17] Ibid.
[18] *The African Daily News*, 1 Jan. 1960.
[19] *The Herald*, 7 Apr. 1961, 1.   [20] Ibid.

removal of Britain's reserved powers without any formal conference. However, when the British Government proposed the convening of such a conference, which was to be attended by all interested political groups in Rhodesia, Sir Edgar Whitehead accepted the proposal as a price for the removal of the offending reserved powers. This could be seen as a triumph for the NDP.

The Conference was held in January and February 1961 and it reached an agreement for a new Constitution for Rhodesia. The new Constitution replaced Britain's reserved powers with two checks on the power of the Rhodesian Legislative Assembly. The first of these was the establishment of a Constitutional Council to examine new laws to ascertain that they did not contain discriminatory provisions. The effect of this device was, however, limited in that the Council's decisions could be overruled by a two-thirds majority vote in the Legislative Assembly, and the whites could easily obtain this vote. Furthermore, the Council could only delay an unwanted Bill by a maximum of six months. Besides, the powers of the Council did not apply to money Bills and other Bills which the Prime Minister certified to be urgent, or if he certified that their delay would be against the public interest. The second check was a justiciable Declaration of Rights which was intended to secure for Rhodesians individual rights irrespective of race, creed, or political opinion. Unfortunately, this Declaration did not apply to existing laws, and since a large body of discriminatory legislation was already in the statute book the Declaration was also of limited use.

Probably the most significant aspect of the 1961 Constitution was the introduction of direct African representation in the Legislative Assembly. This was achieved by creating two voters' rolls, popularly called the A roll for predominantly white voters by virtue of its high property, income, and educational qualifications, and the B roll for Africans because of its low qualification requirements. The membership of the Legislative Assembly was increased from thirty to sixty-five, fifty of whom were elected under the A roll, while fifteen were elected under the B roll. The practical result of an election based on this franchise was the election of fifty white and fifteen black members of Parliament.

Could Africans ever achieve majority rule on the basis of this Constitution? If so, after how many years? Optimists argued that majority rule could come eventually, but on how soon, estimates varied from twelve years to fifty.[21] Soon after the conclusion of the agreement the NDP repudiated it as not being in the interest of the African people and called for a fresh constitutional conference. The British Government ignored this new demand. The Rhodesian Government held a referendum in which the white voters overwhelmingly approved the new Constitution. The NDP boycotted that referendum. There followed a wave of strikes, riots, violence, and general political lawlessness in the main urban centres throughout the country. The NDP was subsequently banned on 9 December 1961. While this represented a setback for Africans it did not destroy their determination to continue the fight for their right to self-determination and independence. Thus, almost immediately, they regrouped in a new party, the Zimbabwe African People's Union (ZAPU).

The objectives of the new party were opposition to the new 1961 Constitution, the abolition of exploitation, the elimination of imperialism and colonialism, and the establishment of a democratic state in Rhodesia. The party's immediate aim was to get Britain to suspend the implementation of the new Constitution and call a fresh conference. In pursuance of this policy it sought international support and pan-African solidarity through petitions to the United Nations[22] and visits to independent African nations. The United Nations became increasingly interested in the Rhodesian problem much to the annoyance of the United Kingdom. The majority members of the General Assembly, responding to petitions of ZAPU delegations, passed Resolution 1747 (XVI) on 12 June 1962 declaring that Rhodesia was a non-self-governing territory within the meaning of Chapter XI of the United Nations Charter. Following this, the General Assembly passed two other resolutions on Rhodesia that year.[23]

ZAPU was also banned in September 1962. The African nationalists decided that they were not going to form another political party again. However, the banning of the ZAPU had

---

[21] Barber, 83–4.   [22] (1962) *YBUN*, 428.   [23] Ibid. 469.

more serious repercussions for the African nationalist movement than appeared on the surface in that it led to a split
which has survived the coming of independence. One wing of
the banned organization formed the Zimbabwe African
National Union (ZANU) and the other formed the Peoples'
Caretaker Council (PCC). This split led to an outbreak of
violence between the two wings, which gave the settler
administration an excuse to ban both movements in August
1964.

It was not until 1971 that African politicians again reorgan-
ized themselves under the African National Council (ANC)
following the signing of proposals for a political settlement
of the Rhodesian problem by Mr Smith and Sir Alec Douglas
Home. Between 1962 and 1971 African political activity
inside Rhodesia seemed to have lost direction. In exile, political leaders had, however, decided that armed struggle was
the only answer to their problems and had already started
infiltrating trained guerrillas back into Rhodesia to wage
that struggle.

It has been argued that the NDP and its leadership mis-
calculated when they rejected the 1961 Constitution and
refused to take part in the December 1962 general election.
Robert Good, for example, maintains that the 1961 Constitution represented a significant concession from the point of
view of the Rhodesian white community which should have
been accepted by Africans so that they could have tipped the
balance in the elections to Sir Edgar Whitehead and against
Mr Field of the Rhodesia Front Party. He believes that had
this happened the African nationalists would have had substantial tactical advantage and a degree of leverage on Sir
Edgar Whitehead to gain further African political advantage.[24]

James Barber also argues in similar vein.[25] He contends, for
instance, that in the Legislative Assembly African nationalists
would have received wide national and international publicity.
In answer to this, it should be pointed out that the nationalists' ideas were already well known at these two levels.
Besides, pronouncements made in Parliament hardly receive
nationwide publicity let alone international coverage. Had

[24] Good, 40.   [25] Barber, 106-9.

African nationalists gone into Parliament they would have been collaborationists in the system they were trying to destroy. The result would have been the birth of a new movement to challenge both the Government and the NDP. This would have weakened rather than strengthened their cause. Internationally also they would have lost rather than gained support, especially from the point of view of independent Africa. In any case, for many years Rhodesian Africans had attempted to work and co-operate with the white leadership in multiracial organizations but this had not significantly advanced their cause. The membership of some African leaders in such organizations as the Capricorn Society, the Central African Party, and the United Federal Party quickly springs to mind.[26]

Barber also argues that by going into the Legislative Assembly, the African leaders could 'have revealed the strength of their support and have exerted pressure on the Government of the day'. The reply here is that no political adversary was unaware of the strength of the support those leaders enjoyed. Had the African leaders participated in Parliament, their numerical inferiority, and their parliamentary inexperience, would have revealed their weakness, not their strength. This would probably have eroded the support they had rather than enhanced it. Barber believes that the 1961 Constitution was a step forward in a phased-out programme of African advancement. Africans would move by stages into higher branches of the civil service and armed forces while acquiring parliamentary and ministerial experience, with Africans enjoying greater responsibility in local government.[27]

Barber should distinguish between ideal and practical conditions. Given Rhodesia's socio-political set-up, the belief that things would move as he describes them is misplaced. The bulk of the white Rhodesians never believed in equality with Africans at any time, let alone eventual control by Africans. Had the Africans accepted the 1961 Constitution they would have given the whites independence gratuitously. The chances are that there would have been no further meaningful African advancement before independence, and after

[26] See Bowman, 46.   [27] Barber, 108.

independence the process of African advancement would most probably have been reversed. It would be unreasonably optimistic to expect white rulers to maintain of their own volition a system which would ultimately deprive them of political control in favour of Africans. The result of the 1962 general election which put the white supremacist Rhodesian Front into office seems to support this argument. That result was a clear rejection of liberalism by the Rhodesia whites. To blame the African leaders for Sir Edgar Whitehead's defeat is to be uncharitable to the Africans.

The crucial question now is what alternative to participation did the Africans have in Rhodesia? With the benefit of hind-sight it would appear that all that had gone on in Rhodesian politics pointed towards a violent racial confrontation. This could have been avoided only if Britain had been prepared to play her full role as an imperial authority in Rhodesia. The white settlers enjoyed an unprecedented autonomy in the territory and Britain stood by and watched, as it were, while these settlers protected themselves with discriminatory legis-lation which they also used to destroy African opposition. They made Rhodesia a white man's country on the basis of 'what we have we hold'. Ndabaningi Sithole aptly observed, 'the average white man in Africa equates his existence with white domination . . . The overall European policy in Africa may be summed up in two words — white supremacy . . . That is, they have a mania to rule Africa.'[28] He maintains—correctly, it would appear—that multi-racialism as practised in Central Africa really meant that 'other races were allowed to participate in government affairs so long as they are satis-fied with a secondary place in the whole system, while the first place is reserved for whites only'.[29]

The victory of the Rhodesian Front and the policies that party pursued subsequently support this assessment. Soon after coming into office the party vigorously demanded independence from Britain, particularly as it became clear that Nyasaland and Northern Rhodesia were to become independent soon after the dissolution of the Central African Federation of Rhodesia and Nyasaland at the end of 1963.

---

[28] N. Sithole, *African Nationalism* (Oxford, 1959), 24.   [29] Ibid.

The British Government was, however, not willing to grant
Rhodesia independence owing to that country's 'franchise
which is incomparably more restricted than that of any other
British Territory to which independence has hitherto been
granted'.[30] The Rhodesian Prime Minister, Mr Field, contended that Britain had undertaken to grant Rhodesia independence on the basis of the 1961 Constitution in the event
of the dissolution of the Federation. This was, however,
categorically denied by Britain.[31] Mr Field was soon replaced
by Mr Ian D. Smith as Prime Minister. Mr Smith's views on
the independence question were more uncompromising. He
soon threatened UDI if Britain could not grant his country
independence on the terms demanded. The British Government warned Mr Smith of the inevitable hostile reactions of
the international community if he took that step. The British
Prime Minister explained that the whole issue would be raised
at the United Nations and Britain would be unable to defend
Rhodesia.

On his part Mr Smith argued that independence was an
absolute necessity in order to restore confidence in the future
of Rhodesia. He claimed that his demand for independence
on the basis of the 1961 Constitution enjoyed the support of
all Rhodesians including Africans. Britain was sceptical about
that claim and challenged Mr Smith to demonstrate that support. The British Prime Minister, however, rejected Mr Smith's
suggestion that African opinion be tested through the chiefs.
In spite of this, Mr Smith called an *Indaba* (meeting) of chiefs
for consultation. The verdict which Mr Smith got from the
chiefs supporting him was rejected by the British Government.

After many exchanges of messages between the two
Governments on the independence issue the Rhodesian
Government requested the British Government to give concrete proposals which must be satisfied before independence
could be granted to Rhodesia. Britain listed the following five
principles:

(i) The principle and intention of unimpeded progress to majority rule,
    already enshrined in the 1961 Constitution, would have to be
    maintained and guaranteed.

[30] Cmnd. 2807, 7.   [31] Ibid. 16.

(ii) There would also have to be guarantees against retrogressive amendment of the Constitution.
(iii) There would have to be immediate improvement in the political status of the African population.
(iv) There would have to be progress towards ending racial discrimination.
(v) The British Government would need to be satisfied that any basis proposed for independence was acceptable to the people of Rhodesia as a whole.[32]

The five principles formed the basis of negotiations which were held in London between 7 and 11 October 1965. At the end of these talks the two sides issued a communiqué showing that a very wide gap existed between them. It concluded with an ominous statement that despite 'intensive discussion, no means have been found of reconciling the opposing views'.[33] Further exchanges of messages took place between 12 and 21 October 1965, before the two sides met again in Salisbury, Rhodesia. At the end of the talks it was tentatively agreed that a Royal Commission be set up to study the 1961 Constitution and suggest amendments which could be made to bring that Constitution into line with the five principles laid down by the British Government. No agreement could be reached, however, on the terms of reference for that Commission. Officials of the two Governments continued to look into that problem while the British Prime Minister returned home. The Rhodesian Government must by then have made considerable progress towards UDI, and it was no longer keen to waste much more time. Thus on 8 November 1965, Mr Smith wrote to Mr Wilson, the British Prime Minister, that '. . . the only conclusion must be that we are back in the position we reached at the end of our talks in London, when we both agreed that the views of our respective Governments were irreconcilable'.[34] Mr Wilson made one last-ditch attempt on 10 November 1965 to forestall UDI by suggesting a further meeting with Mr Smith in Malta. However, his effort was too late, for on 11 November 1965 Mr Smith proclaimed UDI, and overnight Rhodesia became an international outcast for the next fourteen years.

In response to Mr Smith's action the British Government

[32] Ibid. 66.   [33] Ibid. 7.   [34] Ibid.

enacted the Southern Rhodesia Act, 1965, declaring Rhodesia to be still a British territory, and imposed 'economic sanctions'. Britain also took the problem to the United Nations where she found that many other states had raised the question.[35] It should be remembered that at the time of UDI, the Rhodesian question had already been introduced at the United Nations and both the Security Council and the General Assembly had passed resolutions on Rhodesia.[36] The only new factor in the involvement of the United Nations this time was that Britain had at last conceded international jurisdiction over the Rhodesian issue. This facilitated the invocation of the enforcement machinery of the United Nations and the imposition of the non-military enforcement measures described in Chapter V below.

UDI therefore brought about precisely the very thing Britain had done so much to prevent. Within Rhodesia itself, UDI destroyed any further chance of a peaceful resolution of the political problems between the two major races, although, admittedly, Sir Edgar Whitehead had in 1962 reduced that chance to a tiny insignificance by passing the Unlawful Organizations Act which prevented virtually all African politicians from forming political parties. UDI, it could be argued, demonstrated clearly the legitimacy of armed struggle which was soon to unfold in earnest.

The first reported incident of guerrilla war came in April 1966. The areas of initial guerrilla operation were scattered along the Zambezi river, particularly Sinoia (now Chinhoyi), Karoi, Banket, and Wankie (now Hwange). During the period 1966 to 1971 substantial guerrilla attacks came every few months in different parts of the country. In 1971 there was a low-water mark in guerrilla activity.[37] This could have been caused by the problems that the liberation movements were experiencing which, for example, led to the formation of the ill-fated Front for the Liberation of Zimbabwe (FROLIZI) in Lusaka that year.

Guerrilla activity reached its crucial stage in 1972. A statement which was made that year by Mr J. Andrew Flemming,

[35] *UNSCOR*, 1257th mtg.; S/5382; S/5409; S/6897; S/6902; and S/6903.
[36] G. A. Resolutions 1747 (XVI), 1755 (XVII), 1760 (XVII), 1883 (XVIII), and S. C. Res. 202 (1965).   [37] See Bowman, 147.

the so-called Secretary for Law and Order in Rhodesia, is revealing. He admitted the infiltration of a number of guerrillas into Rhodesia to form what he called 'a nucleus for internal subversion'.[38] Large quantities of arms and other offensive weapons were smuggled into the country from Zambia. The regime announced that it held Zambia responsible for acts of subversion which were going on in Rhodesia. On 5 December 1972 it reported killing a number of guerrillas and seizing quantities of arms and explosives of communist origin. It was disclosed that the guerrillas were now receiving support from the local people.[39] On 8 January 1973 explosions were reported in the north-west of the country near the Zambian border, and two South African policemen serving with Rhodesian forces were killed, and two others, as well as three Rhodesian policemen, were injured. Damage was caused to a bridge between Mount Darwin and Bindura. Mr Smith decided to act against Zambia. On 9 January 1973 he announced the closure of Rhodesia's border with Zambia to most traffic except Zambian copper exports. More security measures were taken in the country, including the extension of national service for White, Asian, and Coloured men from nine months to one year.

Meanwhile guerrilla activity continued to mount with reports of deaths of two white inspectors at the Mount Darwin area and the abduction by guerrillas of a third, the death of a number of guerrillas, closure of all shops and about forty schools in Chiweshe Tribal Trust Land, the injury of a farmer and the killing of his wife in the Centenary area, and the killing of a white farm manager in the north-west of Rhodesia. In the face of this insecurity the white farmers began to erect security fences and sandbag barricades to protect their homes. The Smith regime introduced a number of anti-insurgency measures to deal with the situation which was obviously getting out of hand. Among these were powers given to Provincial Commissioners to impose collective fines on the inhabitants of any place where it was found that any person living in that place or area had committed an offence, including the offence of aiding guerrillas.[40] In addition the regime

---

[38] *Keesing's Contemporary Archives*, 25666.
[39] Ibid. 25856.   [40] Ibid. 25856.

built what it termed 'Protected Villages' to prevent African communities giving food and other assistance to guerrillas. The African rural communities suffered untold hardships during this peak period of guerrilla activity. Many of them were killed in what was officially called cross-fire, others had to pay collective fines, and thousands of others led unbearable lives in the 'Protected Villages'.

When Mozambique became independent in 1975 the situation in Rhodesia became unmanageable for the regime. The strategy of the guerrillas seems to have been to subvert the regime's administrative capacity in the rural areas.[41] As a result of this many schools were closed, affecting thousands of children, some of whom decided to cross into the neighbouring independent countries of Botswana, Mozambique, and Zambia either as refugees or as potential guerrillas. Jokow quotes the United Nations High Commissioner for Refugees as stating in May 1979 that there were 19,800 Rhodesian refugees in Botswana.[42] Other figures quoted were 54,000 refugees in Zambia, 80,000 in Mozambique, and 28,000 in Botswana.

The other strategy of the guerrillas was to destroy the morale of the white community without which war against guerrillas would be virtually impossible. The success of this strategy could be seen from the unfavourable immigration figures during the years of severest guerrilla insurgency. For instance in 1973 there was a net loss in immigration for the first time. The main reasons were guerrilla incursions into Rhodesia, and the uncertainty of Rhodesia's future. This could be seen from the regime's efforts to attract immigrants and its subsequent willingness in 1974 to talk to the African leaders who had been languishing in prison, detention, or restriction.

There is no doubt that the combined effect of guerrilla war and the United Nations enforcement action forced the rebel leaders to seek a negotiated solution with Britain. The Smith regime hoped to reach a settlement which would lead to the end of the United Nations action so as to be able to buy arms to prosecute the war against guerrillas. Initially the regime

---

[41] T. J. Jokow, 'The Effect of the War on the Rural Population of Zimbabwe', *Journal of Southern African Affairs*, Apr. 1980, 133.　　　　　[42] Ibid.

had no interest in negotiating with the African nationalist leaders whom it despised. Consequently, the process of negotiation (to be discussed below) was at first held between the rebel leaders and the British Government. However, when the guerrillas proved themselves to be a formidable force it became impossible to get a peaceful settlement which excluded them. Economic enforcement measures created strains on the Rhodesian economy and reduced the country's ability to deal with the natural economic strains. Guerrilla war on its part was expensive both financially and also in taking skilled manpower from the industrial sector to fight the war. It also prevented foreign investment, reduced immigration, and increased emigration. As Harry Strack correctly observes, the 'combined effect of sanctions, Mozambique's hostility, and guerrilla war accomplished what the sanctions programme alone could not do—induce the Smith régime to consider yielding political power to the African nationalists'.[43]

Efforts to Reach a Negotiated Settlement with Mr Smith

When UDI was proclaimed the British Government's position was that it would not negotiate with the rebels. Nevertheless, on 27 April 1966 Mr Harold Wilson, the British Prime Minister, announced to the House of Commons that talks would soon commence between his Government and the leaders of the rebel administration. He, however, hastily said that 'these are not negotiations . . . Her Majesty's Government is not negotiating with the illegal régime . . .'.[44] He insisted that those were only talks to determine whether there was a basis for negotiations. The Rhodesian officials duly arrived in London and the talks got under way on 8 May 1966. The negotiations soon transferred to Salisbury, Rhodesia, in June that year. They were suspended in July without obvious breakthrough, and resumed on 22 August, and again agreement was not possible.

Mr Wilson again met Mr Smith on board HMS *Tiger* on the Mediterranean on 2 December 1966. Mr Smith rejected settlement proposals offered by Mr Wilson at that meeting. However, secret negotiations continued between the two sides

[43] H. Strack, *Sanctions: The Case of Rhodesia* (Syracuse UP, 1978), 238.
[44] Good, 150.

until October 1968 when Mr Wilson again met Mr Smith off Gibraltar on board HMS *Fearless* for further negotiations.

On 24 November 1971, the Conservative Party seemed to have clinched a deal when Lord Home, the Foreign and Commonwealth Secretary, signed an agreement with Mr Smith on a set of proposals for settlement of the Rhodesian problem. The proposals, which were a modification of the rebel Rhodesian Constitution of 1969, were extremely complex. There is no need to go into details of their provisions here. Briefly, they created a new African higher voters' roll with the same qualifications as those of the white voters' roll. The primary objective was ultimate parity of membership in the Legislature between Africans and Europeans. This would be achieved by periodic additions of two African members at a time corresponding to a 6 per cent increase in the number of African voters on the higher African voters' roll. The Constitution would provide that after parity was reached ten Common Roll seats would be created in the House of Assembly. It was anticipated that, as the number of African voters in the higher roll increased, the Africans would influence election to the Common Roll seats. In this way Africans would be able to achieve majority rule with a possible total of sixty out of one hundred and ten seats. How long this process would take no one could say with any degree of precision, perhaps fifty to one hundred years.

As Bowman points out, these proposals reflected British weariness with the entire Rhodesian issue and a desire to get out of it with the slightest excuse. The first four principles which had been laid down by successive British Governments as forming the basis on which independence could be granted were given extremely uncommon interpretation in order to make them fit this Anglo-Rhodesian agreement. Only the fifth principle saved the situation. In order to satisfy this, Britain appointed a commission to test the opinion of the Rhodesians as a whole on the proposals. The Commission, headed by Lord Pearce, reported that the majority of Europeans accepted them, and that the Asians and Coloureds were also broadly in favour, while an overwhelming majority of the Africans rejected them.[45] The overall conclusion of the Commission

[45] Cmnd. 4964, 44–51, 75–8.

was that 'in our opinion the people of Rhodesia as a whole do not regard the proposals as acceptable as a basis for independence'.[46] This finding was accepted by the British Government.

The verdict was hardly surprising. The operation of the agreement depended on too many things which were under the control of the whites. The higher roll qualifications, for example, depended on incomes, property, and education, all of which were under the control of the whites. In any case, nothing could have prevented the white government from simply abandoning the agreement after winning independence and the ending of the United Nations enforcement action. The African voice was very effectively articulated by the African National Council led by two clergymen, Bishop Muzorewa and the Reverend Banana, and their opposition was unmistakably loud and clear.

Following the rejection of the Smith–Home proposals Mr Smith vowed not to negotiate any further because Britain 'has lost the will to settle with us'.[47] He promised to govern the country firmly and not to tolerate 'any attempt to disturb the peace and harmony . . . the country has returned to since the departure of the Pearce Commission'. He held consultative talks with the African National Council hoping to persuade the leadership to accept the proposals just rejected by the people. The ANC was adamant in its refusal to compromise on that issue.[48]

It was not until late in 1974 that another breakthrough seemed possible. It all started with a speech by the South African Prime Minister, Mr Vorster, which he made to the Senate, in which he stated that Southern Africa was at the crossroads and had to choose between peace and escalating conflict. He pointed out that the latter course was too high a price for Southern Africa. He urged those who had influence on the Rhodesian situation in particular to use it to resolve the constitutional crisis there.[49] President Kaunda of Zambia responded warmly to this speech in a public address at the University of Zambia and called it a voice of reason. Following many diplomatic moves between Botswana, Tanzania, and

[46] Ibid. 112.   [47] *The New York Times*, 7 June 1972.
[48] *The Times* (London), 24 May 1972.   [49] *Keesing*, 26909.

Zambia on the one hand and South Africa on the other, Mr Smith released the detained or imprisoned leaders of ZAPU and ZANU on 12 December 1974.[50] On 8 December 1974 the leaders of four Rhodesian nationalist parties, ZANU, ZAPU, FROLIZI, and ANC came together under the umbrella of the ANC. Efforts to negotiate a peace settlement between Mr Smith and the ANC foundered on the latter's demand for majority rule and the Rhodesian Front's rejection of African majority rule.

Diplomatic moves continued, involving Zambia, Botswana, Tanzania (the Frontline States), Nigeria, South Africa, the United States, and Britain. After Dr Henry Kissinger, the Secretary of State of the United States, visited Zambia and South Africa and had talks with the heads of those countries he met Mr Smith in South Africa to discuss Rhodesia. The meeting resulted in an agreement, the terms of which included Mr Smith's acceptance of African majority rule in Rhodesia within two years, and the establishment of an interim government consisting of a council whose membership would be shared equally between the black and white population. This council would rule the country until majority rule was established. There would be a council of Ministers with a majority of Africans and a First Minister. For the period of the interim administration the key ministries of Defence, and of Law and Order would be held by whites. Britain was to enact enabling legislation for the process of majority rule. The United Nations action would be terminated and the guerrilla war would end. Rhodesia would be given economic aid to provide assurance to Rhodesians about the future of the country.[51]

Britain convened a constitutional Conference in Geneva towards the end of 1976 to effect this agreement. Five delegations represented the Rhodesian population. These were led by Mr Smith, Bishop Muzorewa, the Reverend Sithole, Mr Nkomo, and Mr Mugabe. The last two worked together under the umbrella of the Patriotic Front (PF). When the Conference opened under the chairmanship of Mr Ivor Richard, Britain's Permanent Representative to the United Nations, on 28 October 1976, there were varying views

[50] Ibid. 26912. These leaders were already temporarily free on parole.
[51] Ibid. 28197.

as to the purpose of the Conference. Mr Smith's delegation saw the meeting as intended to formalize the Smith–Kissinger agreement, while all the African delegations conceived the purpose of the Conference to be the working out of a Constitution that would transfer power to Rhodesia's African majority.

These differences, however, did not cause as many difficulties as the date of independence and the transitional arrangements between the end of the rebellion and attainment of majority rule. On the first question Mr Smith argued that independence could not be achieved in less than twenty months, or at the earliest, twenty-three months. Britain believed that fifteen months should be adequate to complete all the preparations for independence with sufficient time for the British Parliament to pass the necessary legislation. The Patriotic Front took the view that only twelve months were needed, and therefore named 1 December 1977 as the appropriate independence date for Rhodesia. The parties, however, decided to proceed to the next issue without settling this one.[52] This was not an encouraging start for the Conference.

The next contentious question, the transitional arrangements, proved to be the most difficult to deal with, and it could not be bypassed like the previous problem. The Conference chairman proposed a two tier legislature charged with the drafting of the new Constitution for the country with a council of ministers in which control of the army and the police would remain in white hands.[53] The Patriotic Front proposed a twenty-five member council of ministers with full legislative and executive powers with a clear majority chosen from ZANU and ZAPU.[54] Bishop Muzorewa's delegation insisted on some form of election to set up the interim administration. Mr Smith's group maintained that it was not prepared to discuss anything that was not in the 'Kissinger Plan'. Owing to continued disagreement on this and related issues, the chairman adjourned the meeting until 17 January 1977. As it turned out, the Conference never reconvened. Efforts to salvage what was left of the Kissinger Plan by shuttle diplomacy by British and American officials failed dismally.

[52] Ibid.   [53] Ibid. 28198.   [54] Ibid.

The Kissinger Plan was superseded by another joint initiative made by Britain and the United States. The two Governments put forward new proposals whose main features were the provision of a Constitution for Zimbabwe[55] which would provide for a democratically elected government with the widest possible franchise, an entrenched justiciable Bill of Rights, a six months transition period between the surrender of power by Mr Smith and the establishment of a neutral caretaker administration whose primary role would, in addition to administering the country, be the organization and conduct of elections, and, finally, the establishment of an internationally constituted and managed development fund for Zimbabwe.[56] The British Government was required to place before the Security Council the structure of the transitional administration for the period leading to independence. This would include the appointment by the British Government of a Resident Commissioner, and the appointment by the United Nations Secretary-General on the authority of the Security Council, of a Special Representative to work with the British Resident Commissioner. The Security Council would establish a United Nations Zimbabwe Force which would supervise the cease-fire, support the civil power, and liaise with the existing Rhodesian armed forces and with the liberation forces.[57] Britain appointed Lord Carver as Resident Commissioner designate for Rhodesia, and the Secretary-General appointed Major-General Prem Chand of India as United Nations Special Representative to the territory.[58]

This Anglo-American initiative failed to win the support of either the Smith regime or the liberation movements. The Patriotic Front opposed particularly the enormous power to be enjoyed by the Resident Commissioner, who was charged with the duty to conduct the general election, and was to take command, as Commander-in-Chief, of all armed forces in Rhodesia apart from the Zimbabwe Force which was to be

[55] Zimbabwe had been the name used by Africans for Rhodesia since the early days of African nationalism. Britain and America were also using the name in anticipation of independence.

[56] *Rhodesia: Proposals for a Settlement* (HMS Stationery Office, Sept. 1977).

[57] Ibid. 6–7.

[58] D. Martin and P. Johnson, *The Struggle for Zimbabwe* (London and Boston, 1981) 273–4.

commanded by a United Nations appointee. Mr Smith on his part had already embarked upon a dialogue with three African leaders who had decided to co-operate with him within the country with a view to concluding an 'internal settlement'. These were Chief Jeremiah Chirau, leader of a new party, the Zimbabwe United Peoples' Organization (ZUPO), Bishop Abel Muzorewa, of the United African National Council (UANC), and the Reverend Ndabaningi Sithole who led a faction of the ANC. Mr Smith claimed that these leaders collectively commanded about 85 per cent of Rhodesia's African population, with 15 per cent supporting Mr Nkomo.[59] This necessarily gave Mr Mugabe no support at all according to Mr Smith.

Mr Smith succeeded in his endeavours and signed an agreement with the three African leaders on 3 March 1978.[60] They had promised him to stop the guerrilla war as soon as an agreement was signed. Mr Smith hoped that this internal settlement would be acceptable to Britain and possibly the United States as well. The United Nations would ultimately accept it too, thereby leading to the end of the enforcement action. This was not to be, however. The Security Council rejected the internal settlement while Britain and the United States gave no commitment to support it although they did not condemn it either.[61] Mr Smith's disappointment was complete when the three African leaders failed to get the guerrillas to stop fighting. On the contrary, guerrilla war intensified and affected most of the country.

As Justin Nyoka reported at the time, by August 1978 guerrillas had affected about 90 per cent of Rhodesia's countryside, forcing the regime to extend martial law to more and more parts of the country. On 3 September the guerrillas shot down a Rhodesian Viscount aircraft near the Kariba Dam,[62] in December they used tracer bullets and rockets to set fire to a large fuel depot two miles from Salisbury's city centre,[63] and on 14 February 1979 another Rhodesian aircraft was shot at also on the Kariba route. It was very clear now that the guerrilla war was not only becoming increasingly sophisticated but also that the guerrillas

[59] *Keesing*, 29445.
[61] Ibid.; *Keesing*, 28946–8.
[63] Ibid. 29577.
[60] *The Times* (London), 4 Mar. 1978, 1.
[62] *Keesing*, 29445.

were themselves becoming more daring. South African Airways perceived the dangers on Rhodesian airspace and discontinued its regular flight between Johannesburg and Victoria Falls. It followed this by also stopping its Salisbury-to-London Boeing 747 flight. This was a big blow to the morale of the Smith regime, and it decided to respond with tremendous show of force.

Soon after the shooting down of the Viscount on 3 September, the regime launched a massive invasion into Mozambique and Zambia destroying guerrilla and refugee camps and causing untold deaths. The situation had obviously got out of hand and the whole of the Southern African region surrounding Rhodesia was now an operational area. General Peter Walls, the Head of Combined Operations, stated in 1978 that there was 'no single day in the year when we are not operating beyond our borders'.[64] Certainly this situation could not be allowed to continue.

The question was what was to be done and by whom. The Labour Government seemed to have run out of ideas on how to proceed on Rhodesia. A change of government in the United Kingdom could probably bring a new impetus to the problem. But what was the alternative to the course pursued by the Labour Government? If any change of government did take place it would certainly usher in a Conservative Government. This would be Mr Smith's choice, but it would not mollify the Patriotic Front. Mrs Thatcher, the leader of the Conservative Party, had in the past found it difficult to conceal her animosity towards the Patriotic Front, and her preference for Bishop Muzorewa who had now become the Rhodesian Prime Minister under the internal settlement.[65] It was therefore feared that if her party came to power in Britain, Mrs Thatcher would recognize the Muzorewa (Smith) regime, grant the country independence, stop British participation in the United Nations enforcement action, and request other United Nations members to do the same.

In May 1979 the Conservative Party did come to power. This year also happened to be the year of the Conference of the Commonwealth Heads of Government. The venue,

---

[64] Ibid.   [65] See Boyd Report.

ironically, was Lusaka, Zambia, one of the raiding grounds of the Rhodesian security forces. On arrival in Lusaka Mrs Thatcher was given a deafeningly hostile reception by the press and the public in anticipation of what she would say at the Conference. In line with this expectation Nigeria announced the nationalization of some British oil interests in Nigeria, to the utter disgust of the British delegation to the Conference. In her opening address to the conference Mrs Thatcher confounded virtually everybody. She stated that her Government was 'wholly committed to genuine majority rule in Rhodesia', and that its aim was 'to bring Rhodesia to legal independence on the basis which the Commonwealth and the international community as a whole will find acceptable and which offers the prospect of peace for the people of Rhodesia and her neighbours'.[66] She maintained that the existing Rhodesian Constitution was defective, and 'any solution of the Rhodesian problem must derive its authority from Britain as the responsible colonial power'.[67]

What led to this apparent sudden change of heart by Britain? The answer to this question will be known in time. But certain factors could have played no small part to this end. Mrs Thatcher must have received effective advice from her Foreign and Commonwealth Secretary, Lord Carrington, who was a veteran in dealing with the Rhodesian question, especially at the United Nations. He knew that a mere recognition of the Muzorewa (Smith) regime would not end the Rhodesian crisis. Since Britain was obviously weary of the problem, whatever action undertaken must have some form of finality. All Third World countries had made it clear in varying ways that a recognition of the Smith-manufactured independence for Rhodesia would be unacceptable. Consequently, if Britain flew against all this opposition she would not help Rhodesia but would probably sink with it, especially as far as British economic interests were concerned — the step taken by Nigeria on the eve of the conference served to emphasize this. Probably the most crucial factor was that a recognition of the Salisbury regime would not end the guerrilla war which, as everyone recognized, was far and away

[66] *Keesing*, 29903.   [67] Ibid.

the primary concern of the whole of the Southern African region. Given the position of Rhodesia's neighbours on this issue they would continue to support the war and the Eastern bloc countries would be more than happy to continue their military support to the liberation forces.

Mrs Thatcher, therefore, won many friends and much praise for the stand she declared in her address. This made progress on this item relatively smooth and rapid. At the end of the Conference the part of the Communiqué which dealt with the Rhodesian question carried these major points:

That the Heads of Government—

(i) confirm that they were wholly committed to genuine Black majority rule for the people of Zimbabwe (the new name for Rhodesia);

(ii) recognized, in this context, that the internal settlement Constitution is defective in certain respects;

(iii) fully accepted that it was the constitutional responsibility of the British Government to grant legal independence to Zimbabwe on the basis of majority rule;

(iv) recognized that the search for a lasting settlement must involve all the parties to the conflict;

(v) were deeply conscious of the urgent need to achieve such a settlement to bring peace to the people of Zimbabwe and their neighbours;

(vi) accepted that independence on the basis of majority rule requires the adoption of a democratic constitution including appropriate safeguards for minorities;

(vii) acknowledged that the government formed under such an independence constitution must be chosen through free and fair elections supervised under British Government authority, and with Commonwealth observers;

(viii) welcomed the British Government's indication that an appropriate procedure for advancing towards those objectives would be for them to call a constitutional conference to which all the parties would be invited, and

(a) consequently accepted that it must be a major objective to bring about a cessation of hostilities and end to sanctions as part of the process of implementation of a lasting settlement.[68]

After the Commonwealth Conference, the British Government issued invitations to Bishop Muzorewa and the Patriotic Front leaders to participate in a constitutional Conference at Lancaster House, London, to discuss and reach agreement on the terms of an independence constitution for Rhodesia and

[68] Ibid.

on the elections to be held under British authority to enable Rhodesia to proceed to legal independence.[69] The conference opened on 10 September 1979 under the chairmanship of Lord Carrington who outlined the aim of the gathering as well as the procedure to be followed. He reminded the delegations of an outline of proposals his government had earlier circulated to them requesting a response from them.[70]

Mr Nkomo, replying on behalf of the Patriotic Front, welcomed Britain's readiness to decolonize Rhodesia and warned that over 90 per cent of Rhodesia was already affected by the liberation war and the Patriotic Front had not gone to London to abandon the victories which had been scored by the Zimbabwean people on the battlefield. The Patriotic Front was, however, aware of the rebel regime's destructive ability, hence its leaders had a responsibility to negotiate for genuine independence to put 'an end to the prevailing anarchy and chaos'.[71] The aim of the Conference was thus 'to ensure through an indivisible comprehensive agreement the irreversible transfer of power to the people of Zimbabwe'. Referring to the outlines circulated by the British Government, he pointed out that his delegation needed answers to certain questions raised by the proposals.[72]

In his reply on behalf of his delegation Bishop Muzorewa informed the Chairman of the Conference that his delegation was seeking recognition of his democractically elected government of national unity which fulfilled all the requirements insisted upon by successive British administrations[73] concerning the six principles which had to be satisfied before Britain could consider granting Rhodesia independence. Furthermore, the strength of both the British Government and international action had been directed against a white minority in Rhodesia but now that regime was no longer in existence. He claimed that all racially discriminatory laws in Rhodesia had been repealed, and there was now 'a new Constitution drafted by both black and white members of our four parties to the 3rd March Agreement—it was drawn up by the people of our country to meet the needs of our country . . .'.[74]

All three parties having fired their opening shots the

[69] Cmnd. 7802.   [70] Ibid.   [71] Ibid. 10.   [72] Ibid.
[73] Ibid. 12-13.   [74] Ibid. 14.

Conference proper got under way. It needed a total of forty-
seven plenary sessions between 10 September and 15 December
1979 to agree on an independence Constitution for Rhodesia
thereby bringing to an end the sad Rhodesian rebellion which
cost tens of thousands of lives. The agreement covered such
issues as the legal status of the future republic, the supremacy
of its Constitution, citizenship, Declaration of Rights, the
Executive, Parliament, Judicature, the Defence Forces, and
Finance. It also contained Pre-independence Arrangements,
and the Cease-fire Agreement. Ironically, the Agreement did
not have the signature of Mr Smith, the man who started it
all. The internal settlement of 3 March 1978 saved Mr Smith
from ignominious surrender and enabled him to remain un-
repentant of the blunder he had caused in 1965. The signa-
tories were consequently all Africans except on the British
side of the conference table. Bishop Muzorewa and Dr
Mundawarara signed on behalf of the Rhodesian delegation
while Mr Mugabe and Mr Nkomo signed for the Patriotic
Front and the Liberation Forces.

This book deals in detail with some of the major international legal issues that were raised by the Rhodesian independence crisis, especially after the proclamation of UDI in
1965 and the subsequent imposition of the United Nations
enforcement action. This introductory chapter provides a
brief setting for the subsequent chapters and should not be
regarded as an analytical political comment, which is beyond
the scope of this book. Such an exercise has been effectively
carried out by Robert Good, and David Martin and Phyllis
Johnson who write about the part played by ZANU (PF) in
the liberation war. This book is also not about 'international
sanctions' a subject which is exhaustively covered by Harry
Strack. L. Kapungu also writes on this subject in *The United
Nations and Economic Sanctions in Rhodesia* (Lexington,
1973).

Chapter II examines the principle of domestic jurisdiction
with particular reference to the Rhodesian independence
problem in the light of British opposition to international
jurisdiction in the early stages of United Nations involvement

in the problem of Rhodesian independence. When UDI was proclaimed, however, Britain voluntarily took the problem to the United Nations where UDI was described as illegal by that organization and its organs. Chapter III considers whether UDI was illegal in international law. The answer to this question is to a large extent connected with the problems of international recognition, a subject dealt with in Chapter IV. Chapter V deals with the enforcement action of the United Nations which was imposed in consequence of UDI. Some measures introduced by the United Nations raised special problems, such as measures introduced by Resolution 221 (1966) which related to the freedom of the seas. These are dealt with in Chapter VI.

Chapter VII discusses the effect of Security Council resolutions on non-members of the United Nations. Although the fact that nearly all nations are members of the United Nations reduces the significance of this question, it could be argued that it still remains a problem of considerable importance. In Chapter V an argument is advanced that the binding resolutions of the Security Council were based on Chapter VII of the Charter of the United Nations. Chapter VIII examines the powers of the Security Council under Articles 24 and 25 of the Charter to consider whether these powers could have provided an alternative basis for the enforcement action. The Rhodesian rebel regime was subjected to non-military enforcement measures only (apart from the use of force by liberation forces), however, Chapter IX discusses the use of force by the United Nations. A limited use of force was provided for in Resolution 221 (1966) where Britain was authorized by the Security Council to use force against foreign ships off the Mozambican coast which was at the time under Portuguese control. Portugal challenged the validity of that resolution on the ground that some permanent members of the Security Council abstained when the resolution was adopted. Chapter X examines aspects of the voting procedure in the Security Council. Some commentators have argued that the Rhodesian situation was never at any time a threat to international peace and security, and that therefore the Security Council was wrong in determining that the situation constituted such a threat to the peace. This question is discussed in Chapter XI which deals with the discretionary powers of the Security Council.

Chapter XII is concerned with the objectives and purposes of the enforcement action against the Smith regime. Closely linked to this question is that of the correct procedure for terminating a United Nations enforcement action. This problem is of particular importance in the light of the controversy that followed the unilateral termination of individual participation by Britain and other Western countries. Chapter XIII considers this problem. Finally, Chapter XIV assesses the role of United Nations enforcement action which does not involve use of force. It should be stressed here that this chapter deals with the non-military enforcement measures as opposed to 'economic sanctions' in general. The chapter argues that if non-military enforcement measures of the United Nations are correctly selected and applied they can work despite the difficulties which were experienced in respect of the enforcement action against the Smith regime.

II

Rhodesia and the Principle
of Domestic Jurisdiction

A. The United Nations and Rhodesia: 1962-1965

WHEN in 1952 the Secretary-General of the United Nations
prepared a list of non-self-governing territories Rhodesia was
not included.[1] Although Britain, Rhodesia's administrative
authority, was not immediately challenged by the other
members of the United Nations on this omission, it is doubtful whether those members believed that Rhodesia was a
self-governing territory. It is possible, however, that they did
recognize that Rhodesia had a considerable degree of international existence distinct from that of its mother country,
Britain. This was in keeping with the responsible government
status that Rhodesia had been granted in 1923.[2] Although
international law is primarily concerned with sovereign states,
dependent territories may also enjoy a certain measure of
international personality.[3] It was therefore not surprising that
Rhodesia enjoyed some limited international personality.[4]

The main reasons why Britain was not challenged for not
including Rhodesia on her list of non-self-governing territories
include the fact that the problems related to decolonization
of Africa gained ascendency at the United Nations only in
the 1960s, and the fact that the Africans in Rhodesia were
not seriously organized in mass political parties until the late
1950s. It took the promulgation of the Rhodesian Constitution of 1961 to kindle international interest in the Rhodesian
problem of self-determination. As already noted in Chapter I
African political leaders made a number of petitions to the
General Assembly. As a result of these petitions, the General

---

[1] (1952) *YBUN*, 559.   [2] See Letters Patent of 1 Sept. 1923.
[3] Brierly, *The Law of Nations* (1963), 129.
[4] R. B. Stewart, *Treaty Relations of the British Commonwealth of Nations*
(NY, 1939), 21.

Assembly passed Resolution 1747 (XVI) declaring, *inter alia*, that the Territory of Southern Rhodesia was a Non-Self-Governing Territory within the meaning of Chapter XI of the Charter of the United Nations.[5] Following the adoption of this resolution debate continued in the General Assembly in which many speakers argued that this resolution had effectively established the juridical status of Rhodesia and that Britain therefore had power to intervene to impose a constitutional settlement in the same way as she had previously intervened in Malta and other places.[6]

Britain rejected all attempts to involve her in Rhodesian affairs, arguing that neither she nor the United Nations had power to intervene in Rhodesia. In spite of that, however, the General Assembly passed more resolutions confirming its declaration in Resolution 1747 (XVI) and requesting Britain to take urgent measures to resolve the Rhodesian problem.[7] The important point to note here is that notwithstanding British opposition to United Nations involvement in Rhodesia, the majority of the members of that organization took the view that the principle of domestic jurisdiction did not preclude the United Nations from discussing and passing resolutions on Rhodesia. The principle of domestic jurisdiction is very controversial and has attracted considerable comment from international jurists and other scholars.[8] It has been invoked widely by states in their international disputes to try to escape international condemnation in matters they wish to keep out of the international forum.

Whatever Britain's explanations were for attempting to exclude United Nations jurisdiction from the Rhodesian independence problems, it could be argued that the claim of domestic jursidiction was a doubtful protection that Britain could seek. Probably this is what prevented Britain from making explicit reliance on this principle in attempting to exclude United Nations involvement. Britain merely argued that neither she nor the United Nations had power to intervene

---

[5] See para 1.   [6] (1962) *YBUN*, 428.
[7] Resolutions 1755 (XVII) and 1760 (XVII), see ibid., 469. See also Resolutions 1883 (XVII) and 1889 (XVII).
[8] See M. S. Rajan *United Nations and Domestic Jurisdiction* (London, 1958); H. Kelsen, *The Law of the United Nations* (Stevens, 1950).

in Rhodesia. It would appear that the non-existence of power to intervene in Rhodesia was none the less based on that principle as laid down in Article 2 (7) of the Charter of the United Nations.

The involvement of the United Nations in the Rhodesian problem may be supported on two grounds: the determination of the General Assembly by Resolution 1747 (XVI) that Rhodesia was a non-self-governing territory, and the right of self-determination of the Rhodesian people. The first of these grounds raises the question whether the United Nations has the power to determine issues of this kind independently of what the administering authority of a territory believes to be true. This question is part of the larger one as to who has the power ultimately to determine international jurisdiction in disputes. It is submitted that while an individual state may make the initial determination that a matter is essentially within its own jurisdiction, the ultimate determination of international jurisdiction on the matter rests in international relations.[9] The United Kingdom could therefore not validly claim that Rhodesia's people had attained self-government when 96 per cent of the population were denied any meaningful political voice in their country.

Besides, the question of deciding whether or not a given territory has acquired a self-governing status has been a subject of long study by the General Assembly dating from the late 1940s,[10] and the General Assembly passed a number of relevant resolutions on the subject.[11] For example, in 1953, the General Assembly passed Resolution 742 (VIII) approving a list of factors which may serve as a guide, both to the General Assembly and for the members of the United Nations, in deciding whether a territory has or has not attained a full measure of self-government. One of these factors was the opinion of the inhabitants of the territory concerned. The General Assembly exercised its competence to decide whether a given territory had ceased to be a non-self-governing territory within the meaning of Chapter XI of the

---

[9] Q. Wright, 'Is Discussion Intervention?', (1956) 50, *AJIL*, 105. *Nationality Decrees in Tunis and Morocco* (1922-6), 1 World Court, 156.

[10] (1946-7) *YBUN*, 209-10, and (1950) *YBUN*, 674.

[11] See e.g. Resolutions 222 (III), 334 (IV), 567 (VI), 648 (VII), and 742 (VIII).

Charter on a number of occasions before it considered the Rhodesian problem.[12]

These resolutions have been criticized by some jurists on the ground that the General Assembly lacks authoritative power to interpret the Charter.[13] The most eloquent statement in defence of these resolutions comes from Castañeda who argues:

In postulating the binding character of resolutions that contain determinations, it is obviously not meant that these resolutions in themselves legally oblige an addressee to execute a given act, as is the case with Security Council decisions that contain an order. The function *per se* of these determinations is not to elicit certain behaviour; they do not express a duty, but rather establish in a definitive manner, the hypothesis or condition from which flows a legal consequence, which makes possible the application of a rule. They provide only one element of the rule: the hypothesis. The other, the consequence, may be present in the Charter or in another resolution, or may even be implied in the Organization's decision — making machinery as a whole . . .

The determination as such is a pronouncement of the Organization, which is legally definitive, and against which there is no legal recourse. In as much as it represents the official United Nations position on the existence of a fact or legal situation, it is the only one that the Organization takes into account as the basis for eventual action; thus the individual dissident attitude lacks juridical relevance. In this sense these pronouncements have legal validity, and the resolutions that contain them can properly be characterized as binding in what they determine.[14]

The important point to emphasize in regard to the General Assembly's power to determine whether or not a given territory has attained a sufficient measure of self-government is that such a determination provides international jurisdiction over that territory in so far as matters relating to self-government are concerned. In this sense, although dissenting states are not bound to accept the finding of the General Assembly on the matter, such states cannot, by invoking Article 2 (7) of the Charter, prevent the United Nations making recommendations on the question concerned. Whether or not the finding in any given case is factually justified does not detract from the legal

---

[12] See Res. 748 (VII) relating to Puerto Rico; Res. 849 (IX) in respect of Greenland; Res. 945 (X) on Netherlands Antilles and Surinam.

[13] D. J. Devine, (1973) *Acta Juridica*, 50.

[14] J. Castañeda, *The Legal Effects of United Nations Resolutions* (NY, 1969), 121.

competence of the organ to make the decision. This can be challenged in the same way as the Security Council's exercise of its discretion to determine under Article 39 of the Charter that any given situation constitutes a threat to or a breach of the peace or an act of aggression can be challenged by those states which believe that the discretion has been improperly exercised. Such a challenge would not amount to a questioning of the General Assembly's legal competence or the competence of the Security Council to make the determination concerned.

Apart from what has been said above, the Rhodesian problem was one of the right of self-determination of peoples. Matters relating to the principle of self-determination of peoples have been considered as falling outside the operation of Article 2 (7) of the Charter.[15] Although there is no general agreement among either states or writers on international law about the legal status of this principle, it is safe to say that an ever increasing number of these accept that this principle now constitutes a right given to colonial peoples with a correlative duty on the part of colonial powers to grant it to their dependent peoples.[16] It is submitted, therefore, that whenever matters relating to the right of self-determination of peoples are raised, the colonial power is prima facie not entitled to shelter behind the provisions of Article 2 (7) of the United Nations Charter. On this argument, therefore, the British opposition to United Nations intervention in the Rhodesian independence dispute prior to UDI should fail and it did fail as the other members of the General Assembly refused to acquiesce in the wishes of the United Kingdom.

Thus in 1962 the General Assembly rejected a motion introduced by the United Kingdom to conclude a debate on Rhodesia without a vote, and adopted Resolution 1745 recalling Resolutions 1514 (XV) of December 1960 on the Declaration on the granting of independence to colonial countries and peoples, 742 (VIII) of 27 November 1953 which approved a list of factors to be used as a guide in determining whether a territory is or is not a self-governing

---

[15] Art. 1 (2) and 55 of the United Nations Charter.

[16] (1967) *British Practice in International Law*, 32–4; J. Stone, 'Hopes and Loopholes in the 1974 Definition of Aggression', (1977) 71, *AJIL*, 233–7.

territory within Chapter XI of the Charter, and requesting the Special Committee to consider whether the territory of Southern Rhodesia had attained a full measure of self-government.[17] Following the recommendations of the Special Committee, the General Assembly passed Resolution 1747 (XVI) by which it recalled all relevant previous resolutions and

1. [Approved] the conclusions of the Special Committee on the situation with regard to the Implementation of the Declaration of the Granting of Independence . . . on Southern Rhodesia, and [affirmed] that the Territory of Southern Rhodesia [was] a Non-Self-Governing Territory within the meaning of Chapter XI of the Charter of the United Nations . . .[18]

Thereafter the General Assembly passed Resolutions 1755 (XVII) affirming the determination referred to in the above paragraph, 1760 (XVII) affirming Resolution 1747 (XVI) and requesting the United Kingdom to take urgent measures to resolve the Rhodesian problem.[19]

The Rhodesian problem was then referred to the Security Council, but the British Government vetoed the draft resolution which was introduced. The contents of that draft resolution were subsequently embodied in Resolution 1883 (XVII) of the General Assembly.[20] Until UDI was proclaimed the General Assembly was largely concerned with the question of the right of self-determination of the Rhodesian people and this was an effective basis to found international jurisdiction on the Rhodesian independence crisis. It could be argued, however, that the jurisdiction enjoyed by the United Nations at that stage was not sufficient to support an imposition of an enforcement action by the Security Council. The imposition of an enforcement action became possible only when UDI was proclaimed.

B. *Unilateral Declaration of Independence*

The Unilateral Declaration of Independence of Rhodesia by Mr Ian Smith on 11 November 1965 brought a completely

---

[17] Adopted on 23 Feb. 1962.
[18] Passed by 73 votes in favour, one against, and 27 abstentions.
[19] (1962) *YBUN*, 469.   [20] (1963) ibid. 473.

new complexion to the independence crisis of that country. The most significant change was in the attitude that the British Government now took on the question of international jurisdiction in that dispute. Britain now abandoned the already worn-out argument that the Rhodesian situation was a matter of domestic jurisdiction in which United Nations intervention was precluded. Britain quickly saw a role for the international community and took the Rhodesian problem to the United Nations.[21]

Addressing the Security Council Mr Stewart, the British Foreign Secretary, explained the reasons for his Government's decision to refer the question to the United Nations in these terms:

Southern Rhodesia is a British possession and the responsibility lies on Britain. Nevertheless, we have thought it right, for two main reasons, to bring this matter now before this council. The first reason is this. An attempt to establish in Africa an illegal régime based on minority rule is a matter of world concern . . . The second reason . . . is a very practical reason. I am about to describe the measures which the United Kingdom Government has taken to deal with this illegal declaration and to restore the rule of law in Southern Rhodesia. If these measures are to be fully effective we must ask for the goodwill, the co-operation and the active support of all those who accept the principles set out in resolution 2012 (XX)[22] adopted by the General Assembly . . . We believe that we have the right to ask for this support.[23]

A full reason why Britain referred the Rhodesian case to the United Nations was given by the British Prime Minister of the day, Mr Harold Wilson (as he then was) in the House of Commons in answer to a question when he stated, *inter alia*:

We assert that this is our responsibility. For that reason, it was we who took it to the United Nations to prevent other people doing so. The Honourable member must know perfectly well that, whatever we had done in the Security Council, the matter would have been transferred to the Assembly and there would have been no doubt whatever of the

[21] The British Foreign Secretary went to address the Security Council on the matter. *UNSCOR* 1257th mtg. para. 10 *et seq.*

[22] Reference to this Resolution by the United Kingdom is curious because it was adopted at the time that country still denied that the United Nations was entitled to intervene in the Rhodesian problem.

[23] *UNSCOR* 1257th mtg. para 10 *et seq.*

overwhelming desire of members of the Assembly . . . for the use of military force . . .[24]

In his statement to the Security Council Mr Stewart emphasized that UDI was responsible for the changed British attitude and that from then onwards Rhodesia had lost its self-governing status which it had hitherto enjoyed. He stated that now 'that this illegal declaration has been made, the only lawful Government of Southern Rhodesia is the Government of the United Kingdom'.[25]

In fact, immediately following the proclamation of UDI, the Governor of Rhodesia, Sir Humphrey Gibbs, acting on instructions of Her Majesty the Queen, dismissed Mr Smith and his colleagues from office.[26] On 16 November the British Parliament passed the Southern Rhodesia Act, 1965 declaring that Rhodesia continued to be part of Her Majesty's dominions, and conferring executive and legislative authority to be exercised on behalf of the British Government by a Secretary of State. The Act further empowered the British Government to make orders in Council with reference to Rhodesia as appeared necessary and expedient. In pursuance of this power, the British Government made the Southern Rhodesia (Constitution) Order, 1965.[27]

In the light of UDI and the measures Britain had to take in consequence of it, the British Government conceded international jurisdiction on the Rhodesian independence question. This was welcomed by nearly all the other members of the United Nations. In the Security Council only France spoke against that international jurisdiction. Her Representative stated:

The very fact that a rebellion is involved seems to my Government's view, to set a limit to United Nations action in this affair. The issue is not between states and the conflict between the United Kingdom and Southern Rhodesia is therefore an [internal] one . . . For that reason, the French Government considers that the Security Council should take no decision on the matter . . . .[28]

France refused, therefore, to vote for any resolution on

---

[24] *Weekly Hansard*, No. 673, 23 Nov. 1975.
[25] *UNSCOR*, 1257th mtg.   [26] *The Times* (London), 12 Nov. 1965.
[27] SI 1965 No. 1952.   [28] *UNSCOR*, 1257th mtg. paras. 10 and 11.

Rhodesia in the United Nations and sought refuge in abstentions.[29]

The position adopted by France on this issue was shared by a considerable body of opinion in the United Kingdom itself as reflected in many letters to the press. For example, Sir Lionel Heald and Sir Derek Walker-Smith, in a letter to *The Times* (London), argued that Rhodesia:

is not a sovereign state in dispute; and because she is not a sovereign state in dispute the matter is not within the jurisdiction of the United Nations, but is essentially within the domestic jurisdiction of the United Kingdom in accordance with Article 2 (7) of the Charter. It appears therefore that on a proper interpretation of the Charter the Government should never have referred the matter to the United Nations.[30]

Similarly, Mr Ronald M. Bell complained:

. . . Article 2 (7) of the Charter makes it clear that the United Nations has no authority to intervene in matters essentially within the domestic jurisdiction of any State. Since the passing of the Southern Rhodesia Act 1965, and the making under it of the Southern Rhodesia Constitution Order in Council, Rhodesia is, legally, ruled directly from Whitehall, and is within our jurisdiction.[31]

The argument presented by France and the two letters to *The Times* quoted above is without any legal basis. The fact that Rhodesia was legally a British responsibility is beyond doubt and has never been challenged by any state. This fact is borne out by the United Nations resolutions on Rhodesia which were always directed at the United Kingdom as the administering authority. The important point which was overlooked by the critics of the involvement of the United Nations in the Rhodesian problem is that while Article 2 (7) says that states are not obliged to submit to the United Nations matters which are essentially within their domestic jurisdiction, that Article does not prevent states which want to do so from submitting such matters. Consequently, Britain was perfectly

---

[29] France deviated from this practice in 1968 when the Security Council adopted Res. 253 (1968) on 29 May. Her Representative explained that he supported that resolution without prejudice to the stand already taken by his Government on the matter, but that France wanted to help Britain prevent international recognition of the illegal declaration of independence.

[30] 12 Jan. 1967.   [31] *The Times* (London), 11 Apr. 1966.

entitled to submit the problem to the Security Council as she did.[32]

A further point which needs attention is the apparent view of the United Kingdom that it was the Unilateral Declaration of Independence which provided ground for international jurisdiction in the Rhodesian independence question. It is submitted that this is a misconception. When UDI was proclaimed the United Nations had already effectively assumed jurisdiction over the question of Rhodesia and, as already seen, had passed a number of resolutions making recommendations to the British Government on how the problem should be solved. It is submitted, therefore, that the significance of UDI was that it facilitated the implementation of enforcement action under Chapter VII of the Charter, and not that it established international jurisdiction.

In the eyes of the Afro-Asian nations, when UDI was proclaimed the situation in Rhodesia became a threat to international peace and security which warranted imposition of enforcement measures under Chapter VII of the Charter. This was, however, rejected by the United Kingdom which described the situation merely as a matter of 'world concern'[33] which did not fall under Chapter VII of the Charter. The Security Council thereafter passed Resolution 216 (1965) and Resolution 217 (1965) recommending the application of a number of enforcement measures against the Smith regime, but these were not based on Chapter VII, as can be seen from the debate that preceded the adoption of these resolutions. Their legal basis could have been the doctrine of international concern, which originated from the Spanish case concerning the implications of the existence of the Franco regime in Spain.[34]

Referring to this doctrine J. M. Howell points out:

The idea of international concern appears to be based on the authority of the Security Council to recommend appropriate procedures or methods of adjustment in disputes 'the continuance of which is likely to endanger the maintenance of international peace and security'. Any

---

[32] R. Higgins, 'International Law, Rhodesia and the United Nations', (1967) 23, *World Today*, 94; J. M. Howell, 'A matter of International Concern', (1969) 63, *AJIL*, 722 (footnote).　　　　　[33] *UNSCOR*, 1257th mtg. para. 10.
[34] Ibid. 1st year, *Special Supplement*, 1 and 2, para. 4.

matters which constitute a potential threat to the peace are declared to be of international concern and consequently, outside domestic juris- diction . . .[35]

In addition to the doctrine of international concern it may be possible to find a legal basis for the Security Council action from some provisions of the Charter. As already pointed out, this could not have been Chapter VII of the Charter because the Security Council deliberately stopped short of invoking it owing to the opposition of the United Kingdom. The legal basis could not be Chapter VI either because it deals with pacific settlements of disputes between states and Rhodesia was not a state in dispute with Britain. The most probable legal basis found in the Charter was the Security Council's general powers under Article 24 and 25 of the Charter.[36]

It was not until 1966 that the Security Council determined that Rhodesia did constitute 'a threat to the peace'.[37] All further measures imposed by the Security Council against the Smith regime after that year were clearly based on Chapter VII of the Charter.

By the way of a summary, it is submitted that international jurisidiction in the Rhodesian problem was originally founded on the international community's concern with questions of human rights and self-determination of peoples of non-self-governing territories under Chapter XI of the Charter. Until 1963 only the General Assembly was concerned with the Rhodesian question. In 1963, however, the Security Council attempted to make recommendations on the question but this attempt was thwarted by the British veto. However, as the threat of UDI loomed high, the Rhodesian problem assumed a new air of importance as the members of the United Nations recognized that it was connected with the question of the maintenance of international peace and security. Even the United Kingdom did not lose sight of that connection, and thus refrained from using her veto, thereby making it possible for the Security Council to adopt Resolution 202 (1965) on 6 May 1965 which endorsed all the resolutions of

[35] J. M. Howell, 'Domestic Jurisdiction' (1954) *Proceedings: ASIL*, 92-3.
[36] These powers are discussed fully in Chapter VII below.
[37] Resolutions 221 (1966) adopted on 9 Apr. 1966, and 232 (1966) passed on 16 Dec. 1966.

the General Assembly which had already been passed. The adoption of this resolution effectively established the jurisdiction of the Security Council to deal with the Rhodesian independence crisis.

When UDI finally came, the Security Council merely exercised jurisdiction it already had. The difference between the pre-UDI period and the post-UDI period is that the latter enabled the Council to impose enforcement measures under Chapter VII of the Charter after determining the existence of a threat to the peace. The fact that the Council did not invoke Chapter VII immediately after UDI was proclaimed is not inconsistent with this conclusion. If this proposition is correct, it should be concluded, as already submitted, that when the Council determined that the Rhodesian situation constituted a threat to the peace it was not to found international jurisdiction, but to provide a basis for specific enforcement measures which were then imposed.

III

Was the Unilateral Declaration of Independence an Illegal Act?

THROUGHOUT its fourteen years of existence, the Smith regime (and its successor Muzorewa regime) was referred to as an illegal regime by members and organs of the United Nations, and by all commentators who were opposed to its existence. What is not clear is whether this tag 'illegal' referred to illegality under British constitutional law, or under international law, or both. What is well recognized is that unilateral declarations of independence by dependent entities seeking to establish their sovereign status have a long history in international relations. Examples that may be cited include the declaration of independence by the Dutch Republics from Spain by the Act of Abjuration of 1581;[1] that of Portugal from Spain in 1641;[2] that of North American colonies from Britain in 1776;[3] those of various Latin American colonies from Spain between 1810 and 1826.[4] Similarly, Brazil broke away from Portugal in 1822, while Belgium broke away from the Netherlands, and Greece from Turkey, in 1830.[5] Montenegro, Romania, and Serbia broke away from Turkey in 1878; Cuba broke away from Spain in 1898, and Panama from Colombia in 1903; while after the First World War Finland, Latvia, Lithuania, and Estonia declared their independence from Russia, as did Poland from Germany, Russia, and Austria.[6] All these rebellions were successful. As can be seen, therefore, the Rhodesian UDI was by no means a unique event, yet unlike the others it was termed illegal and was frustrated by all the might on which the international community could reach a consensus.

The legal significance of a declaration of independence has been commented upon by a number of jurists. Lauterpacht,

---

[1] Oppenheim, *International Law*, vol. i, 579. [2] Ibid. 570.
[3] D. J. Devine, (1973) *Acta Juridica*, 73. [4] Oppenheim, 124–5.
[5] Ibid. 579. [6] Ibid.

for example, states that international law does not condemn
rebellion or secession aimed at the acquisition of independence.[7] This is generally accepted as the correct statement of
the law on this question. When an entity makes a declaration
of independence, it is inviting members of the international
community at large to accord it international recognition so
as to join the family of nations. This announcement *per se*
has no legal significance. Its importance lies in the reaction of
the international community to it. Normally this reaction
varies from state to state. Some states may immediately
accord recognition to the putative state. For example, on
26 September 1973, the African Independence Party of
Guinea and the Cape Verde Islands (PAIGC) formally proclaimed the independence of Guinea-Bissau. This declaration
was quickly recognized by a large number of states.[8] At the
United Nations, the General Assembly adopted a resolution
welcoming 'the recent accession to independence of the
people of Guinea-Bissau, thereby creating the sovereign state
of the Republic of Guinea-Bissau'.[9] Portugal, the former
colonial administrative power of Guinea-Bissau, however,
dragged her feet in recognizing the new state, and actually
recognized the new state only after the Portuguese Revolution
of 1974.[10] Other states may refuse to recognize the new
entity claiming statehood or independence. For example,
when the MPLA Government came to power in Angola
following the departure of the Portuguese administration in
1975 the majority of the members of the international community recognized the statehood and independence of the
new state of Angola. The new state was admitted to the
United Nations on 1 December 1976. The United States,
however, refused to recognize Angola on the ground that
there was foreign intervention in the civil war which led to the
establishment of the MPLA Government in the territory.[11]

The important point which needs emphasizing is that the
act of declaration of independence itself is neither legal nor

[7] Lauterpacht, *Recognition in International Law*, (1947). See also (1928) 22,
AJIL, 105–30; J. Crawford, *The Creation of States in International Law* (Oxford,
1979), 267; D. J. Devine, (1967) *Acta Juridica*, 40; D. Anzillotti, *Cours de Droit
International*, vol. i (Paris, 1929), 169.   [8] See Crawford, 260.
[9] G.A. Res. 306 (XXVIII), 2 Nov. 1973.   [10] Crawford, 260–1.
[11] Ibid. 136.

illegal. It does not even change the status of the entity concerned. Nevertheless the declaration provides the basis for recognition by the existing members of the family of nations. This should be borne in mind in considering whether or not the Rhodesian UDI was illegal. Was the Rhodesian UDI illegal in international law? At first sight this question does not seem to present any difficulties since as we have seen, unilateral declarations of independence are not illegal.

Indeed this is the line Devine adopts in his analysis of the Rhodesian problem on this question. He states:

The Rhodesian Unilateral Declaration is . . . not illegal in international law. Nor can the situation which results therefrom be illegal. But neither is the situation legal in the sense that it acquires a basis in international law. The matter is simply extra-legal. In the same way as international law refused to condemn it, that law also refuses to put the stamp of legality upon it until recognition is afforded . . .[12].

He argues further that the situation resulting from UDI was not unlawful since it conflicted with no established norm of international law. When the organs of the United Nations persisted in referring to the UDI and the resulting situation as being illegal, it is extremely doubtful whether this linguistic usage correctly reflects the international law position seeing that international law does not condemn rebellion.[13]

This statement is a logical conclusion of the argument adopted by the author quoted above. With the greatest respect, it is submitted that this is a simplistic approach which can only produce misleading results. While UDI as an act is not illegal, it can have illegal results. For example, while acquisition of territory as an act is not an illegal act, acquisition of territory by force is illegal. It is submitted that to reach a decision whether the Rhodesian UDI was or was not illegal, all relevant facts connected with that case should be carefully examined.

Before examining the legal question of UDI, it will assist our discussion to remind ourselves of certain essential points here. In 1965 (the UDI year) the population of Rhodesia was probably around the 5 million mark.[14] The population of the

---

[12] D. J. Devine, (1973) *Acta Juridica*, 74.   [13] Ibid.
[14] The estimated population in 1969 was 5,190,000 of whom 234,000 were Europeans: W. Laqueur, *A Dictionary of Politics* (Pan, 1973), 411.

Europeans was about 4 per cent of that total. As already seen
in Chapter I above, the Europeans controlled the Government
and the whole way of life of Rhodesia. Although in the 1961
Constitution Africans were allowed representation in Parliament for the first time, two factors made this change virtually
meaningless. Firstly, Africans could hope to put in Parliament
only 15 members out of a 65 member house. Secondly, owing
to this inequitable allocation of seats in the Constitution,
African nationalists rejected that Constitution, and when
they protested their parties were banned and their leaders
imprisoned, detained, or restricted.[15] When UDI was proclaimed, therefore, the Africans who formed the overwhelming
majority of the population were voiceless and constitutionally
helpless. UDI was proclaimed to entrench this undemocratic
state of affairs. UDI, therefore, did not mean independence
of the people of Rhodesia as a whole, but independence of
the white minority.

The proclamation of independence itself is revealing. It
states that the people of Rhodesia (white people) had demonstrated their loyalty to the British Crown and to their
kith and kin in the United Kingdom and elsewhere through
two World Wars in defending 'what they believed to be the
mutual interests of freedom-loving people'. Furthermore,
the people of Rhodesia had remained steadfast when the
principles of Western democracy, responsible government,
and moral standards crumbled elsewhere. Although the
people of Rhodesia supported their Government's requests
for independence, Britain had refused to grant this on the
terms acceptable to the people of Rhodesia, but had persisted
in maintaining an unwarrantable jurisdiction over Rhodesia.
In the light of that the Rhodesian Government was adopting,
enacting, and giving 'to the people of Rhodesia' the new
Constitution.[16]

One point that comes out of what the proclamation says
is that Britain had refused to grant Rhodesia independence
on the terms acceptable to the people of Rhodesia. This was
true. Britain had not refused to grant Rhodesia independence.
As pointed out in Chapter I above, the British position on

---

[15] See Chapter I above.   [16] Full text in (1966) 5, *ILM*, 230-1.

independence since 1963 when the Federation of Rhodesia and Nyasaland came to an end had been that Rhodesia could proceed to independence if the franchise was widened to allow more Africans to participate in the electoral process.[17] As Akehurst points out: 'Everyone expected Southern Rhodesia to become independent soon; the only uncertainties related to the date and the constitutional changes which would have to be made first.'[18] It is clear, therefore, that UDI was made to perpetrate an undemocratic system which prevented Africans from exercising their right of self-determination. As Akehurst again observes, the 'real dispute has never been between Southern Rhodesia and the United Kingdom, but between the two races in Southern Rhodesia itself . . .'.[19] In this dispute the whites wanted Britain to be on their side, while the Africans also suspected 'with some justification, that the sympathies of the United Kingdom [were] directed primarily towards its own kith and kin in Southern Rhodesia'.[20]

The following are some of the major provisions of the UDI Constitution. Section 143 referred to the attainment of independence by Rhodesia; section 2 (1) (b) made provisions for the appointment of the Officer Administering the Government to act as the representative of the Queen. The executive government was vested in the Queen acting on the advice of the Rhodesian Government.[21] The Rhodesian Parliament was empowered to make laws for the peace, order, and good government of Rhodesia.[22] No legislation of the United Kingdom Parliament would extend to Rhodesia unless it was extended thereto by an Act of the Rhodesian legislature.[23] The Colonial Law Validity Act, 1865 was not to apply to Rhodesia in the future.[24] Section 26 (5) provided that no future law of Rhodesia was to be void on the ground that it was repugnant to the law of Britain or future Act of the United Kingdom Parliament. The Rhodesian Legislature might repeal or amend any such Act of the United Kingdom.

As can be seen, section 26 of the Constitution purported to give the 'Rhodesian Parliament' supremacy over any United

[17] Cmnd. 2807, 5. [18] M. Akehurst, (1968-9) 43, *BYBIL*, 51.
[19] Ibid. [20] Ibid.
[21] S. 47. [22] S. 26 (1).
[23] S. 26 (3). [24] S. 26 (4).

Kingdom law. This, as Devine points out, amounted to a constitutional revolution where 'the Government' had the support
at least of important powerful elements among the public.[25]
Had this revolution succeeded it would have meant that the
Africans would have been condemned to perpetual servitude
which they could have changed only by a counter-revolution,
a daunting task if Rhodesia had been accepted as an independent state entitled in international law to seek and receive
assistance of all kinds from friendly countries. The right of
self-determination of the African population of Rhodesia
would have been suppressed for a long time to come.

With this background in mind we may examine the question
whether the Rhodesian UDI was or was not illegal in international law. A declaration of independence by an unrepre-
sentative government whose composition is based on race in
which a small white minority in the middle of Africa domin-
ates an overwhelming black majority is surely a matter of
interest to international law. The Rhodesian UDI is therefore
not an ordinary UDI of the kind we have seen in other countries
where the declaration of independence was a popular move
by the representatives of the people of a territory as a whole.
As Higgins maintains, the Rhodesian UDI is: 'Anomalous . . .
in that while rebellion is not itself contrary to international
law, or anything contained in the Charter, the Charter is
concerned with the maintenance and promotion of human
rights . . .'[26].

It is for this reason that it is to miss the point completely to
argue that because international law does not forbid rebellion,
or even, the fact that many rebellions and secessions have
occurred throughout history, the Rhodesian unilateral declaration of independence, like the ones that have occurred before
it, is not illegal in international law. It is submitted that there
is more to this question than appears on the surface. While it
is correct to say that rebellion or secession is an extra-legal
act upon which international law has no pronouncement the
Rhodesian UDI formed a category of its own; it was, so to
speak, *sui generis*. The Rhodesian UDI was a violation of the
right of self-determination of the Rhodesian African majority,

[25] D. J. Devine, (1973) *Acta Juridica*, 65.
[26] R. Higgins, (1967) 23, *World Today*, 95.

and a violation of that right is illegal in international law.[27] As an illegal act UDI was therefore also void and a nullity in the sense that it had no legal effect on the status of Rhodesia. Consequently, notwithstanding UDI, Rhodesia remained a dependent territory of the United Kingdom and the regime that ruled the territory in defiance of that status was itself illegal.

Because of this, some members of the United Nations did indicate clearly that they considered the Rhodesian UDI illegal not only in the eyes of the law of the United Kingdom but also in international law. For instance, Mr Diop, the representative of Senegal, told the Security Council:

> the unilateral declaration of independence by the Smith Government is a veritable act of rebellion in the eyes of British law; [it is also] an act of rebellion under the Charter of the United Nations, since by making such a declaration Mr Smith has violated the right of self-determination of the four million African Rhodesians . . . and also violated General Assembly resolution 1514 (XV) on the granting of independence to colonial countries and peoples.[28]

Similarly, the United States representative considered that the rebellion had violated the rights of Rhodesians under Chapter XI of the Charter, pertaining to the rights of inhabitants of non-self-governing territories.[29]

Failure to distinguish the Rhodesian UDI from earlier declarations of independence may produce misleading conclusions about the legality of that act. This distinction is necessary especially if one takes into account the fact that the United Nations on a number of occasions recommended, in effect, that secessionist movements should succeed against colonial powers in order to enable the colonial peoples to exercise their right to self-determination. Resolutions of the General Assembly on Algeria[30] and on Angola[31] are good illustrations of this policy. Probably the most striking case was the question of the independence of Indonesia, a Dutch territory.[32] In that case the Netherlands opposed the

---

[27] See G.A. Resolutions 1514 (XV) and 2625.
[28] *UNSCOR*, 1257th mtg. para. 96.
[29] UN. Doc. S/PV 1333, 12 Dec. 1966; cf. the opinion of the French representative, *UNSCOR*, 1258th mtg. para. 11.   [30] Res. 1573 (XV).
[31] Res. 1819 (XVII).   [32] See Res. 67 (1949).

establishment of the Republic of Indonesia.[33] In the middle of hostilities between the Netherlands and Indonesia, the Security Council established a Committee of Good Offices to initiate a dialogue between the parties. Throughout the negotiations the Security Council treated the problem as a dispute between equals. The reason for this was that the declaration of independence by Indonesia was an exercise of the right of self-determination of the majority of the Indonesians.

Unlike the Indonesian case, the Rhodesian UDI was condemned by the same Organization and its organs. This was because in Rhodesia a minority declared independence for precisely the opposite purpose to that of the Indonesian independence. At the United Nations this position was very firmly stated by Mr Paÿsse Reyes, the representative of Uruguay, who told the Security Council:

> I place great emphasis on one point which I think is of importance. The declaration of independence does not shock us because it is unilateral — it shocks us, fundamentally, because it is made by a racist minority. Throughout history declarations of independence have always been unilateral acts. The declaration we are considering is therefore not evil because it is unilateral — it is evil because it has been made by a racist minority to oppress and coerce a huge majority . . . Therefore we point out that the legal aspect of the condemnation of the declaration arises . . . from the fact that it was made by a racist minority in furtherance of political goals which should be condemned.[34]

In order to determine which declarations of independence are legal or illegal it is essential to know who may claim the right of self-determination. Although paragraph 2 of the Declaration on the Granting of Independence to Colonial Countries and Peoples says that all 'peoples have the right to self-determination', it is doubtful if this means that every ethnic entity in a given territory may legitimately claim a separate right to self-determination and independence, or the right to secede from the larger state. Thus, although paragraph 2 of the Declaration on the Granting of Independence to Colonial Countries and Peoples states that all 'peoples have the right to self-determination', that paragraph should be read

---

[33] (1947–8) *YBUN*, 212; Fawcett, 'Security Council Resolutions on Rhodesia', (1965–6) 41, *BYBIL*, 114. [34] *UNSCOR*, 1258th mtg., para. 19.

together with paragraph 6 of the same Declaration which forbids any 'attempt aimed at the partial or total disruption of the national unity . . . of a country . . .'. Furthermore, the Annex of General Assembly Resolution 2625 of 1970 also prohibits 'any action which would dismember or impair, totally or in part, the territorial integrity of political unity of sovereign and independent states conducting themselves in compliance with the principles of equal rights and self-determination of peoples . . .'.[35]

This interpretation seems reasonable in the sense that most new nations are composed of many ethnic groups which, if the right of self-determination were interpreted widely, would validly claim the right of secession. This would obviously endanger the territorial units of many of these countries. The right of self-determination should, as Crawford suggests, be interpreted to reinforce 'the effectiveness of territorial units created with the consent of the former sovereign'[36] when the respective territorial units achieved independence. That is why in 1960 the secession by the Congo (now Zaïre) province of Katanga was strongly opposed and crushed mercilessly.[37] The attempted secession by the Eastern Region of Nigeria as the new state of Biafra also received little encouragement from Africa, for instance, although it was an indigenous secession with much less involvement of external forces than was the case in the Katangese secession.

It seems that to be a true exercise of the right of self-determination, two conditions must be satisfied. Firstly, the people claiming the right must exercise their claim within the colonial context, and secondly, that claim of the right must not be a violation of the right itself. The second of these two requirements is no doubt the more important. That is why, for example, the purported granting of independence to Bantustans by the South African Government has been rejected as illegal[38] because it is an attempt by the South African Government to strengthen apartheid by depriving the

---

[35] See also Akehurst, *A Modern Introduction* (4th edn.), 253.
[36] Crawford, 102.
[37] Ibid., 263; R. Higgins, *The Development of International Law Through the Political Organs of the United Nations* (Oxford 1963), 104.
[38] Crawford, 222–8.

Africans whose ethnic groups inhabit the affected Bantustans of their right to self-determination within the larger South Africa. Similarly, the Smith regime declared UDI in Rhodesia in violation of the right of self-determination of the African majority. Such a declaration was therefore illegal and a nullity in international law.

Devine argues that the Rhodesian UDI could not be illegal because an 'act which is unlawful in international law can be committed only by an entity which enjoys personality in that system'.[39] Similarly Crawford maintains that the Smith regime could act illegally in international law only if it was a subject of international law, the very status the United Nations sought to deny that regime.[40] These views suggest that only states may violate international law. This is no longer accepted as even a half truth.[41] Even traditional international law long recognized that non-sovereign entities can and do violate international law. For instance, it is a long established rule of international law that piracy, which can only be committed by individuals, is an unlawful international act.[42] Again, war crimes and crimes against humanity may be mentioned as examples of unlawful international acts which may be committed by individuals, as was seen in the Nuremberg Trial in 1945.[43] Such individuals are surely not full subjects of international law. In the same way, the fact that the Smith regime lacked full international personality was not inconsistent with its capacity to violate the right of self-determination of the bulk of Rhodesian people. It is submitted, therefore, that it was legally sound to hold the Rhodesian UDI illegal, null and void.

[39] Devine (1973), 77–8.   [40] Crawford, 267.
[41] M. S. McDougal and M. W. Reisman (1968) 62, *AJIL*, 10–12.
[42] See (1935) 29, *AJIL*, Suppl., p. 440.
[43] Judicial Decisions, (1947) 41, *AJIL*, 174, 770.

IV

International Recognition

THE unilateral declaration of independence by the Rhodesian Government was an invitation to the world community to recognize Rhodesia as a full member of the family of nations with rights and duties in international law. The legal effect of international recognition has been a subject of considerable debate centring on two schools of thought referred to as the constitutive and declaratory theories. The constitutive theory states that an entity claiming to be a state does not exist as a state in international law until it is recognized. The declaratory theory on the other hand stipulates that recognition has no legal effect on the creation of a state. Whether an entity is or is not a state is a matter of fact and not of law. Therefore, when recognition is accorded an entity, this is merely a response to an already existing fact.[1]

The controversy between these two schools of thought has nearly been done to death and will therefore not be examined in any detail here. Nevertheless it is important to point out that in practice recognition may have different effects on different situations. In any case, Crawford is probably right when he suggests that neither theory satisfactorily explains the modern state practice in this area.[2] For example, when constitutivists argue that recognition brings about the statehood of new territories, it should be pointed out that recognition depends for its proper operation on the cognition of certain factual situations such as the physical existence of the entity with all the attributes of statehood save only that which depends on recognition itself — rights and duties under international law. In the light of this, therefore, it is clear that although states have a discretion in according or withholding recognition of a new entity, this discretion is not absolute but is based on general rules. That is why, for example,

---

[1] For a detailed study of this subject see Lauterpacht, *Recognition* (Cambridge, 1947); Schwarzenberger, *International Law*, vol. i. (Stevens, 1957), 134; and Kelsen, (1941) 35, *AJIL*, 605-17.   [2] Crawford, 4.

there is a rule against premature recognition. Similarly, the supporters of the declaratory theory, by suggesting that a state may exist whether or not it has been recognized provided it satisfies the criteria of statehood, overlook the fact that the determination of those criteria in any given case should, surely, be a matter of rules or law. If this is so, it follows that the determination of statehood of an entity cannot be only a matter of fact but a matter of both fact and law.

Without deciding in favour of one or the other of the two schools of thought referred to above, it should be stated that there are cases where recognition has a constitutive effect. This is particularly so in cases where an act which is otherwise illegal may be rendered legal by recognition. Thus an illegal acquisition of territory does not give title to that land to the state concerned. However, if that acquisition is subsequently recognized, that recognition may cure the illegality and turn an act which was a nullity into a valid title. In the last chapter we argued, for instance, that if a putative state comes into being in violation of the right of self-determination, it is illegal and a nullity. If, however, it subsequently receives inter-national recognition, the illegality may be cured by that recognition in that entity's relations with the recognizing states.[3]

In the previous chapter we also submitted that the Smith regime was illegal and a nullity because it was created in violation of the right of self-determination of the Rhodesian Africans. If, on the strength of the proposition given above, Rhodesia was ever recognized as a state by any member of the international community, the illegality of its creation would be cured as between Rhodesia and the recognizing state. Therefore, we may now examine whether Rhodesia was ever recognized. Before doing that, however, we should first determine whether the territory ever became a state.

A. *Did Rhodesia Ever Become a State?*

The meaning of the word 'state' for the purposes of

[3] Akehurst, *A Modern Introduction* (Allen and Unwin, 4th edn.), 255.

international law is more difficult to give than it appears. J. B. Moore says that a state may be defined as:

a people permanently occupying a fixed territory . . . bound together by common laws, habits, and customs into a body politic, exercising, through the medium of organized government, independent sovereignty and control over all persons and things within its boundaries . . .[4].

According to Article One of the Montevideo Convention on the Rights and Duties of States, 1933, a state as a subject of international law should possess a permanent population; a defined territory; government; and capacity to enter into relations with other states.

The last-mentioned criterion is probably merely a qualification of the third criterion. In any case, capacity to enter into relations with other states is not an independent fact but one whose exercise depends on the co-operation of other states. Therefore it may be argued that there are really only three criteria which have to be satisfied before an entity may be accepted as a state for the purposes of international recognition — population, territory, and government. In a discussion of whether or not Rhodesia ever became a state the first two criteria cause no difficulty. Rhodesia did have a permanent population living in a defined territory with definite boundaries. No further discussion of this need be pursued.

The criterion that causes some difficulty is that of government. The possession of a central government by an entity claiming statehood appears to be the major criterion of statehood. The government in question must not only exist, but must also be an effective government in the maintenance of internal law and order to make it possible for a certain level of political stability to prevail. For example, it is through the government that the putative state claims recognition of its assumed status. Under traditional international law the most significant fact about the existence of a government was its effectiveness in maintaining law and order in the territory. To a certain extent this position remains the same today, except that now the principle of self-determination will be set against the concept of effective government. Consequently, a putative

[4] J. B. Moore, *A Digest of International Law* (Washington, 1906), 14–15.

state may have an effective government, yet that government may not succeed in winning international recognition if its existence serves to perpetuate a colonial, or possibly, a neo-colonial situation in the territory claiming statehood.[5] As Brownlie maintains, the 'relevant question may now be: in whose interest and for what legal purpose is the government "effective"?'[6]

As regards the Rhodesian case, it has been argued that that territory not only had a government but that it had a demonstratively effective administration as was recognized by the Rhodesian judges in *R. v. Ndhlovu.*[7] Devine argues, for example, that effectiveness may be demonstrated if the government is able to exercise its functions without substantial resistance.[8] He further maintains that the absence of resistance need not rest on free consent of the population, and that *de facto* submission is enough whether it is given happily, indifferently, grumblingly, voluntarily, or out of fear.[9] In the light of this, therefore, he concludes that there is no doubt that Rhodesia did have an effective government. It follows from this argument, then, that Rhodesia did satisfy all the criteria of statehood and the territory deserved to be recognized as a state, and that the failure of Rhodesia to win international recognition was due only to the use of discretion by other states to withhold that recognition.[10]

Fawcett also suggests that Rhodesia did satisfy the traditional criteria of statehood. However, he adds:

. . . to the traditional criteria for the recognition of a régime as a new State must now be added the requirement that it shall not be based upon a systematic denial in its territory of certain civil and political rights, including in particular the right of every citizen to participate in the government of his country, directly or through representatives elected by regular, equal and secret suffrage. This principle was affirmed in the case of Rhodesia by virtually unanimous condemnation of the unilateral declaration of independence by the world community, and by the universal withholding of recognition of the new régime which was a consequence . . .

---

[5] I. Brownlie, *Principles of International Law* (Oxford, 2nd edn.), 75.
[6] Ibid.
[7] D. J. Devine, (1973) *Acta Juridica*, 82; the citation of *R. v. Ndhlovu* is 1968 (4) SA 515 (RAD).		[8] Devine (1973) *Acta Juridica*, 82.
[9] Ibid.		[10] Devine, (1971) 34 *MLR*, 418.

It would follow then that the illegality of the rebellion was an obstacle to the establishment of Rhodesia as an independent State, but that the political basis and objectives of the régime were, and that the declaration of independence was without international effect.[11]

This statement has been criticized by Devine, who argues that this amounts to asserting that to the traditional criteria already examined should be added the criterion that before a new state can qualify for recognition it must have a 'good government'.[12] In reply to this criticism Fawcett points out that Devine misreads his conclusions, which are not that there should be a good government in a state seeking recognition but that all the citizens of that state must 'have effective representation . . . in their government'.[13] In other words, Fawcett is referring to the exercise of the right of self-determination.

This is how Crawford also interprets Fawcett's proposition.[14] The position seems to be that the establishment of a state in violation of the right of self-determination of peoples is illegal and therefore the existence or non-existence of the traditional criteria of statehood is irrelevant. However, as already proposed above, if the traditional criteria of statehood are present and a state recognizes the new regime, that may cure the illegality which previously existed in relation to the recognizing state.

As already submitted in Chapter III above, the proclaimed independence of Rhodesia was a violation of a legal norm — the right of self-determination — and therefore illegal, the existence or otherwise of the traditional criteria of statehood being probably of no significance. Therefore the question of Rhodesia's statehood, which depended on the application of international rules of acquiring that status, could be of importance only if some members of the international community had accorded Rhodesia recognition. That is why some members of the United Nations were anxious to appeal to the rest of the membership of the Organization not to grant Rhodesia recognition.[15]

It may be added here too that in spite of the fact that the

---

[11] J. E. Fawcett, (1965–6) 41, *BYBIL*, 103–21.
[12] Devine, (1971) 34, *MLR*, 410.   [13] Ibid. 417.
[14] Crawford, 106.   [15] See Chapter V below.

Smith regime claimed that Rhodesia was independent, it continued to behave as though it accepted that the territory's statehood depended on approval to be given by the United Kingdom. In pursuance of this stand, the Smith regime continued to negotiate with Britain with a view to reaching a constitutional agreement which would lead to legitimate independence in Rhodesia with African participation in government. It could be argued that such negotiations were inconsistent with independence as it is generally accepted that constitutional matters are questions of domestic jurisdiction of states. The constitutional agreement which was ultimately concluded between the British Government, the rebel regime in Salisbury, and the African liberation movements confirms this argument. Although on 11 December 1979 the Rhodesian Legislative Assembly went through the motions of dissolving itself and asserting that Rhodesia 'shall cease to be an independent state and shall become part of Her Majesty's dominions', such assertion had no legal significance outside Rhodesia.

B. *Rhodesia and International Personality*
Before and After UDI

Although international law is primarily concerned with independent states,[16] the latter are not the only entities which enjoy international personality. Consequently, the fact that an entity is not an independent state does not necessarily preclude it from possessing some measure of international personality, be it of very restricted kind, and which depends on the agreement or acquiescence of recognized legal persons and opposable on the international plane only to those agreeing or acquiescent.[17] What may be emphasized from the very beginning is that the international personality of a dependent territory emanates from that of its mother state. Such personality is thus limited in that its donee receives as much international personality as the mother state (donor) is

---

[16] Brierly, *The Law of Nations* (Oxford, 1963) 129; Brownlie, *Principles of International Law* (Oxford, 1973), 61.

[17] Brownlie, *Principles of International Law*, 60.

prepared to entrust to it.[18] This limited international personality 'must naturally always coincide with the degree of
personality which the mother state retains, each ... supporting
the personality of the other'.[19]

To find out whether a given entity has an international
personality, and if so, the extent of that personality, one has
to look at the facts of the case concerned. If a territory is in
certain respects, though not in other respects, a separate
political actor, it is clearly endowed by international law with
the necessary faculties of legal action to give effect to this
political reality.[20] For example, Laos, Kampuchea, Vietnam,
Egypt, Tunisia and Morocco all had considerable autonomy
in the conduct of external affairs before independence.[21]

An examination of the constitutional history of Rhodesia
shows that the United Kingdom delegated to that territory
some measure of international personality from the time the
territory became a British colony in 1923.[22] This enabled
Rhodesia to gain an increased voice in both Commonwealth
and international affairs. For example, in 1932 Rhodesia
attended the Imperial Economic Conference at Ottawa and
concluded bilateral trade agreements with Canada and
Britain.[23] In 1937 Rhodesia had an observer status at the
Imperial Conference.[24] 'By 1939 ... Rhodesia could be quite
legitimately regarded as a separate member of the Commonwealth for some and as a dependency of the United Kingdom
for other purposes. Thus it could communicate directly
with other members of the Commonwealth but could not
communicate with foreign governments except through
the ordinary channels of the British diplomatic service.'[25]

Between 1953 and 1963 Rhodesia was a member of the
Federation of Rhodesia and Nyasaland. This membership
froze for some time the growth of Rhodesia's international
personality. The Federation took over what international

---

[18] O'Connell, *International Law* (Stevens, 2nd edn.), 82-3.
[19] Ibid.; Akehurst (4th edn.), 56.
[20] Broderick, (1968) 17, *ICLQ*, 396.
[21] *Whiteman's Digest of International Law*, vol. i. (Washington, 1968), 287, 289.
[22] Devine, (1973) *Acta Juridica*, 41.
[23] Stewart, *Treaty Relations of the British Commonwealth of Nations*, (New York, 1939), 21.   [24] Ibid.
[25] Devine, (1973) *Acta Juridica*, 41.

personality had been enjoyed by Rhodesia in addition to receiving its own international personality from Britain. For example, the Federation received from Britain authority to negotiate directly with foreign states and to sign and ratify certain classes of treaties without intervention of the United Kingdom.[26] When the Federation was dissolved in 1963 the limited international personality it enjoyed probably devolved to Rhodesia, the only member of the Federation to which the dissolution of the Federation did not bring independence.[27] These powers were detailed in a statement issued by the Federal Prime Minister. They included:

The right to conduct all relations and to exchange representatives with Commonwealth countries without consultation with the United Kingdom; the right to appoint representatives to the diplomatic staffs of Her Majesty's embassies; the right to conduct negotiations and agreements with foreign countries subject to the need to safeguard the United Kingdom Government's international responsibilities; the right to appoint its own diplomatic agents, who will have full diplomatic status and who will be in charge of federal missions, in any foreign countries prepared to accept them, and to receive such agents from other countries; the right, on its own authority, to acquire the membership of international organizations for which it is eligible.[28]

In the exercise of its delegated powers, the Federation concluded trade and customs agreements with the United Kingdom and a number of other countries.[29] It joined a number of international organizations including the International Telecommunications Union (ITU), World Meteorological Organization (WMO), General Agreement on Tariffs and Trade (GATT), the African Postal Union (APU), the African Telecommunications Union (ATU), the Commission for Technical Co-operation in Africa South of the Sahara, the Foundation for Mutual Assistance in Africa South of the Sahara, International Red Locust Central Service, International Union for the Protection of Industrial Property, International Wheat Council, Universal Postal Union (UPU), and International Monetary Fund (IMF).[30]

Its diplomatic capacity which in 1953 included the power

---

[26] Broderick, 378.
[27] Fawcett, (1965–66) 41 *BYBIL*, 107.
[28] Ibid., 106.   [29] Ibid.
[30] Devine, (1973) *Acta Juridica*, 43.

to exchange representatives with Commonwealth countries, subject to the agreement of the United Kingdom, was increased in 1957 to include the power to conduct all manner of representations with Commonwealth countries directly. Thus it appointed High Commissioners in London and Pretoria.[31] It also attached representatives to British Embassies in Washington, Tokyo, Lisbon, and Bonn. It received diplomatic representatives from both foreign and Commonwealth countries.[32] It also had power to protect its nationals under the Federal Citizenship Act, 1957, and could bear international responsibility for wrongs suffered by foreigners in the Federation.[33]

That these powers devolved upon Rhodesia on the dissolution of the Federation was made clear by the Secretary of State for Commonwealth Relations who stated that the powers entrusted to Rhodesia in the conduct of external affairs would be the same as those entrusted to the Federation.[34] The enjoyment of these powers was, however, subject to the ultimate responsibility of the United Kingdom Government. In addition to these powers, Rhodesia had consular relations with a large number of countries inside and outside the Commonwealth of Nations. These countries included the United Kingdom, Australia, Japan, Sweden, Turkey, West Germany, Switzerland, Belgium, Denmark, Norway, the United States of America, France, Greece, the Netherlands, South Africa, and Portugal including Portuguese Mozambique.

In keeping with the powers formerly enjoyed by the Federation, Rhodesia exchanged High Commissioners with Commonwealth members on the basis that the 'unity of the Crown entailed that British territories could not be foreign to each other and that the principles of international recognition were not applicable between them . . .'.[35] Rhodesia had, in addition, diplomatic relations with South Africa, a non-Commonwealth country. This anomalous situation assumed international signficance in 1965 when UDI was proclaimed. Mr Arthur Bottomley, the Commonwealth Secretary,

---

[31] Ibid. [32] Ibid.
[33] Fawcett, (1965–66) 41 *BYBIL*, 107. [34] Ibid.
[35] Fawcett, *The British Commonwealth in International Law* (Stevens, 1963), 194.

explained it as a creation of history which should not be regarded as a precedent.[36] These relations were established before 1961 when South Africa was still a member of the Commonwealth.

As can be seen from the foregoing, Rhodesia did have a considerable measure of international personality before UDI was proclaimed. It now remains to determine whether UDI affected this international personality in any way. If the international personality of a dependent territory is delegated by the mother state, it is pertinent to ask whether, once such delegation has been made, the mother state retains the power to revoke it. Broderick doubts that this is possible once delegation is made.[37] Palley holds the view that it is possible because the dependent territory possesses no international personality of its own at all.[38] It is submitted that Palley's position is probably a better explanation. It would appear that there is a difference between a grant of power, such as for example a grant of independence, which is irrevocable, and a delegation of power, which is revocable. Rhodesia's international personality was only delegated to it by the United Kingdom who could revoke it if she so pleased. As Devine argues, this 'is probably what happened after the Unilateral Declaration of Independence when the United Kingdom passed the Southern Rhodesia Act 1965.'[39] It means, therefore, that if any foreign country wished to continue to have international relations with Rhodesia after the Southern Rhodesia Act, 1965 deprived Rhodesia of its limited international personality, it could maintain only such relations as were consistent with British legal authority in Rhodesia or else such a country would have had to recognize Rhodesia's capacity in international affairs in its own right. Consequently, when the Smith regime declared Rhodesia a Republic on 2 March 1970, there was a mass withdrawal of consular representation of those countries which had maintained this form of external contact with Rhodesia since UDI; these

[36] *Weekly Hansard*, vol. 717, No. 667, 23–29 July 1965.
[37] Broderick, 'Associated Statehood—A New Form of Decolonization' (1968) 17 *ICLQ*, 378.
[38] C. Palley, *The Constitutional History and the Law of Southern Rhodesia* (Oxford, 1965), 730.   [39] Devine, (1973) *Acta Juridica*, 41.

included the United Kingdom itself. Since the republican status of Rhodesia represented a complete break with Britain, any official international contacts with Rhodesia could be construed as amounting to some form of recognition of the declared changed status of Rhodesia.[40]

The first countries to end their consular relations with Rhodesia were Australia, the United Kingdom, Canada, Finland, Japan, Sweden, and Turkey, which announced the complete withdrawal of their missions on 2 March 1970.[41] West Germany and Switzerland withdrew their consular officers but allowed their administrative officers to remain in Salisbury. Belgium and Denmark replaced their career officers by honorary consuls. But on 4 March 1970 Denmark and Norway also closed their consulates. During the rest of the month, Italy, France, West Germany, Sweden, Australia, Greece, the Netherlands, and the United States also closed down their consulates.[42] On 10 March 1970, South Africa announced that it would not withdraw its consular representation, and Portugal made a similar announcement the following month.[43]

The withdrawal of the United States consular relations presents an interesting point which needs a comment. The announcement was made on 9 March 1970, with the intended date of actual withdrawal being 17 March. According to press reports this announcement was preceded by both a strong British representation and that of some of President Nixon's White House advisers. On 27 February Mr Ronald Ziegler, the White House Press Secretary, had stated that the Consulate would remain open without in any way implying recognition of the Smith regime. But later that day, after a meeting of the National Security Council during which Mr William Rogers was reported to have vigorously protested, Mr Ziegler amended his earlier statement and announced that the status of the mission was being reviewed in the light of Rhodesia's decision to become a Republic.[44] When Mr Rogers announced the closure of the Consulate the following month, he stated that the implementation of the Rhodesian Republican Constitution represented the 'final and formal break' with Britain, and that

---

[40] *Keesing*, 24005.   [41] Ibid.   [42] Ibid.   [43] Ibid.
[44] Ibid.

the United States 'has regarded and continues to regard the United Kingdom as the lawful sovereign' in Rhodesia.

The question whether or not the maintenance of consular relations amounts to implied recognition of the state issuing the exequatur will be considered below. What is important for the present purpose is that since the exequatur on the basis of which the United States operated was issued by Britain, any continued maintenance of the mission after the exequatur had been withdrawn would have meant that the government concerned recognized, if not full international capacity on the part of the Smith regime, certainly some limited international capacity, or *de facto* authority. As O'Connell points out, the consul derives his authority from the exequatur and not from the commission.[45] If, therefore, the United States in the case referred to above had maintained its Consulate in Rhodesia after Rhodesia declared itself a Republic in defiance of the United Kingdom authority, it could have been regarded as doing so under the authority given to it by the Smith regime notwithstanding that no new exequatur had been issued.[46] This presumption could, however, be rebutted by the United States showing contrary intention. It could show this by making a statement to that effect or by acting in such a way that it was clear that it did not regard the Smith regime as having authority in Rhodesia. Be that as it may, it was wiser for the United States to pull out its Consulate altogether to avoid comforting the illegal regime in Salisbury.

All the pieces of evidence examined so far point to the rejection by the international community of all claims of the Smith regime based on UDI or the proclamation of the republican status of Rhodesia. As already seen, South Africa and Portugal decided to keep their consular missions in Salisbury open. Of what legal significance were those decisions? Furthermore, was the proclaimed independence of Rhodesia ever recognized by any state? These questions will be examined in the following section.

---

[45] O'Connell, 917.   [46] Ibid.

C. *Was Rhodesia Ever Recognized?*

When a new state is born, a new government is established, a territory changes its status, or a legally established position is altered, a question often arises whether the new situation has been recognized by the members of the international community.[47] Recognition of new states and governments usually causes no difficulties in the majority of cases, especially where the new states are created in a constitutional manner such as, for example, a grant of independence by the colonial power. Exceptions may, however, occur in cases where a grant of independence to an entity is seen as a violation of some legal norms such as for example, a violation of the right of self-determination of peoples. The South African Bantustan policy has been internationally rejected on this basis.[48] The major controversy on international recognition arises in cases where an entity is created by revolution.

Probably the most controversial aspect of recognition is the extent of its legal effect. This controversy has, as already seen, been dominated by the two theories of recognition – the constitutive and declaratory theories. So much has been written about this debate that little can be added by indulging in further detailed analysis of the two theories in a discussion which is primarily concerned with the practical question of whether Rhodesia was ever recognized by states.[49] This discussion will therefore only make a passing reference to the two theories in so far as this may be relevant to the central points being considered on the international status of Rhodesia at the end of this section.

Recognition of a new government or state may be express or implied.[50] When it is expressly granted there is generally no dispute about the juridical status of the recognized entity *vis-à-vis* the recognizer. However, it should be noted that there is no uniform type of recognition or non-recognition as the official communications invariably employ different forms

[47] Sorensen, *Manual of Public International Law* (Macmillan, 1968), 267.

[48] Akehurst (4th edn.), 255; Crawford, *The Creation of States in International Law*, 222–7.

[49] See e.g. Lauterpacht, *Recognition in International Law* (Cambridge 1947).

[50] Schwarzenberger and Brown, *A Manual of International Law* (Stevens, 1968), 267.

of terminology. This is particularly so since the word 'recognition' may not even be used in the communication, as for example, where the recognizing state merely declares its intention to establish diplomatic relations, or merely sends the new state a congratulatory message on attainment of independence. Whatever form the communication between the recognizing state and the new state, there is usually little problem in determining whether recognition has been accorded.

Difficulties arise, however, where one state is deemed to have recognized another by implication. This depends on the ascertainment from conduct of the true intention of the recognizing state. A state 'cannot stumble unwittingly into recognition (of another state) by making some false step'.[51] Consequently, a state sometimes may formally announce that its conduct is not to be taken as a recognition of a new entity with which it has had some dealings.[52] What helps, however, is that recognition will not be implied lightly.[53] Therefore, there 'is, as a rule, no conduct, however conclusive in ordinary circumstances, the normal legal consequences of which cannot be averted or interpreted by a clear manifestation of a contrary intention'.[54] Recognition is implied solely when the circumstances unequivocally indicate an intention to establish formal relations with the new state or government as the case might be.[55]

To examine whether or not Rhodesia was ever recognized it will be convenient to examine first whether there are statements to that effect which were made by states. This should be relatively easy. Thereafter, an examination will be made of the conduct of existing states in their relations with Rhodesia throughout the independence crisis to determine whether there was implied recognition.

Up to the time that the independence crisis was resolved in December 1979, no state had expressly recognized the independence of Rhodesia. On the contrary, virtually all states

---

[51] O'Connell, vol. i (2nd edn.), 153.   [52] Ibid.
[53] Schwarzenberger, *International Law*, 71.
[54] Lauterpacht, *Recognition in International Law*, 369.
[55] Starke, *An Introduction to International Law* (London, 1972), 147; Oppenheim, *International Law* (8th edn.), 146–8; Lauterpacht, *Recognition in International Law*, 395–6.

had expressed their non-recognition of both Rhodesia and its rebel government.[56] The first statement of non-recognition came from the British Government; it was produced in the case of *Madzimbamuto* v. *Lardner-Burke*,[57] which declared *inter alia*:

... I, the Honourable Arthur Bottomley, O.B.E., M.P., Her Majesty's Secretary of State for Commonwealth Relations, hereby certify as follows:

(a) Southern Rhodesia has since 1923 been and continues to be a colony within Her Majesty's dominions and the Government and Parliament of the United Kingdom have responsibility for jurisdiction over it.

(b) Her Majesty's Government in the United Kingdom does not recognize Southern Rhodesia or Rhodesia as a state either *de facto* or *de jure*.

(c) Her Majesty's Government in the United Kingdom does not recognize any persons whomsoever as Ministers of the Government of Southern Rhodesia and does not recognize any persons purporting to be such Ministers as constituting a government in Southern Rhodesia either *de facto* or *de jure*.

The United Kingdom stated substantially the same position in the Security Council of the United Nations.[58] A large number of states also reacted to UDI almost immediately in a similar fashion. Mr Robert McCloskey, speaking for the State Department of the United States, said that 'no request for recognition had been received from Salisbury, none was expected and it would not be granted if it were sent'.[59] The Canadian Prime Minister, Mr Lester Pearson, said that Canada 'would not recognize an independent Rhodesia'.[60] Mr Holyoake, the New Zealand Prime Minister, also stated that his country 'could not accord recognition to the illegal government'.[61] The Prime Minister of India, Mr Shastri, said that so 'far as India is concerned, we have made it quite clear that we will not recognize [Rhodesia]'.[62] Similar reactions came from Japan, Denmark, Kenya, Norway, Sweden, Israel, Czechoslovakia, and the Soviet Union.[63] Other countries which made

---

[56] Reference to recognition should henceforth be taken to refer to both Rhodesia and the Smith regime.
[57] [1969] 2 AC 645. [58] *UNSCOR*, 1257th mtg. para. 10 *et seq.*
[59] *The Times* (London), 12 Nov. 1965, 8.
[60] Ibid. [61] Ibid.
[62] Ibid. [63] Ibid. 12 Nov. 1965, 8.

similar statements included Malaysia, Nigeria, Pakistan, Australia, Turkey, and Botswana.[64]

The Portuguese Foreign Minister, Dr Nogueira gave an ambivalent statement to the effect that his Government would consider whether or not to recognize the Rhodesian independence only after studying the terms of the declaration.[65] A West Germany spokesman stated that the future action of his Government would be determined by friendly relations with Britain, possible United Nations decisions, and Germany's belief in the principle of self-determination. Dr Verwoerd, the South African Prime Minister, declared that his country would maintain 'normal relations' with Rhodesia as his Government did not wish to be involved in the constitutional dispute between the United Kingdom and her rebel colony.[66]

The South African statement could mean one of two things. Firstly, it could mean that since South Africa did not wish to be involved in this constitutional dispute, it would not regard UDI as having altered the legal position of Rhodesia, in which case South Africa continued to regard Rhodesia's international personality as that entrusted to it by the United Kingdom. In that case South Africa could be considered as continuing to recognize the dependency of Rhodesia and ultimate British responsibility for her rebel colony. This, of course, would be in conflict with the British claims which aimed at withdrawing any international personality which Rhodesia might have had. Secondly, if Britain could be regarded as having effectively withdrawn the limited international personality she had entrusted to Rhodesia, South Africa's continued relations with Rhodesia could be regarded as being based on a fresh grant of some form of recognition of Rhodesia which was independent of ultimate British responsibility.

It would appear that the first of the two interpretations is the more likely since it is evident that South Africa refused to recognize British claims of enhanced sovereignty over her

---

[64] *Die Burger*, 3 Mar. 1970.

[65] *The Times* (London), 12 Nov. 1965, 8. Subsequently Portugal adopted a policy of non-recoꞡ ᵗion when the Smith regime declared Rhodesia a 'Republic'. The Portuguese Prim. Minister pointed out that Portugal recognized the legal sovereignty of the Briti h Crown. See *The Times* (London), 20 Apr. 1970.

[66] *Keesing*, 21245.

rebel colony. South Africa thus recognized the status quo ante UDI. This was confirmed by Dr Verwoerd's refusal to grant Rhodesia *de facto* recognition as that would have raised the measure of international personality of Rhodesia in her relations with South Africa above that which she enjoyed prior to UDI. Those states which recognized increased British sovereignty over Rhodesia could be regarded as having either withdrawn or suspended the limited recognition they had previously accorded Rhodesia prior to UDI.

It remains now to examine Rhodesia's practical relations with members of the international community to determine whether or not any state could be deemed to have impliedly recognized Rhodesian independence. It should be remembered that recognition may not be implied lightly. It will usually be implied in cases where a state may lay itself open to the inference of having recognized another state or government.[67] What conduct leads to such a conclusion is open to question, but rules of thumb have developed in respect of certain conduct from which, when it prevails between two states, recognition will or will not be implied. A number of these forms of conduct will now be considered.

1. *Conducting Negotiations*

As a general rule, initiating or conducting negotiations with an unrecognized entity does not necessarily imply recognition.[68] The exception to this rule is when intention to recognize such an entity is manifested by the recognizing state. Thus, the negotiations that took place between the United Kingdom and the Smith regime did not imply that the United Kingdom had recognized the rebel regime. In spite of this fact, Britain was at first reluctant to admit that she was engaged in negotiations with the rebels.[69] Furthermore, British statements of non-recognition also operated against any possible implied recognition of UDI. In any case implied recognition would have been inconsistent with the British claims over Rhodesia.

---

[67] Starke, 147.   [68] Schwarzenberger, *International Law*, 71.
[69] See Chapter I above.

2. *Maintenance of Trade Relations*

We have seen that when UDI was proclaimed the Security
Council imposed a trade embargo against the Smith regime.
In spite of the fact that the generality of the members of the
United Nations, and the international community generally,
proclaimed their support for that trade embargo, South Africa
and Portugal maintained trade relations with Salisbury.[70]
For example, on 28 February 1966, the South African Prime
Minister stated that the policy of his Government on the
Rhodesian independence crisis was to maintain what he
termed normal trade relations with Rhodesia.[71] These trade
relations continued until the solution of the Rhodesian independence dispute, and have by and large been maintained
by the newly independent Government of Zimbabwe, which
is now scaling them down. A point worth noting in the first
instance is that trade between two countries is primarily
carried on by private individuals living in those countries.
Conversely, recognition of one country by another is a
government to government action. Consequently, actions of
private individuals by way of, for example, maintaining trade
relations with other private individuals in a country seeking
recognition cannot be interpreted as implying international
recognition by the government·of those individuals. In any
case, even where trade is carried out between the two governments of such states, the rule of thumb is that such relations
do not constitute implied recognition.[72] Consequently, the
trade relations which South Africa maintained with Rhodesia
throughout the Rhodesian independence crisis could not by
themselves be regarded as constituting implied recognition.
This argument is strengthened by the statements of non-
recognition made by the government of that country to the
effect that South Africa's international relations with Rhodesia
did not exist beyond those which existed before UDI. These
related to limited recognition of Rhodesia's international
personality established under the *inter se* doctrine of the
Commonwealth of Nations when South Africa was still a
member of that family of Nations and which were maintained

---

[70] *The Times* (London), 21 Dec. 1965, 4.   [71] Ibid.
[72] Bot, *Non-recognition and Treaty Relations* (Leiden, 1968), 31.

even when South Africa was forced out of the membership of the Commonwealth.[73]

3. *Maintenance of Consular Relations*

According to Starke, an issuance of a consular exequatur by the admitting state for a consul of an unrecognized state may conclusively imply international recognition.[74] This, however, does not include the mere maintenance of a consular mission without formal relations with the central 'authorities'. This is so because a 'consul' while an agent of the commissioning state, is not a diplomat and hence has no diplomatic status.[75] It would appear that although the maintenance of a consular mission does not import *de jure* recognition, it could imply some form of limited recognition. This could explain the mass withdrawal of consular relations by foreign countries when the Smith regime declared Rhodesia a republic, an act which effectively severed Rhodesia's connection with Britain. One could imagine that this is the argument which Britain might have used in persuading the United States to change its position after having earlier declared that its consulate would remain open in Rhodesia without in any way implying any form of recognition of Rhodesia's independence or her declared republican status.

An examination of the American practice and that of Britain in regard to this issue may be instructive. As regards the American practice, it would appear that the United States does not regard the maintenance of consular missions as such in an unrecognized country as implied *de jure* recognition.[76] If, however, a consular mission is established in an unrecognized country with the authority of the ruler in that country, it would appear that the United States regards this as implying *de facto* recognition of that foreign state and government.[77] If an unrecognized government issues exequaturs which are accepted unconditionally, such acceptance, in the American view, will 'have the effect of recognition of that Government'.[78] However, this is rebuttable by contrary intention.

[73] Weekly Hansard, vol. 717, No. 667, 23–9 July 1965, col. 469.
[74] Starke, 147.   [75] O'Connell, 918.
[76] Hackworth, *Digest of International Law*, vol. iv (Washington, 1940), 684.
[77] Ibid.   [78] Ibid., 688.

This is what the United States told Chile in 1924 when it maintained that the United States would be pleased to have her officers accept the exequaturs provided it were understood that such acceptance did not involve recognition of the existing regime. The Chilean authorities expressed their willingness that the exequaturs should be issued with that understanding.[79]

The United Kingdom seems to follow a different practice. For example, during a debate on the admission of immigrants to Hong Kong, the British Under-Secretary of State for Commonwealth Relations and Colonies stated in relation to British consulates in Formosa (Taiwan):

The existence of a British consulate in Formosa does not mean that we have diplomatic relations. As my honourable friend knows, consuls are not diplomatic representatives: their duty is simply to look after British interests . . .[80].

On another occasion the British Foreign Secretary was asked, in regard to British consular missions in Vietnam, whether he would apply for an exequatur for the British Consul-General in Hanoi. He replied that he would not. The Prime Minister added:

Her Majesty's Government do not recognize *de jure* or *de facto* the Democratic Republic of Vietnam. Our Consul-General therefore exercises purely consular functions although there have been occasions . . . when [he] has been able to transmit messages, and indeed to get a reply . . .[81].

It would appear therefore that the United Kingdom holds the view that the maintenance of consular missions implies neither *de jure* nor *de facto* recognition even if there is some measure of official contact between the authorities of the two countries. This position is different from that of the United States as we have already seen. Both Governments, however, agree that the maintenance of consulates *per se* does not imply recognition of any kind.

But if this is the case, how can one explain the mass withdrawal of consulates from Rhodesia in 1970 when the Smith

---

[79] Ibid.
[80] E. Lauterpacht (ed.), (1964) 1, *British Practice in International Law*, 25.
[81] (1965) 2, ibid. 124–5.

regime declared that country a republic? It will be remembered that the United States had initially intended to keep its consulate in Salisbury open but changed her mind when Britain put pressure on her to withdraw her consular offices.[82] This question should be viewed against the background of two distinct considerations. The first, which was probably paramount, was that of the United Nations enforcement action. The declaration of a republic by the Smith regime demonstrated that instead of the United Nations enforcement measures forcing the rebel regime to adopt a more conciliatory position in its relations with Britain, the Smith regime was moving even further from Britain and completely severing whatever ties remained between the two parties. For that reason, it was obvious that more pressure was needed to demonstrate the aversion of the international community to the attitude of the Smith regime. That is why most governments stated that their reason for closing their consulates was the complete break with Britain that the Smith regime had made. These closures could be seen therefore as political acts to demonstrate the rejection of the action of the Smith regime. These actions were given a legal seal by Resolution 277 (1970) adopted on 18 March 1970.[83]

The second consideration is a legal one, already adverted to above. This is that, as long as Britain itself maintained a consular office in Salisbury and did not object to other states doing the same, the question of implied recognition of the Smith regime did not arise since the exequaturs, on the basis of which the consular relations in Rhodesia were established, were issued on the authority of the British Government. As soon as Britain withdrew her own consular offices and requested other nations to do the same, failure on the part of a state to close its consular office could be regarded as inconsistent with the British claims in Rhodesia and, in turn, inconsistent with recognition which the state concerned had accorded to the British claims of overall sovereignty over Rhodesia.

4. *Maintenance of Official Relations*

Devine urges that an act from which recognition may be

---

[82] *Keesing*, 24055.   [83] See para. 9(a).

implied should be formal and official.[84] He also indicates, however, that it is possible to have intensive and even official relations which may not imply recognition. Such official relations may include:

giving relief to victims of disaster; informal calls on officials; informal diplomatic approaches; informal communications; conduct of routine matters; postal agreements; maintaining an agency; protesting because of an outrage, and dealing with postal orders issued by the unrecognized entity.[85]

In view of the expressed policies of non-recognition of the various members of the international community in relation to Rhodesia, and as members of the United Nations were under an obligation not to recognize the declared Rhodesian independence, it would need very clear evidence to imply recognition of that country.

The countries which had some official relations with Rhodesia were South Africa and Portugal. The Portuguese official relations with Rhodesia at diplomatic representation level were terminated on 17 March 1975 following the Portuguese Revolution of 1974.[86] South Africa continued not only to maintain but, in some cases, also to expand her official contacts with the Smith regime. For example, South Africa had the practice of endorsing subpoenas issued in Rhodesia for service in South Africa.[87] It usually surrendered escaping criminals to Rhodesia.[88] It also recognized passports issued by the Smith regime as valid documents.[89] Officials of South Africa, including that country's Prime Minister, visited Rhodesia, and Rhodesian officials including Mr Smith himself also visited South Africa to discuss issues of mutual interest.

Some of these acts, especially the recognition of Rhodesian passports, could under normal circumstances amount to implied recognition of the issuing country. In this particular case, however, it would appear that the presumption of recognition was rebutted by the expressed contrary intention

[84] Devine, (1974) *Acta Juridica*, 114.
[85] Ibid.; *Whiteman's Digest*, vol. II. 526, 529, 544.
[86] *Keesing*, 27087. This was the only diplomatic mission Smith had in Europe.
[87] See *S.v. Charalambous* (1970) SA 599 (T); Devine, (1974) *Acta Juridica*, 115.
[88] See *S.v. Eliasov* (1967), (2) SA 423 (T); Devine, (1974) *Acta Juridica* 115.
[89] Devine, (1974) *Acta Juridica*, 115.

of South Africa as already seen. This is not the first time a state has refused to grant full recognition to an entity while recognizing passports issued by that entity. For example, although the United States did not recognize the Order of Malta, it did accept passports issued by the latter as valid travel documents in terms of United States municipal law.[90]

5. *Maintenance of Diplomatic Relations*

Among the official relations maintained by South Africa and Portugal with Rhodesia was diplomatic representation.[91] The South African diplomatic mission was under the direction of an accredited diplomatic representative.[92] Rhodesia had a reciprocal mission in South Africa. The general rule of international law is that the maintenance of accredited diplomatic representation does imply recognition. However, these general rules are subject to the existence of contrary intention, and in this particular case it would appear that South Africa never intended to recognize Rhodesian independence. Firstly, these diplomatic relations were established at the time South Africa and Rhodesia were in the Commonwealth of Nations and were continued when South Africa left the Commonwealth in 1961.[93] The conclusion, therefore, seems to be that South Africa granted Rhodesia no more international recognition than she had done before UDI. It seems that all relations which existed between South Africa and Rhodesia could be explained on those terms. These included the bilateral agreements under which South African military police operated in Rhodesia during the liberation war.[94] In any case, the Smith regime itself never claimed to have been formally recognized by South Africa.

It has also been argued that the imposition of economic enforcement measures against the Smith regime by the United Nations might amount to a recognition of Rhodesia as a sovereign state.[95] This assertion is based on a misconception that the United Nations can take enforcement action only

[90] Turack, 'Passports Issued by Some non-State Entities', (1968–9) 43, *BYBIL*, 209.   [91] Devine, (1974) *Acta Juridica*, 119.

[92] *Die Burger*, 11 Mar. 1970.

[93] *Weekly Hansard*, vol. 717, No. 667, 1965, col. 469.

[94] Devine, (1974) *Acta Juridica*, 120; (1969) 86, *SALJ*, 112 at 113–14.

[95] Higgins, 'International Law, Rhodesia, and the United Nations', (1967) 23, *World Today*, 105.

against sovereign states. There is, on the contrary, no legal basis for this claim. Article 39 of the Charter makes it clear that enforcement action may be imposed to deal with a threat to the peace, breach of the peace, or acts of aggression against states or other lesser entities such as Rhodesia.

From 1970 the principle of non-recognition of Rhodesia was made mandatory on all United Nations members by Resolution 277 (1970) of the Security Council.[96] In view of this resolution it is even less likely that recognition could have been implied in the absence of compelling reasons, and no such compelling reasons existed.

Before UDI Rhodesia appointed representatives to the diplomatic staffs of British Embassies in foreign countries which were not members of the Commonwealth. When UDI was proclaimed the attitude of those representatives towards UDI was sought. Where the representatives disassociated themselves from UDI, they were sometimes retained in their posts as members of the British Embassy staff. Where they failed to disassociate themselves from UDI, they lost their diplomatic status. The former treatment befell the Rhodesian representative in Greece, and the latter befell Mr Henry Hooper, Rhodesian representative in Washington.[97] In the United Kingdom itself, the Rhodesian High Commissioner in London, Brigadier Andrew Skeen, was informed on 11 November 1965 by the Commonwealth Relations Secretary that in the absence of any statement from him declaring his opposition to UDI, he was requested to leave the country. Brigadier Skeen accordingly left the following day and the Rhodesia High Commission was closed down.[98]

From the foregoing it would appear that Rhodesia was never recognized as a state. This was a shattering blow to the Smith regime, which had hoped to be accorded recognition by at least its closest friends, Portugal and South Africa, at the time UDI was proclaimed. Instead of being recognized the regime found itself having to deal with the economic embargo sponsored by the United Nations.

---

[96] Para. 2 stated that the Security Council 'Decides that Member States shall refrain from recognizing this illegal regime or rendering any assistance to it.'
[97] *The Times* (London), 1 Mar. 1966, 11.   [98] *Keesing*, 21127.

V

Non-Military Enforcement Measures

WHEN UDI was proclaimed in 1965, the British Government had at least two choices open to it. It could apply whatever measures were at its disposal to crush the rebellion; alternatively, it could surrender the problem to international action, especially to the United Nations which had already shown considerable interest in the matter. The British Government chose to follow a combination of the two alternatives but to exclude the use of force. It believed that Rhodesia was economically vulnerable and that an imposition to an economic embargo would quickly bring about a political change in the territory which would enable Britain to regain full control of the country.[1] Thus Mr Wilson's Government took the initiative to impose a number of economic measures on the rebel administration. Explaining these measures to the United Nations Security Council, the British Foreign Secretary, Mr Stewart, stated that 'the Prime Minister and other ministers of Southern Rhodesia' had been dismissed from office, and that his Government had prohibited all exports of arms to Rhodesia. He also stated that his Government had imposed exchange control restrictions and prohibited exports of United Kingdom capital to Rhodesia and denied Rhodesia access to the London capital market. It denied Rhodesia all advantages in trade, through Commonwealth preference, through export credits which it would have enjoyed if UDI had not been proclaimed. He added that the Government proposed to ban the importation into the United Kingdom of Rhodesian tobacco and sugar.[2]

In theory these measures could have had a considerable impact on the economy of Rhodesia because her domestic exports concentrated on one product, tobacco, which accounted for 33 per cent of the country's income and Britain, being one of Rhodesia's largest trading partners, imported a

---

[1] H. Strack, *Sanctions: The Case of Rhodesia* (Syracuse), 15–16.
[2] *UNSCOR*, 1257th mtg., paras. 25–30.

large slice of this. The success of this economic strangulation of course depended to a large extent on the participation in it by the other countries. African members of the United Nations, however, did not believe that economic measures by themselves were capable of bringing down the rebel administration. Their scepticism was at least supported by intellectual opinion regarding the efficacy of economic sanctions to induce the targets or receivers to comply with the wishes of the senders. The position is summarized by Strack in these words:

[First], aside from purely punitive or symbolic considerations, sanctions have not been useful devices to induce, persuade, or compel the target to comply; second, sanctions may be dysfunctional by serving to make the target less rather than more compliant; and third, while some of the effects of sanctions may be very beneficial and desirable for the target, enhancing its internal political and economic situation in ways not foreseen by the senders.[3]

All these weaknesses manifested themselves in the Rhodesia economic embargo. Although African nations insisted that the economic embargo should be reinforced by military measures, the British Government was not persuaded that military force was necessary. Inevitably, the debates that were to follow in the Security Council were often very heated. However, the members were anxious to be seen to be capable of taking quick action on the pressing problem before them. Consequently, in spite of the differences between the Afro-Asian nations on the one hand and the British Government on the other, the Security Council was able on 12 November 1965 to pass Resolution 216 (1965), by which it condemned UDI and called upon all states not to recognize the illegal administration in Rhodesia and to refrain from rendering any assistance to it.

This resolution could be regarded as having introduced the first non-military enforcement measures, namely non-recognition. Although the resolution used the word 'decide' in both paragraphs, and 'decisions' of the Security Council are binding on the members of the United Nations by virtue of Article 25 of the Charter, it is doubtful whether this resolution

---

[3] Strack, 13.

was intended to be binding. It was probably only a recommendation. For example, there is no evidence that it was
based on Chapter VII of the Charter which is the major basis
of mandatory enforcement measures. It is possible that the
resolution was based on the doctrine of international concern
which is discussed in Chapter II above. Mr Stewart, the British
Foreign Secretary, for example, merely described the
Rhodesian rebellion as 'a matter of world concern' rather
than as a threat to the peace within Chapter VII of the
Charter. Alternatively the resolution could have been based
on Article 24 of the Charter which gives the Security Council
general powers in respect of the maintenance of international
peace and security. (These powers are discussed in detail in
Chapter VIII below.) The same is probably true of Resolution
217 (1965) which was passed after an exhaustive debate. The
original draft resolution introduced by the United Kingdom
had a preambular paragraph which stated that the Security
Council determined that the continuance of the rebellion in
Rhodesia was likely to endanger the maintenance of international peace and security.[4] This paragraph was heavily
criticized for its similarity with Article 33 in Chapter VI
of the Charter, which deals with disputes between states,
since Rhodesia was not a state and the situation there was
not a 'dispute' within the meaning of that Chapter.[5]

One suspects that Britain, indeed, intended to bring the
Rhodesian situation within the provisions of Chapter VI
because of her conception of how the Rhodesian problem
could be solved. She believed that the solution to the rebellion
was best sought through negotiations between the British
Government and the Smith regime. For that reason, she saw
the Security Council's action as a means necessary to create
an atmosphere in which meaningful negotiations between the
British Government and the Smith regime could take place.
This explains why, as will be seen later, Britain insisted on
the enforcement measures being introduced on a piecemeal
fashion,[6] while the British Government engaged in a series of
negotiations with the rebels throughout the United Nations
action. These negotiations began with the 'Tiger Talks' in

---

[4] *UNSCOR*, 1259th mtg. para 31; S/6928.   [5] Ibid.
[6] See Chapter XII below.

1966 when Mr Harold Wilson, the British Prime Minister, and Mr Ian Smith, the rebel leader, met on board HMS *Tiger* in the Mediterranean.[7] These talks were followed twenty-two months later by further talks between the two sides on board HMS *Fearless*.[8] In between these sea-borne talks there were also some protracted secret negotiations between the two parties. When the Conservative Party took over power in Britain in 1970, it also pursued the same line of reasoning and came close to a settlement in 1971.[9]

The African members of the Security Council, however, saw the Rhodesian problem differently. They believed that the Smith regime should be forced into submission since by seizing power illegally it had forfeited its right as a party whose views should be taken into account in the solution of the problem. For this reason they condemned the British Government for its willingness to negotiate with the rebels, and called for stronger measures against the rebel regime. They argued that the appropriate chapter for dealing with the rebellion was Chapter VII. Owing to Britain's adamant refusal to allow the invocation of that chapter of the UN Charter, Mr Reyes of Uruguay introduced a compromise resolution which he described as not being based on either Chapter VI or Chapter VII of the Charter. That draft resolution was thus accepted by both sides, and was adopted as Resolution 217 (1965).

The resolution determined both that the situation resulting from the proclamation of UDI was extremely grave and requested Britain to put an end to it, and that its continuance would in time constitute a threat to international peace and security. It further reaffirmed Resolution 216 (1965) and General Assembly Resolution 1514 (XV). It also called on all states not to recognize the illegal regime or to entertain any diplomatic or other relations with it. It called for the revocation of the 1961 Constitution of Rhodesia and the granting of the right of self-determination to the people of Rhodesia. All states were urged to refrain from any action which would assist and encourage the illegal regime, in particular to desist from providing it with arms, equipment, and military material,

---

[7] See Chapter I above.   [8] Ibid.   [9] Ibid.

and to break all economic relations, including an imposition of an embargo on oil and petroleum products. It called upon the Organization of African Unity to assist in the implementation of the measures imposed by the resolution.

Like other compromise solutions this resolution was neither satisfactory to the British Government nor to the Afro-Asian states. However, whatever its weaknesses, and they were many, this resolution laid a solid foundation for the policy of international non-recognition. Although formal recognition is of doubtful practical significance, it is of vital importance where a regime has been established by revolutionary means as was the Smith regime. There is no doubt that Mr Smith attached considerable importance to international recognition, as that would have had both practical and symbolic benefits. Be that as it may, however, the biggest preoccupation of the rebel administration at the time was the economic embargo that had been imposed by the resolution. Of the measures introduced the most important was the oil embargo. If properly enforced, it could have brought down the Smith regime within a relatively short time. Unfortunately the multinational oil companies of the Western world continued to supply the rebels with oil by covert means. This was made easier by the fact that the resolution which imposed the oil embargo was not mandatory, and was not even based on Chapter VII of the Charter, as already indicated. This was made clear by the British Prime Minister in the House of Commons.[10]

It is difficult to say precisely which provision of the Charter formed the legal basis of this resolution. The British Prime Minister merely said, in answer to a question, that it fell between Chapter VI and Chapter VII. This is not a very helpful statement. It is possible that this resolution was based on the doctrine of international concern, or more likely, the general powers of the Security Council found in Article 24, which are discussed below.[11] Alternatively the resolution could be based on some sort of extension from Chapter VII. This could be implied power, in addition to express power under Article 39, to deal with situations which are potential threats to the maintenance of international peace and security.

[10] *Weekly Hansard*, No. 673, vol. 730/1, col. 250-1.
[11] Chapter VIII.

Such power may be commensurate with the powers of the Secretary-General under Article 99 by which he may bring to the attention of the Security Council any matter which in his opinion may threaten the maintenance of international peace and security.

It will be noticed that these powers are broader than those of the Council under Article 39 in that the Secretary-General may raise matters which not only threaten but also those which 'may threaten' the peace.[12] If the Secretary-General has power to raise such issues before the Council, it seems to follow that the Council equally has power to deal with those matters, although its powers are probably restricted only to making recommendations. Consequently, Resolution 217 (1965), like Resolution 216 (1965) before it, was not binding on the member states of the United Nations. If the Council had intended to bind the members, it would have acted under Chapter VII as demanded by the African states, or would have specifically invoked Article 25 of the Charter. The United States representative was probably expressing a consensus when he referred to the resolution merely as 'an important statement by the Council of its unanimous desire to condemn this rebellion in . . . Rhodesia . . .'. No member of the Security Council ever thought the resolution binding. Virtually all of them believed that further and stronger action was necessary, especially the imposition of a mandatory oil embargo under Chapter VII.

The need for this soon became obvious when reports were received of two Greek-registered tankers near the Mozambique territorial waters; one, the *Joanna V*, had already arrived at the Mozambican coast while the second, the *Manuela*, was approaching the same destination. Both vessels were believed to be carrying large quantities of oil destined for Rhodesia. This clearly demonstrated that the recommended oil embargo was being ignored. At the request of the British Government the Security Council passed Resolution 221 (1966) to deal with the new situation. The provisions of this resolution will be discussed fully in Chapter VI below.

Seven months after the adoption of Resolution 221 (1966),

[12] Schwebel, 'The Origins and Development of Article 99 of the Charter', (1951) 27, *BYBIL*, 371 at 377.

it became clear that further stronger action was still required as the Smith regime showed no signs of weakening. On 16 December 1966 the British Government called for another meeting of the Security Council to consider those measures. They were introduced by Resolution 232 (1966). They included the banning of the export of petroleum, arms, ammunition and military equipment, vehicles, and aircraft to Rhodesia, and the prohibition of importation by members of tobacco, sugar, meat and meat products, asbestos, copper, chrome ore, hides, and skins from Rhodesia. From the words of the resolution it was clear that these measures were mandatory on the member states of the United Nations.

For instance, the Council explicitly invoked Articles 39 and 41 of the Charter. In paragraph 2 of the resolution it stated that it decided that all states members of the United Nations 'shall' apply the measures stipulated therein. 'Decisions' of the Security Council are binding on the members. Anyway, to make clear the mandatory nature of the resolution the Security Council reminded member states that failure or refusal by any of them to implement the 'present resolution shall constitute a violation of Article 25 of the United Nations Charter' which obliges the members 'to carry out the decisions of the Security Council in accordance with the Charter'. Notwithstanding its obligatory nature, this resolution was largely ignored by Rhodesia's traditional trade partners. This became apparent when on 13 June 1968 the Secretary-General of the United Nations issued his progress report on the implementation of the resolution. This report showed that imports from Rhodesia in 1967 amounted to $40 million as against $330 million in 1965. About 79 per cent of this went to West Germany, Switzerland, Portugal, the Netherlands, Belgium, Luxembourg, France, and Japan.[13]

The exports of the importing countries to Rhodesia amounted to $54 million as against $187 million in 1965. About 68 per cent of this came from Japan, West Germany, the Netherlands, France, the United States, the United Kingdom, Belgium-Luxembourg, Portugal, Austria, Italy, and Australia.[14] None of the reporting countries provided data

---

[13] (1968) *YBUN*, 127.   [14] Ibid. 131.

involving the supply of petroleum products to Rhodesia, and the Middle-East suppliers of petroleum had not reported their trade data to the Secretary-General. The African members of the United Nations expressed general dissatisfaction with the implementation of Resolution 232 (1966) and called for the introduction of a comprehensive trade embargo against the rebels. This call increased when in March 1968, the Smith regime defied international public opinion and the intervention of the British Queen and executed three African political prisoners. Five powers, Algeria, Ethiopia, India, Pakistan, and Senegal, introduced a draft resolution calling for comprehensive economic measures. Britain, who feared losing the initiative on Rhodesia, quickly introduced a counter draft resolution diluting that already tabled. The British argument was that the Security Council must not unduly raise hopes of the Rhodesian people which it had no power to satisfy, but that it should offer them effective action within the Council's clear capacity. It could do this, the argument went, by limiting its enforcement measures to those in which there was a consensus among the members. But if the Afro-Asian nations insisted on measures which were totally unacceptable to the United Kingdom there would be a deadlock and an opportunity to solve the problem would be lost.

This British argument never failed although some members saw it more or less as blackmail. Britain was saying in essence that if these states insisted on unacceptable measures she would veto their draft resolution and no action could be taken by the Security Council. It was a matter of half a loaf being better than no bread at all. This use or threat of use of veto power was made by Britain to good effect throughout the enforcement action. This suggested that African nations needed action in Rhodesia more than did Britain. While this was probably true, one should not lose sight of the fact that Britain had failed to solve the Rhodesian problem single-handed and was thus seeking international co-operation. It could be argued, therefore, that Britain was as keen as were the African nations to find a solution to the problem. The difference there was related to the nature of the solution each side had in mind. While the British Government sought the end of the Rhodesian rebellion, the African nations sought the end of the regime and white supremacy and the introduction of majority rule. Consequently they were not interested in the soft approach adopted by Britain.

In spite of this, however, the African nations always found themselves accepting half-measures which were acceptable to Britain. In that same spirit they supported the adoption of Resolution 253 (1968) imposing comprehensive mandatory economic measures. This resolution was not only mandatory, but its scope was wider than anything that had been passed by the Security Council on the question of Rhodesia. It covered the widest spectrum of Rhodesia's economic activity. As it turned out, it proved difficult to widen the economic measures any further after this resolution. As Zacklin correctly recognized, this resolution marked a watershed 'political consensus on Rhodesia'.[15] It was not approached until the Rhodesian settlement was reached when the United Nations agreed to terminate the enforcement action. It was even regarded, with some justification, as 'the effective ceiling of collective measures' on Rhodesia.[16] The resolution determined that the Rhodesian situation was a threat to the peace, and invoked the mandatory provisions of the Charter. By this resolution the Security Council 'decided' that member states shall prevent imports from or exports to Rhodesia of all products and commodities regardless of prior contracts or licences. Specially mentioned items included the transfer of all funds except for specified purposes including those for medical, educational, and informational purposes, and funds sent strictly for humanitarian reasons. Member states were enjoined from permitting shipment by whatever conveyance of Rhodesian exports or imports or from allowing air traffic to or from Rhodesia or flights that would connect with Rhodesian aircraft. Anyone carrying a Rhodesian passport or ordinarily residing in Rhodesia or anyone who had furthered or was likely to further the unlawful actions of the illegal regime was to be denied entry into any member state. The resolution further recommended a number of additional measures including the cutting of consular and trade representation in Rhodesia.

[15] Zacklin, *United Nations and Rhodesia: a Study in International Law* (Praeger, 1974), 51–2. [16] Ibid.

The resolution also covered two important areas in the United Nations action against the rebels. Firstly, it recognized the predicament of states like Zambia which depended on trade routes which passed through Rhodesia. Consequently, paragraph 15 of the resolution requested member states of the United Nations, specialized agencies of the Organization, and other international organizations in the United Nations system to extend assistance to Zambia as a matter of priority with a view to helping it solve such special economic problems as it might be confronted with arising from the carrying-out of the decisions of the Security Council. Secondly, the resolution recognized the legitimacy of the liberation struggle of the Zimbabwean people against the oppressive system in Rhodesia.

Two years after the adoption of this resolution the Rhodesian problem had still not gone away. It was necessary, therefore, to be seen to be doing something about it. The difficulty was, however, that having previously passed so comprehensive a resolution as Resolution 253 (1968), the Security Council could hardly find anything concrete to do in order to expand the enforcement action. All that could be done, was merely to undertake a topping-up ˙operation coupled with the re-iteration or reaffirmation of the already existing measures and the re-exhortation of members to observe them. On 18 March 1970, the Security Council passed Resolution 277 (1970) which had precisely that effect. This was a very lengthy resolution of twenty-four paragraphs which added very few measures. Paragraph 2 made non-recognition of the Smith regime mandatory.[17] Paragraph 9 also decided that member states must sever all diplomatic, consular, trade, military, and other relations they might have with the illegal regime. Members were also ordered to terminate any representation they might have maintained with the rebels, and to interrupt any existing means of transportation to or from Rhodesia.

Prior to the adoption of this resolution the United Kingdom had resisted all attempts to condemning South Africa by name for violating the United Nations enforcement action. This resolution, however, did condemn South Africa and

---

[17] This was the most significant part of this resolution.

Portugal for their non-co-operative stand on Rhodesia. Other paragraphs of the resolution referred to a variety of matters connected with the implementation of the measures already in force. The other paragraph worth a special mention is paragraph 11 by which the Security Council requested member states to take all possible further action under Article 41 of the Charter to deal with the situation in Rhodesia, not excluding any of the measures provided in that Article. It is interesting to note that this paragraph does not bind member states. Had it attempted to bind them it is certain that the United Kingdom would have insisted that it be excluded because member states would have had to be bound to apply Article 41 in its entirety, a thing which Britain had steadfastly resisted. Britain was not prepared to interrupt the 'postal, telegraphic, radio, and other means of communication' as provided for in Article 41. Britain had always argued that as the administering authority in Rhodesia, it had to keep open the channels of communication with the rebel colony. This was obviously in keeping with the British policy of trying to get a negotiated settlement with the Smith regime.

As indicated above, hardly any of the resolutions which were passed after the adoption of Resolution 253 (1968) added anything new. This was true of Resolution 314 (1972) passed on 28 February 1972, which merely reaffirmed Resolution 253 (1968), and by implication criticized the United States for resuming the importation of Rhodesian chrome. Similar resolutions were 318 (1972) and 333 (1973). In pursuance of a special report of 15 December 1975 from the 'Sanctions Committee', the Security Council adopted Resolution 388 (1976) further widening the enforcement measures to include insurance, trade names, and franchises. It 'decided', *inter alia*, that all member states should take appropriate measures to ensure that their nationals and persons in their territories did not insure any imports from or exports to Rhodesia, in contravention of Resolution 253 (1968). The resolution also prohibited such persons from granting to any commercial, industrial, or public utility undertaking in Rhodesia, the right to use any trade name, or from entering into any franchising agreement involving the use of any trade name, trade mark, or registered design in connection with the sale or distribution of any products, commodities, or services of such an undertaking.

During the debate in the Security Council this draft resolution was regarded as being of considerable significance because it represented the first time a draft resolution was sponsored by all the fifteen members of the Security Council. This was seen as a reflection of unanimous concern of the entire membership, over the apparent ineffectiveness of the measures already taken. This unanimity was, however, illusory in that it did not mean that the new resolution would be better respected by the members than the previous one. It is submitted that the ineffectiveness of the United Nations action in Rhodesia had less to do with the number of items included in or excluded from the Security Council resolutions than the application of what was included. The important thing, it would appear, was to select the most vital economic targets and enforce them effectively, and these could have brought the desired political results in Rhodesia speedily. For instance, a properly observed oil embargo by itself could have had better results than a loosely observed wide spectrum of economic measures.

Without getting involved with arguments of what made the enforcement action ineffective, it should be stated that this ineffectiveness was, by and large, due to the non-observance of the selected economic measures. For instance, South Africa and Portugal overtly declared at the outset that they were not prepared to observe the decisions of the Security Council, and they never observed them. These two countries were, however, not the only culprits. Economic ties were maintained by a large number of states even after the enforcement measures were made mandatory. In most cases the states which were shown to be contravening the enforcement action argued that these violations were committed by private individuals or companies and that their governments were doing their utmost to stop these illegal actions without success. Indeed, a number of states reported to the Security Council that certain individuals and firms had been prosecuted in their municipal courts for violating the Untied Nations resolutions.[18]

[18] *UN Monthly Chronicle*, Jan. 1974, 21.

These prosecutions were in accordance with the general principle of responsibility of states to take reasonable steps to ensure that their inhabitants act in accordance with the states' international obligations. However, in the Rhodesian case, it would appear that the prosecutions that did take place were those of unlucky individuals and firms, while many other companies, especially multinational oil companies of the Western powers, acted in similar fashion with impunity. It could be argued, therefore, that what was crucial for the success of the United Nation enforcement action was not who was prosecuted but how many violations went unpunished.

In any case, a state which fails to prevent its nationals from ignoring international rules is itself guilty of breach of those rules. The situation is worse where a state by its own laws permits a violation of international law. This is what happened in the United States in 1971 when that country promulgated the Arms Procurement Appropriations Authorization Act on 3 November. Senator Byrd initiated an amendment to this law which effectively barred the President of the United States from prohibiting the import of Rhodesian chrome and other strategic materials into the United States. This amendment thus permitted United States firms to violate Security Council decisions which were binding on the United States.[19]

As a result of this amendement, figures released in Washington in February 1973 showed that in 1972 the United States imported nearly three times as much chrome from Rhodesia as it did in 1965.[20] While the firms which ordered this chrome from Rhodesia did nothing illegal by United States law, the United States was clearly in violation of its obligations under international law and could not justify its actions by relying on its own domestic law.[21] Whatever reasons the United States had for this conduct that country remained guilty under international law. These violations increased African nations' demand for use of force against the Smith regime. Britain, however, remained unmoved in her opposition to

---

[19] See *Head Money* (112 US.580 (1884) US) *Supreme Court*, cited in Harris, *Cases and Materials on International Law* (London, 1973), 80.

[20] Zacklin, 82-3.

[21] See *Free Zones* case (1932), PCIJ Ser. A/B, case No. 46.

that course of action. The position taken by the United States on this matter is revealing. It shows that when there are strong vested interests, states are prepared to breach international law.[22] Where economic 'sanctions' are concerned, there are always vested interests between the target state and some states. This is why so many commentators have little faith in this system of international behaviour control. The problem is whether there are any alternative coercive methods short of military force. The question of the future of United Nations enforcement action is discussed in the last chapter of this book. Suffice it to say here that the United Nations action against the Smith regime suffered from many weaknesses and it is difficult to regard it as a success story of the non-military enforcement action of the United Nations. This accounts to a large extent for the enormous number of resolutions which had to be passed by the Security Council over the fourteen years of the Rhodesian rebellion.

[22] Zacklin, 82–3.

VI

Resolution 221 (1966)
and the Freedom of the High Seas:
Incidents relating to
Joanna V and *Manuela* at Beira

A. *Events Leading to the Adoption of*
Resolution 221 (1966)

AMONG the measures imposed by Security Council Resolution 217 (1965) was the oil embargo, which was rightly regarded by all the member states of the United Nations as the crucial single measure in determining how long the Rhodesian rebellion would hold out. Mr Corner, New Zealand's Permanent Representative to the United Nations, for instance, referred to oil as 'figuratively and literally, the lubricant of a modern economy . . .'.[1] The oil embargo was also a subject for intensive and sometimes heated debate in the British House of Commons shortly after the Rhodesian situation was referred to the United Nations in November 1965.[2] Members of Parliament sought an explanation as to whether the British Government contemplated imposing an oil embargo. In answer to these demands Mr Wilson, the British Prime Minister, stated that Britain would not go in for an embargo on its own or seek the imposition of an oil embargo.[3]

In conformity with this statement, the original draft resolution presented by the representative of the United Kingdom to the Security Council did not include an embargo on oil. The other members criticized this omission,[4] and as a result the compromise resolution which was finally adopted as Resolution 217 (1965) did include a recommendation for an oil embargo. As this oil embargo was not mandatory it was largely ignored, and five months following its introduction,

---

[1] *UNSCOR*, 1277th mtg., para. 17.
[2] *Weekly Hansard*, No. 673, vol. 720/1, cols. 250–1. [3] Ibid.
[4] *UNSCOR*, 1258th mtg., para. 80.

unconfirmed reports were received by the Security Council that two oil tankers were approaching Beira with substantial quantities of oil to be pumped through a pipeline in Beira to Rhodesia.[5]

Early in March, the British Government had issued strong warnings to the British directors of the Mozambique-Rhodesian Pipeline Company, owners of the pipeline from Beira to the Feruka oil refinery in Umtali in Rhodesia, not to receive oil for Rhodesia. They had also ordered a strict surveillance of the seaward approaches to Beira by British naval and air forces.[6] Accordingly the British Government had stationed their aircraft carrier, *Ark Royal*, and two frigates, supported by two supply ships, to keep watch on the Mozambican coast. The British Government had also obtained landing and fuelling rights and other facilities in Madagascar for the Royal Air Force reconnaissance aircraft.

These moves by the British Government sparked off protests from the Portuguese Government which argued that there were increasingly frequent reports of interference with merchant shipping of various nationalities by 'the powerful British aeronaval concentration in the international waters of the Mozambique channel'.[7] In reply the British Ministry of Defence stressed that 'neither the Royal Navy nor the Royal Air Force were intercepting ships and that they were merely "keeping observation" on vessels, asking for their identity and destination . . .'.[8]

The unconfirmed reports related to a South African firm working with a Greek-owned concern who had arranged for large-scale oil supplies for Rhodesia by chartering two Greek-registered tankers, the *Arietta Venizelos* (later renamed *Joanna V*), and the *Charlton Venus* (later renamed *Manuela*), to carry oil to be secretly pumped through the Mozambique-Rhodesia pipeline at Beira.[9] When this became public knowledge, King Constantine of Greece signed a royal decree on 14 March 1966, prohibiting the transport of vessels flying the Greek flag of petroleum products to Rhodesia via ports in Mozambique or South Africa. The Greek Government then

[5] Ibid. 1340th mtg.   [6] (1965–6) *Keesing*, 2141.
[7] *The Times* (London), Apr. 1966, 12.   [8] (1965–6) *Keesing*, 21417.
[9] Ibid.

issued several warnings to George Vardinoyannis, the captain of the *Arietta Venizelos*, not to proceed to Beira, but these warnings were ignored by the captain, whose vessel was by now known as *Joanna V.*[10]

At this stage, the British Government lost patience with the *Joanna V*, which was reported to be only about 600 miles from Beira, and suggested to the Greek Government that the ship be stopped by force from reaching Beira. The Greek Government, however, rejected this suggestion arguing that 'no Government would consent to a foreign power intercepting or intimidating merchant ships under its flag'.[11] However, the Greek Under-Secretary also assured the British Government that his Government was 'using all our influence to get the tanker not to go to Beira', and that he hoped that it would not be necessary to use force. He added, nevertheless, that 'if the United Nations authorizes the British Government to intercept the vessel, we shall respect the decision. However, we cannot give our permission without a United Nations ruling.'[12]

In spite of the Greek Government's refusal to allow this, on 4 April 1966, the British frigate, *Plymouth*, intercepted the *Joanna V* on the high seas, when it was clearly heading for Beira. The master of the tanker received the captain of the frigate on board. The latter alleged that 'the British action in intercepting the tanker was taken in conformity with the United Nations resolution of 20 November (1965) and with the knowledge of the Greek Government'.[13] When questioned, the captain of the *Joanna V* admitted that his vessel was sailing to Beira 'for bunkering and provisions', before proceeding to Djibouti to discharge her cargo. The tanker was thereupon allowed to enter Beira where it anchored about a mile from the oil storage tanks which had been quickly constructed to receive oil for Rhodesia from tankers which arrived in Beira.

Thereafter, the British Government maintained that the responsibility for the ship lay with the Portuguese authorities to see that no oil was unloaded by the *Joanna V* in Beira. As may be expected, Portugal denied any responsibility and

---

[10] *The Times* (London), 4 Apr. 1966, 10.
[11] Ibid.; (1965-6) *Keesing*, 21417.   [12] Ibid.   [13] Ibid.

reiterated in a formal statement her non-participation in economic enforcement measures against the Smith regime. She also emphasized that she had no intention of interfering with the transport of merchandise for any African country through Portuguese territory.[14]

Meanwhile, the Greek Government struck the *Joanna V* off the Greek register and the master of the tanker forfeited his licence for life. The owners of the vessel were held liable to a fine of £30,000. While this was going on, the other Greek-registered tanker, the 11,022 ton *Charlton Venus*, which had now been renamed *Manuela*, was reported to be in the Mozambican Channel and heading for Beira.[15] The Greek Ministry of Merchant Marine twice sent a signal to the master of the ship drawing his attention to the severe penalties to which he would be liable if his ship sailed to Beira.

By this time the British Government was convinced that more drastic measures were required to prevent this threat of what it considered a major breach of the oil embargo in Rhodesia. However, Britain argued that whatever action was taken should be strictly within the law of nations.[16] The point at issue was how Britain could use force without breaking international law. Five months earlier, in December 1965, Mr Wilson had stated in answer to a question posed by the Leader of the Opposition, Mr Edward Heath, that Britain did not contemplate a military blockade of Beira unless 'there should be any seepage or leakage by one or two spivs'. He added that whatever Britain did would be decided internationally. However, he assured the House that Britain had no intention of imposing a naval blockade, but, if the embargo failed, it would be because it did not have sufficient international support, and this would cause the question to be raised at the United Nations.

Mr Wilson went on to say that if:

there is a decision under Chapter VII in which it is suggested that a couple of frigates be placed outside Beira to stop oil tankers going through, this is what will happen, and it will happen by international decision. We do not ourselves propose to seek such a resolution. We certainly do not propose to take individual unilateral action to blockade Beira.

[14] *The Times* (London), 7 Apr. 1966, 12.   [15] Ibid.
[16] *UNSCOR*, 1276th mtg., para. 19.

We are dealing with a hypothetical situation, but members opposite entirely misconceive the whole feeling of Africa and in the United Nations if they think that in the event of such seepage nothing would be done about it. It would happen, and it would happen under Chapter VII which would be mandatory on all countries. I do not believe that it would be a particularly notable use of force in the sense of bloodshed such as military force against Rhodesia would have been. I believe that it would be one of the simpler operations. But we do not seek it, and we shall not promote it.[17]

The incidents of the *Joanna V* and the *Manuela* were seen by Britain as representing the 'seepage and leekage' to which Mr Wilson had referred in December 1965. Mr Wilson's prediction seemed to be coming true, except that while he had expected that states other than Britain, presumably African states, would raise the issue of that seepage at the United Nations, this did not materialize. Britain therefore had no choice but to raise the matter herself in spite of the assurances Mr Wilson had given to the House of Commons to the contrary. The African nations were not likely to raise this matter of only two ships which they considered less significant than the much larger quantities of oil which reached Rhodesia on land through South Africa, which Britain did not intend to do anything about. In a way the breach of this oil embargo was viewed by African states as proving their argument that economic measures without the use of force could not work. One representative even sarcastically expressed sympathy with Portugal for being singled out for this rough treatment by Britain, while South Africa was allowed to support Rhodesia unchallenged. It was for this reason that the President of the Security Council for that month, an African,[18] was reluctant to call an emergency meeting of the Council requested by Britain to discuss the incidents of the two tankers.

The Security Council met after two days' delay, which led to criticisms of the President of the Council by Britain and the United States. Arguing his case for using force to stop those ships, Lord Caradon told the Council that the problem was not merely one of two tankers, but that if nothing was done about those vessels many others would follow. Britain

[17] *The Times* (London), 11 Apr. 1966, 5.
[18] Mr Moussa Leo Keita of Mali.

thus introduced a draft resolution spelling out the measures she wished the Council to adopt. Supporting this draft resolution, Mr Goldberg of the United States emphasized the legal implications inherent in the draft resolution:

The question of intercepting vessels on the high seas, the question of arresting and detaining them is a matter that has a long history in the field of international law. Indeed, if we refer to history, my own country once went to war with Great Britain on the question of arresting and detaining vessels on the high seas. We are asked in the Security Council, and it should be a matter of deep consideration and concern for all of us, to put our sanction upon what will be a rule of international law — that when this Council acts vessels on the high seas can be arrested and detained in the interest of the international law which we will be making here today, if we adopt the draft resolution as I hope we will do . . . [19].

Some representatives were not convinced, however, that Britain could not act against those tankers without the authorization of the United Nations. For example, the Soviet representative, Mr Morozov, argued rhetorically:

Is it not strange that the United Kingdom authorities, who have more than adequate naval contingents in the area, have suddenly found themselves unable to prevent an oil tanker from reaching the shores of Mozambique?

He maintained that Britain could use her power over the British company Lonrho which had a 62.5 per cent interest in the Companhia do Pipeline Mozambique–Rhodesia pipeline, to prevent oil being pumped through it.[20] He also referred to a press communiqué issued by the Portuguese Ministry of Foreign Affairs on 8 April 1966 which stated that the oil aboard the tanker in Beira was supplied by large international companies whose names were known and who could have been stopped at the source of the oil, if Britain had intended to do that. The communiqué had further indicated that with their naval strength in the area of Beira, the British authorities could have prevented the ship from entering Beira, but they 'deliberately refrained from doing so, for reasons best known to Her Majesty's Government and which cannot but give rise to a number of different questions'.[21]

The strongest criticism from Africa of the British decision

[19] *UNSCOR*, 1276th mtg., para. 69.   [20] Ibid. para. 119.
[21] Ibid. para. 121.

to seek United Nations authorization before taking action, came from Mr Collier of Sierra Leone, who also referred to the Portuguese communiqué quoted by the Soviet representative. He quoted the following passage from the communiqué:

In so far as it concerns the above-mentioned concrete case, the Portuguese Government wishes to observe that what is in question is a Greek ship hoisting the Greek flag, and commanded by a captain who is supposed to be of the same nationality, transporting oil which is said to belong to a South African company. Openly and without any disguise, the oil tanker crossed the entire vast area intensely patrolled by the aero-naval British forces concentrated there, which, even though they interfered with the ship by sending two officers on board, did not consider it proper or deliberately did not wish to impede its advance . . .

The powerful British aero-naval forces, even though they obviously had adequate means for the purpose, preferred not to impede the entrance of the oil tanker in question, for reasons which may be appreciated by the British Government.[22]

It should be noted that these criticisms of the United Kingdom were not backed by legal arguments. They were sustained almost entirely by reference to the Portuguese communiqué which was in turn based on the physical strength Britain could have utilized against the two vessels in question. Nevertheless, it is submitted that there are some questionable incidents in the way the British authorities handled the *Joanna V*. Firstly, if the United Kingdom Government needed Security Council authorization to prevent the two tankers entering Beira, on whose authority was the *Joanna V* intercepted by the frigate *Plymouth* on 4 April 1966? The captain of the frigate told the master of the *Joanna V* at the time that 'the British action . . . was taken in conformity with the United Nations resolution of 20 November [1965], and with the knowledge of the Greek Government'.[23] If this was true, was that authority limited only to the interception of the tanker, without extending to preventing the tanker from entering Beira? According to *The Times* (London), the British officials were reported to have said that force was not used to stop the tanker because of the serious danger of loss of life.[24] This implies that Britain did have authority to intercept and prevent the *Joanna V* from entering Beira. If that was the case, it could be argued

---

[22] Ibid. 1277th mtg., para. 59.
[23] *The Times* (London), 5 Apr. 1966, 10.   [24] Ibid.

that Britain went to the United Nations only in order to buy time to allow the problem to sort itself out somehow. But did Britain have that legal power forceably to stop the *Joanna V* from entering Beira? This question will be examined below.

There is yet another criticism which was mentioned by Mr Morozov, Mr Collier, and the representative of Bulgaria. The point in question may be found in a statement quoted by Mr Morozov from the France–Presse Agency, viz. that it was 'stated in Portuguese circles at the United Nations that, when the tanker *Joanna V* entered the port of Beira ten days ago, it was steered by technical officers of the British Navy, members of the British harbour service'.[25] This suggested that British officers not only refrained from preventing the *Joanna V*, but positively assisted it to attempt to breach the oil embargo. Lord Caradon in the Security Council did not make reference to this accusation in his speech and the other representatives did not press the question further. Consequently, whether or not it was well founded has never been established.

Whatever reservations the other members might have had about the need for Britain to seek a mandate of the Security Council, the Security Council did give her that authorization in a resolution adopted on 9 April 1966 by ten votes in favour, none against, and five abstentions.[26] The relevant operative paragraph of this resolution stated that the Security Council

5. *Calls upon* the Government of the United Kingdom of Great Britain and Northern Ireland to prevent, by the use of force if necessary, the arrival at Beira of vessels reasonably believed to be carrying oil destined for Southern Rhodesia and empowers the United Kingdom to arrest and detain the tanker known as the *Joanna V* upon her departure from Beira in the event her oil cargo is discharged there.

The paragraph quoted above raises two major legal questions which will be discussed in the next two sections of the present chapter. The first question is concerned with the freedom of the high seas, and the second with the constitutional basis of the Security Council's authorization of the

[25] *UNSCOR*, 1277th mtg., para. 163.   [26] Res. 221 (1966).

United Kingdom to use force. The discussion will also consider the question raised in the preceding pages as to whether or not Britain had power to intercept the tankers at Beira without the authorization of the United Nations.

Before that is done it should be remembered that the resolution which gave this authorization of use of force also contained provisions which related to some non-military enforcement measures. These measures will be discussed in the present chapter before an examination of paragraph 5 quoted above is considered.[27]

B. *Non-Military Provisions of Resolution 221 (1966)*

This resolution states *inter alia*:

The Security Council,
Gravely concerned at reports that substantial supplies of oil may reach Southern Rhodesia as a result of an oil tanker having arrived at Beira and the approach of a further tanker which may lead to the resumption of pumping through the Companhia do Pipeline Mozambique Rhodesia pipeline with the acquiscence of the Portuguese authorities,
Considering that such supplies will afford great assistance and encouragement to the illegal régime in Southern Rhodesia, thereby enabling it to remain longer in being,
1. *Determines* that the resulting situation constitutes a threat to the peace;
2. *Calls upon* the Portuguese Government not to permit oil to be pumped through the pipeline from Beira to Southern Rhodesia;
3. *Calls upon* the Portuguese Government not to receive at Beira oil destined for Southern Rhodesia;
4. *Calls upon* all states to ensure the diversion of any of their vessels reasonably believed to be carrying oil destined for Southern Rhodesia which may be en route for Beria . . .

It would appear from paragraph one that the Security Council invoked Chapter VII of the Charter which had hitherto been resisted by the United Kingdom. Although the paragraph did not mention that Chapter by name, it is clear from the wording that the Council was now acting under that Chapter. What is not clear from the wording of this resolution, however, is whether its provisions were meant to be binding on the

---

[27] These are paras. 2–4.

members. If one considers the fact that Britain had up to that time resisted the invocation of Chapter VII of the Charter mainly because she did not want the Security Council to pass binding resolutions, it could be argued that her decision to allow Chapter VII to be applied in this particular instance was symbolic of her willingness to let the Security Council pass a mandatory resolution, and that therefore, at least some paragraphs of Resolution 221 (1966) could be binding. It should be remembered also that on 20 December 1965, Mr Wilson did tell the British House of Commons that when there was seepage and leakage in the oil embargo a mandatory resolution would be passed to take care of the situation.[28]

At the Security Council itself some members took the view that the non-military measures of Resolution 221 (1966) were binding. For instance, the representative of the Netherlands, after referring to previous Council resolutions on Rhodesia, stated:

A mandatory call upon Portugal not to receive oil at Beira destined for Rhodesia, or to permit oil to be pumped through the Beira–Umtali pipeline, linked with the calls designed to prevent a repetition of the situation which is immediately confronting us, represents a further turning of the screw of sanctions.[29]

The representative of Nigeria also said that there was need for the imposition of 'mandatory sanctions'.[30] Unfortunately, the text of this resolution does not help much.

Some commentators have taken the view that the resolution imposed no 'order' on member states.[31] J. W. Halderman, for instance, argues that the remarks that Resolution 221 (1966) was mandatory are based on the 'persistence of the view that collective measures must be mandatory'.[32] He argues for example that the resolution could not be binding on any state because the Security Council cannot 'order' a member state to use armed force in the absence of an Article 43 agreement between the Council and the member concerned.[33]

The flaw in Halderman's argument is that he fails to distinguish between the provisions of this resolution which

[28] See *Weekly Hansard*, No. 673, vol. 720/1, cols. 250–1.
[29] *UNSCOR*, 1277th mtg., para. 18.   [30] Ibid., para. 28.
[31] J. W. Halderman (1968) 17, *ICLQ*, 687.
[32] Ibid.   [33] Ibid.

applied to the United Kingdom authorizing her to use force off Beira, and those which applied to Portugal and other members generally. He treats the resolution as if all its provisions applied to Britain. If the distinction referred to here is made, it would appear that there could be ground for arguing that while the paragraph which applied to Britain could not be mandatory, those paragraphs which were addressed to the members generally could. This distinction is clearly drawn by J. E. S. Fawcett.[34] Having done that, however, he does not commit himself one way or the other as to whether Resolution 221 (1966) had any mandatory provisions. He merely refers to the Portuguese complaint that the resolution could not have mandatory provisions since no proof was shown that there existed a threat to the peace in the Rhodesian situation.[35]

The Portuguese argument seems to suggest that before the Council declares that a situation is a threat to the peace, it should first set out fully its reasons for making that determination. There is no evidence that this is the proper interpretation of Article 39 of the Charter. This Portuguese argument should therefore be dismissed out of hand. It is submitted that the non-military provisions of Resolution 221 (1966) might have been binding on member states of the United Nations. Since Britain was authorized by paragraph 5 to use force to prevent ships taking oil to Beira for Rhodesia, it would appear that those ships must have been deemed to be engaged in doing that which was prohibited under the Charter. If therefore, the provisions which applied to such ships were mere recommendations, it is difficult to find the legal basis for the Council to authorize Britain to use force against ships which were engaged in undesirable but none the less lawful business. Furthermore, if those provisions were merely recommendatory it is difficult to see why, if states were unwilling to comply with the recommendatory provisions of Resolution 217 (1965) they should have been expected to treat the provisions of Resolution 221 (1966) with any more respect. In that case, therefore, if those provisions were also non-mandatory, it could be argued that they were superfluous.

[34] Fawcett (1965-6) 41, *BYBIL*, 118.
[35] Ibid. 116. For Portuguese comment, see (1965-6) *Keesing*, 21417-18.

Finally, the determination in paragraph one that the situation constituted a threat to the peace is surely an invocation of Chapter VII of the Charter. Since, as already seen, the United Kingdom had previously resisted the application of that Chapter largely because she did not want the Security Council to pass mandatory resolutions, her acceptance of the need for the application of that Chapter in that instance suggests that she was ready to allow the Council to pass orders in respect of that situation. This conclusion is further strengthened by the fact that after the adoption of Resolution 221 (1966) the British Government never again tried to prevent the adoption of mandatory resolutions by the Security Council. This is also consistent with Mr Wilson's statement in the British House of Commons in 1965 that if the oil embargo imposed under Resolution 217 (1965) was not complied with, there would be an irresistible demand for a mandatory resolution to make sure that the oil embargo was observed.[36]

C. *The Constitutional Basis of Paragraph 5 of Resolution 221 (1966)*

When the Security Council adopted Resolution 221 (1966) the Portuguese reaction was predictably hostile and the government spokesman announced formally that his government had 'grave and serious observations' to make on that issue.[37] Some of these observations pertained to the voting procedure in the Security Council following the abstention of France and the Soviet Union, and these will be dealt with in Chapter X below. The one that needs to be considered here is what Portugal called 'a clear denial of the principle of . . . free access to the sea by landlocked countries . . .'.[38] This point will be examined below, but in the meantime, the present discussion centres on paragraph 5 of Resolution 221 (1966).

This paragraph has already been quoted above and need not be repeated here. Its essence is that it authorized Britain

---

[36] *The Times* (London), 11 Apr. 1966, 5.
[37] *The Times* (London), 12 Apr. 1966, 8.
[38] (1965-66) *Keesing*, 21419.

to use force if necessary against merchant ships on the high seas if she believed those ships to be carrying oil to Beira destined for Rhodesia. What is necessary is to determine the constitutional basis for this paragraph which involved the use of military force.

The United Nations had in the past authorized the use of armed force in the Korean situation in 1950 and in the Congo (now Zaïre) crisis in 1960. However, the Rhodesian case was unique in that, while in the other two cases the use of force was undertaken by forces technically contributed by member states to the United Nations and operating under the United Nations flag, in the Rhodesian case the United Nations authorized a single member state to use military force on behalf of the Organization.

The purpose of examining this paragraph is to determine under which Charter provision the Security Council acted. It has already been submitted that the resolution itself was based on Chapter VII of the Charter. The basis of this paragraph could therefore only be an article or articles in Chapter VII. Article 40 lays down provisional measures to be adopted by the Council. The use of force under discussion could not have been a provisional measure, as the resolution itself clearly indicates that the force was to deal on a final basis with a pressing problem. Article 40 was, therefore, it is submitted, not the basis of paragraph 5 of this resolution. Article 41 lays down measures not involving the use of armed force, and it would appear therefore that it could not have been the basis of this paragraph either, despite the fact that the measures it contains include the interruption of sea communication. Article 41 refers by implication to flag states which are enjoined to take such a step against their own vessels.

The most likely basis for paragraph 5 seems to have been Article 42 which deals with military enforcement measures. It provides:

Should the Security Council consider that measures provided for in Article 41 would be inadequate or have proved to be inadequate, it may take such action by air, sea, or land forces as may be necessary to maintain or restore international peace and security. Such action may include demonstration, blockade, and other operations by air, sea, or land forces of Members of the United Nations.

Did the action taken against the two Greek tankers amount to a use of armed force? Owing to the adoption of Resolution 221 (1966) the *Joanna V* remained anchored in Beira until it left without discharging its cargo and no further interference with it was made by the British authorities.[39] The *Manuela*, on the other hand, was boarded by British officers while it sailed south to Durban. In neither case was there any physical violence. In spite of that, however, it should be pointed out that the use of armed force does not necessarily mean that physical force must be actually used. An unmistakable display of a determination to use physical force in appropriate circumstances may be sufficient to amount to the use of armed force. As Fawcett points out, a blockade, which according to Article 42 is a use of force, 'may be effective without a shot being fired'.[40] Similarly, a demonstration is also, as indicated in Article 42, a use of force. Thus in the *Corfu Channel* case[41] the International Court of Justice held that the passing of ships 'with crews at action stations, ready to retaliate quickly if fired upon . . . must have been not only to test Albania's attitude, but at the same time to demonstrate such force that she would abstain from firing again on passing ships'.[42] The court held this to amount to use of armed force. On this basis there can be little doubt that armed force was used against those tankers, and paragraph 5 could, therefore, properly be said to be based on Article 42. In any case, whatever was or was not done, the fact remains that use of force was authorized and provisions for using force are contained in Article 42.

This conclusion is not accepted by Fawcett, who argues that the Security Council could not have invoked Article 42 before applying mandatory measures under Article 41 and testing their efficacy, or before ascertaining that non-military measures under Article 41 would be inadequate.[43] The answer to this is that the Security Council does not need to apply non-military measures by a mandatory resolution before it resorts to military measures if it is satisfied that the situation

---

[39] See section D below.
[40] Fawcett, 'Security Council Resolutions on Rhodesia', (1965–6), 41 *BYBIL* 118.   [41] (1949) *ICJ Rep.*, 31.
[42] Ibid.   [43] Fawcett, (1965–6) 41, *BYBIL* 119.

calls for immediate use of force. The Security Council has wide discretionary powers in making this decision.[44] It could be argued that the incidents of the two oil tankers needed such immediate application of Article 42.

In any case, it is difficult to see what a mandatory resolution, for instance, ordering the Government of Greece to stop the *Joanna V* or the *Manuela* going to Beira would have achieved since the Greek Government had clearly demonstrated its willingness to co-operate with the United Nations by striking the registration of the *Joanna V* from the Greek register, forfeiting the licence of its captain for life, and imposing a fine on the owners of the vessel.[45] The Greek Government had also indicated that it would have no objection if Britain used force against the tankers if she obtained the authorization of the United Nations.

Having concluded that paragraph 5 of Resolution 221 (1966) was based on Article 42, it should also be pointed out that as Britain had signed no special military agreement with the United Nations as required by Article 43, this paragraph was not binding on Britain to use force off the Mozambican coast. The paragraph was therefore only a recommendation or authorization which Britain could apply to her discretion.[46]

If this was the case, Fawcett asks whether the Security Council can recommend or empower a single member of the United Nations to use 'on its behalf force, which is in itself unlawful'.[47] While he answers this question himself in the affirmative, he, however, regards it as objectionable.[48] It will be remembered that the United Nations had also recommended the use of force in the *Korean* case in 1950 as already seen. In that case, however, the armed forces were contributed by a number of states, although the bulk of the forces were contributed by the United States. Furthermore, it has been suggested by some commentators that since in the *Korean* case there had been a 'breach' of the peace while in the Rhodesian case there was only a 'threat' to the peace, it was

---

[44] Goodrich and Hambro, 279.
[45] *The Times* (London), 7 Apr. 1966, 12.
[46] Akehurst, *A Modern Introduction to International Law* (George Allen and Unwin, 4th edn.), 184.   [47] Fawcett, (1965-6) 41 *BYBIL* 119.
[48] Ibid.

appropriate to use force on the strength of a recommendation in the former and not in the latter because 'breach' of the peace is more serious than a mere 'threat' to the peace. The Charter does not support this attempted distinction. It is submitted that 'recommendations' of the Security Council apply equally to either case.

It remains now to comment briefly on the Portuguese observation which was mentioned at the beginning of the present section, that Rhodesia was being denied the right of access, as a land-locked country, to the open seas. In the first place, as the Security Council enforcement measures were directed against the Smith regime, it would look absurd at the same time to provide that regime with the means of defeating the measures imposed against it. Even if this were not the case, the Convention on the Transit of Land-Locked States, 1965,[49] Article 14 provides that 'this Convention does not impose upon a contracting state any obligation conflicting with its rights and duties as a member of the United Nations'.[50]

By virtue of this provision it appears that the Portuguese Government's responsibility lay in observing the resolutions of the Security Council imposing an embargo against the Smith regime. Besides, this right could only be claimed by the legal authority of Rhodesia who in that case was the United Kingdom. Since the United Kingdom herself required that this right be suspended in order to end the rebellion of the Smith regime, any assistance given by Portugal or any other state to the regime would amount to unlawful intervention in British territory. Apart from that, if the proposition offered here that the paragraphs of Resolution 221 (1966) other than paragraph 5 were mandatory is correct, such assistance would also have amounted to a breach of Charter obligation by Portugal. In that case, Portugal's duties arose from both general international law prohibiting states from interfering in each other's internal affairs, and from Article 25 of the Charter which binds member states to accept the decisions of the Security Council.

[49] See (1966) *Australian YBIL*, 96.
[50] In any case the right Portugal referred to applies only to states, and Rhodesia was not a state.

It is submitted finally, that whether Britain could have used force against the two Greek tankers without going to the United Nations for authority[51] was really not a crucial issue. What was important was whether Britain could treat every other ship that came into that area in the same way without being challenged. It was therefore correct for Britain to seek the authority of the United Nations so as to eliminate any lingering doubt about the lawfulness of the use of that force. This action also had a deterrent effect on other tankers which might have attempted to violate the oil embargo.

D. *Freedom of the High Seas*

The use of force by the United Kingdom on the high seas against foreign shipping would in peacetime normally conflict with the well-established rule of the freedom of the high seas laid down in Article 2 of the Geneva Convention on the High Seas, 1958. Since this use of force was sanctioned by the United Nations, an explanation of this apparent conflict is therefore necessary here. Before that is undertaken it would be helpful to explain briefly what the principle of freedom of the high seas entails.

Although this principle is very well established, its scope is still uncertain.[52] It means that no state can exercise authority over any vessels on the high seas except those flying its own flag. Put positively, the 'principle means that in time of peace every state and its inhabitants may make use of the high seas for navigation, fishing, the collection of its fauna and flora, the laying of submarine cables, and flying above it'.[53] Article 2 of the Convention on the High Seas 1958 provides:

The high seas being open to all nations, no state may validly purport to subject any part of them to its sovereignty. Freedom of the high seas is exercised under the conditions laid down by these articles and by the other rules of international law. It comprises, *inter alia* both for coastal and non-coastal states:

[51] See section D below.
[52] Hackworth's *Digest of International Law*, vol. 11 (1941), 654.
[53] Colombos, *The International Law of the Sea* (Longmans 6th edn., 1967), 314; Hall, *International Law* (8th edn., 1924), 328.

(1) Freedom of navigation;
(2) Freedom of fishing;
(3) Freedom to lay submarine cables and pipelines;
(4) Freedom to fly over the high seas.

Those freedoms, and others which are recognized by the general principles of international law, shall be exercised by all states with reasonable regard to the interests of other states in their exercise of the freedoms of the high seas.

The term 'high seas' is defined in Article 1 as 'all parts of the sea that are not included in the territorial sea or in the internal waters of a state'. As can be seen, Article 2 of this Convention does not purport to codify all existing rules of international law relating to the freedom of the high seas.

As to the apparent conflict between the authorization of Britain to use force against foreign ships on the high seas and the freedom of those ships on the high seas, two explanations may be offered. Firstly, Article 103 of the Charter stipulates that obligations of a state under the Charter shall prevail over those founded on any other international agreement. Fawcett points out, however, that 'Article 103 of the Charter would not over-ride High Seas Convention, Article 22, unless a decision covered by Article 25 of the Charter was in issue'.[54] It will be remembered that the argument presented in the previous section of the present chapter is that paragraph 5 of Resolution 221 (1966), on the basis of which Britain used force on the high seas, was not mandatory, but only a recommendation of the Security Council since Britain had signed no special military agreements required by Article 43. This recommendation, therefore, necessarily fell outside Article 25 of the Charter under which states are bound to comply with the decisions of the Security Council. Fawcett, therefore, argues that because of this, Article 103 of the Charter did not apply in the case of those two ships. Fawcett is probably right in this conclusion. Furthermore, it could be argued that there was no conflict at all as regards Britain's interference with the *Joanna V* and the *Manuela* because those vessels were not engaged in lawful shipping but in activities which violated the United Nations mandatory enforcement measures, as already submitted, for the maintenance

---

[54] Fawcett (1965–6) 41, *BYBIL*, 120.

of international peace and security. Such ships could therefore not claim any right of the freedom of the high seas. A conflict could, however, have arisen in respect of other ships which were engaged in innocent shipping. In such a situation also, it is doubtful if Britain could have justified her action on the basis of Article 103 in the light of what has been said about there being no obligation for her to act against the ships.

Secondly, the conflict referred to above could be resolved by reference to the main exception to the freedom of the high seas, in Article 22 of the Convention on the High Seas 1958 which permits 'acts of interference derived from powers conferred by treaty . . .'. The powers of the United Kingdom under paragraph 5 of Resolution 221 (1966) could be said, therefore, to have been derived from the Charter of the United Nations. For that reason, Article 2 of the Convention on the High Seas could not have been used against the United Kingdom even if she had interfered with ships engaged in innocent shipping on the high seas.

At this point, it will be useful to return to the criticisms which were raised by the various members of the United Nations in the Security Council that Britain could have acted against the *Joanna V* and the *Manuela* without resorting to the Security Council. It will therefore be necessary to determine if Britain could have used any of the existing general exceptions to the principle of the freedom of the seas to justify her interference with those two tankers. A cursory look at all the exceptions under general international law shows that the only possible relevant exception in connection with these two Greek-registered oil tankers is the right of self-defence.[55]

There are a number of marine cases where this exception or right has been claimed by states to justify their interference with foreign ships. The classical example is the *Caroline* case in 1837 which involved an American vessel of the same name which was seized by the British authorities during a Canadian rebellion which set it on fire and sent it adrift down the Niagara Falls for allegedly carrying supplies to rebels. When the American Government complained about this, Britain

---

[55] Colombos, 314; Brierly, *The Law of Nations* (Oxford, 6th edn., 1963), 316; Hall, *International Law* , 328.

'asserted that her act was necessary in self-preservation . . .'.[56]
Another example is the case of the *Virginius*, also a vessel
flying the American flag, which was captured by the Spanish
authorities on the high seas[57] for carrying men and ammun-
itions to Cuban insurgents. Several people, some of whom
were British, were summarily tried and executed. Britain
complained to Spain, not against the capture of the ship,
which she was disposed to accept as justified in self-defence,
but about the execution of her citizens.[58] A number of cases
involving France occurred in the 1950s. These included the
cases of the *Slovenija*, a Yugoslav vessel; the *Las Palmas* and
the *Bilbao*, two German vessels. The flag states protested,
arguing that the French action was illegal.[59]

It should be pointed out that the extent of the application
of this right on the high seas is more controversial than the
application of the same right on land.[60] The examples cited
here should not therefore be seen as illustrating unanimity of
states on this subject. As a matter of fact, these cases came
about precisely because there were disagreements between
the state exercising the right and the flag state of the affected
vessel. The controversy is, however, less serious where the
foreign vessel concerned has been involved in some accident
on the high seas and is subsequently destroyed by a coastal
state which is in imminent danger of oil pollution from the
damaged ship. This may be illustrated by the case of the
Liberian-registered tanker, the *Torrey Canyon* which was
bombed by Britain in 1967 when it ran aground on a reef
in the English Channel.[61] The Liberian Government did not
protest about the destruction of the vessel.

In spite of the controversy referred to here, there is none
the less some general agreement in theory as to what situations could give rise to the exercise of the right of self-defence.

---

[56] Oppenheim, *International Law* (8th edn., 1955), 300.
[57] The United States protested about the capture of the ship. See Moore's
Digest vol. 2, 895-903; Brierly, *The Law of Nations*, 316.
[58] Brierly, *The Law of Nations*, 316.
[59] Ibid.; *Whiteman's Digest*, vol. 4, (Longmans), 513-14.
[60] Van Zwanenberg, 'Interference with ships on the High Seas', (1961) 10,
ICLQ, 785, 817.
[61] Akehurst, *Modern Introduction* (3rd edn.), 175; Akehurst suggests that
perhaps the distinction lies in the differing degrees of urgency in the two situations.

According to the decision in the *Caroline* case, there must exist a 'necessity for self-defence, instant, overwhelming, leaving no choice of means and no moment for deliberation'.[62] In the case of the *Joanna V* it would appear that the facts fell far short of those which could justify an exercise of the right of self-defence by the United Kingdom within the criterion laid down in the *Caroline* case. In the eyes of the United Kingdom, the situation resulting from the arrival of the *Joanna V* and the *Manuela* at Beira only threatened a breach of the oil embargo against the Smith regime, and this could have helped lengthen the life of the Rhodesian rebellion, thereby increasing the risk of military intervention by third states. This, therefore, was seen as an issue related to the maintenance of international peace and security. Matters of threats to the peace are not matters of unilateral action by states and should be referred to the Security Council which has primary responsibility in this field.[63] It could be argued, therefore, that Britain was right in seeking the authorization of the Security Council. Whether or not Resolution 221 (1966) was adequate, as questioned by the African States at the United Nations, need not be considered here.

Following the adoption of this resolution it was reported that a British frigate, the *Berwick*, had intercepted the *Manuela* about 150 miles south-east of Beira. The captain of the tanker having acknowledged his intention to proceed to Beira according to his sailing instructions, the *Berwick* sent a boarding party which met no resistance.[64] The authority given to the British Navy was not to seize the tanker but to prevent it reaching Beira by ensuring that she sailed on a different course. The boarding party remained on board the *Manuela* until it was clear that she was sailing south to Durban in South Africa.

Meanwhile, the *Joanna V*, which was still anchored in Beira, had its registration cancelled by the Greek Government. The tanker subsequently hoisted the Panamanian flag until the Panamanian Government also announced that it had cancelled its registration of the tanker. Therefore, the tanker left

---

[62] D. J. Harris, *Cases and Materials on International Law* (London, 1973), 642-3.
[63] H. L. Cryer, 'Legal Aspects of the *Joanna V* and *Manuela* Incidents' (1966), *Australian YBIL*, 90.   [64] *The Times* (London), 11 Apr. 1966, 5.

without discharging its oil cargo at Beira and the British authorities took no further interest in it. The *Manuela* was also reported on 18 April 1966 to have left Durban for an unknown destination.[65]

In the aftermath of the interception of the *Manuela*, the agent of the vessel threatened to sue the British Government for the action the Royal Navy had taken against the ship. But at about the same time the Secretary-General of the Ministry of Merchant Navy of Greece announced that the master of the vessel would be committed before a disciplinary court over the *Manuela* incident in Beira. And a statement from the Greek Foreign Affairs Ministry also approved of the British action against the *Manuela* as being in accordance with the United Nations Resolution 221 (1966). It added that 'Greece has always respected United Nations resolutions'.[66]

The significance of the position adopted by Greece in this dispute is that she had effectively deprived the tanker of its right to the protection of a ship by its flag state. This affected the claim the agent of the ship intended to bring against the British Government as the ship would be without representation in any international claim unless its individual owners or the charterers made their claims through their respective governments for the protection of their interests, if they were not Greek nationals themselves. Even so, such an action could not succeed in view of the Security Council resolution which made the British action lawful.

The vessel that faced an even more difficult position was the *Joanna V* which had been rendered stateless by the cancellation of its registration by both the Greek and the Panamanian Governments. The fate of a stateless ship was the subject of a decision by the Privy Council in London in 1948.[67] According to that Court, which cited Oppenheim, a stateless ship 'enjoys no protection whatever' on the high seas, 'for the freedom of navigation on the open sea is freedom for such vessels only as sail under the flag of a state'.[68] It is submitted that this proportion is too wide. As Fawcett points out, 'a ship without nationality is not *res nullius*, and the fact

[65] Ibid. 18 Apr. 10.   [66] Ibid. 11 Apr. 1966.
[67] *Molvan v. A-G. for Palestine*, [1948] AC 369.
[68] Oppenheim, *International Law*, vol. vi. 546.

that it is not under the jurisdiction of any state does not mean that the rights and interests of the owners or charterers in the ship or its cargo may be infringed without lawful excuse'.[69]

It is worth noting in conclusion that in the case of the *Joanna V* and the *Manuela* the British Government acted with dispatch and resolution. The effect of this decisiveness was that no further threat of a major violation of the oil embargo through Beira was posed. This should have been a lesson to be learnt and applied in all cases of violation of this embargo through other oil routes such as by road through South Africa. Be that as it may, it would appear that, having examined the only possible exception Britain could have invoked to justify unilateral military action on the high seas to deal with the two vessels under discussion, and having found the exception inapplicable, the inevitable conclusion is that Britain acted correctly in seeking a mandate from the Security Council. Such an action was not only desirable, but also probably the only legally correct course of action in the circumstances.

[69] Fawcett, (1965–6) 41, *BYBIL* 119.

VII

The Effect of United Nations Resolutions on Non-Member States

A. *Introduction*

ONE aspect which could be singled out as a probable major contributory factor in the weakness and ultimate collapse of the League of Nations system was the failure on the part of one of the world's major powers, the United States, to join the Organization. The United Nations, on the other hand, claims the membership of not only all the major world powers but also of nearly the whole of the membership of the international community. Margaret Doxey, however, believes that the United Nations also 'suffers from many of the disabilities of the League' in that, among other things, 'it has serious gaps in membership which limit its relevance as a rule-making body . . .'.[1]

Although this is probably an overstatement of the truth, it is pertinent to examine the relevance of the question of lack of universality of membership of the United Nations in relation to the extent to which non-members of the United Nations are affected by the Organization's binding resolutions. Particular attention will be paid to an examination of the juridical status of Article 2 (6) of the United Nations Charter and its relevance to resolutions addressed to non-member states.

The need for this examination cannot be over-emphasized. When there exists an organization in the international milieu, enjoying an almost universal membership of the whole international community, charged with grave international responsibilities whose significance might be of relevance to the entire international community, it is imperative that the relationship of the members of that organization and non-members as far

---

[1] M. Doxey, 'The Rhodesian Sanctions Experiment', (1971), *YBWA*, 147.

as the decisions of the organization are concerned should be clearly established. This is particularly true of the United Nations, which was formed as a forum to help prevent the occurrence of a cataclysmic war of the magnitude experienced in the previous two World Wars. The members would certainly not want to see their organization fail simply because its efforts were torpedoed by non-members.

B. *The Charter and Non-Member States of the United Nations*

There are very few states which are not members of the United Nations. The present chapter will attempt to establish how, if at all, these few states are affected by the decisions of the United Nations, especially the binding decisions of the Security Council. The discussion will make a brief general survey of the effects of treaties on third states, examine generally the nature of Article 2 (6) of the Charter, which refers to non-members and the decisions of the Security Council, and finally, look at the practice of the Security Council in the Rhodesian case.

Effect of Treaties on Third States

The purpose of a treaty is to lay down rights and duties of the parties to it in accordance with the agreement it represents. How far non-parties to the treaty are affected by any provisions of that treaty is a matter for jurisprudential argument which has now almost been done to death. No lengthy examination of this question will therefore be made here.

The general rule is that a treaty creates neither rights nor obligations for third states. This principle is expressed by the maxim *pacta tertiis nec nocent nec prosunt*. It is now declared in the Vienna Convention on the Law of Treaties, Article 34, which provides that a 'treaty does not create either obligations or rights for a third state without its consent'. The only exception to this general rule is where the parties to the treaty intend the treaty to establish obligations for the third party, which in turn accepts those obligations in writing.[2]

---

[2] Art. 35; Art. 36 creates rights for third parties to a treaty.

Except probably for the requirement that the third party's acceptance be in writing, this exception accurately reflects customary law.[3]

The important point to note here is that the obligation of the third state arises only with the consent of the state concerned. Similarly, Article 37 (1) also states that if that obligation which has arisen as provided in Article 34 is to be revoked or modified the consent of the parties and the third party should be obtained unless all the parties have otherwise agreed. The need for this consent emanates from the sovereignty of states and the resulting principle that international law does not as yet recognize an international legislative process which would enable dissenting states to be bound by rules created by the majority.[4]

Oppenheim, however, believes that international society has been transformed into an integrated community, thus making inevitable a departure from this principle as stated above.[5] He points out that the Covenant of the League of Nations, without expressly imposing obligations upon non-members, in fact asserted the right of the League to compel them to assume some of the obligations of the Covenant with regard to the settlement of their disputes with members of the League. It also asserted the right of active intervention of the League in disputes between non-member states.[6]

He also refers to article 2 (6) of the United Nations Charter which lays down that the Organization is under the obligation to ensure that non-members of the Organization act in accordance with the principles of the United Nations so far as may be necessary for the maintenance of international peace and security, and concludes:

Both the Covenant of the League of Nations and the Charter of the United Nations must therefore be regarded as having set a limit, determined by the general interest of the international community to the rule that a treaty cannot impose obligations upon states which are not parties to it.[7]

The present chapter is mainly concerned with the effect of

[3] Akehurst, *A Modern Introduction* (3rd edn.), 163.
[4] Oppenheim, 928.   [5] Ibid.
[6] Art. 17 of the Covenant.
[7] Oppenheim, *International Law*, vol. 1, 8th edn. 929.

Article 2 (6) on non-members of the United Nations. This is made necessary by the fact that a large number of resolutions on Rhodesia purported to be addressed to all states which, it would appear, included non-members of the United Nations. Before discussing that provision, however, it seems necessary first to dispose quickly of Oppenheim's argument that Article 17 of the League Covenant marked a departure from the general rule that treaties create neither rights nor obligations for non-parties to it.

Article 17 (3) provided that in a dispute which involved non-members those non-members would be 'invited to accept the obligations of membership in the League for the purposes of such a dispute'. Surely this is not language that imposes obligations on these non-members. Use of such expressions as 'invited to accept the obligations' makes this very clear. It is true that if these non-members rejected the invitation, they risked the application against them of sanctions listed in Article 16 if they resorted to war against a member of the League. This, however, did not create a right–duty relationship between members and non-members but, in Hohfeld's terminology, one of liberty – no-right.[8] Treaties of this kind are well known in international relations. An example of such a treaty is the Convention for Limiting the Manufacture and Regulating the Distribution of Narcotic Drugs, opened for signature on 13 July 1931.[9] The nature of such treaties is that their efficacy depends on the contracting parties being able to constrain the non-contracting powers to comply with what is laid down in the treaty.[10] Thus while non-contracting powers are not legally bound by the provisions of the treaty, they are none the less subject to a power arrangement imposed by the contracting powers as long as the latter do not violate the rights of the non-contracting states.

Article 2 (6) and Non-Members of the United Nations

Article 2 (6) of the Charter provides:

The Organization shall ensure that states which are non Members of the

---

[8] See Lloyd, *Introduction to Jurisprudence*, (London, 1972), 248.
[9] See e.g. Art. 14 (2).
[10] Full text is in Hudson (1929–31) V, No. 294, *International Legislation*, 1048.

United Nations act in accordance with these Principles so far as may be necessary for the maintenance of international peace and security.

It is not clear whether this provision was intended to create obligations for non-members. If this was the intention of the drafters of the Charter, this would amount to an attempt to legislate for other sovereign states. As already seen, international law has refused to accept this. Thus, if the relationship created by a treaty concluded between states A and B, is to bind state C, a non-signatory of the treaty, state C's consent must be sought and obtained, and that consent must be given in writing.[11]

Kelsen appears to argue that Article 2 (6) is in fact binding on all states. He suggests that if this is the case, the Charter could be regarded as representing a departure from the maxim *pacta tertiis nec nocent nec prosunt.*[12] Kelsen further suggests that if the Charter is binding on all states it could be argued that the membership of the United Nations is universal. The weakness of this argument is that if the United Nations membership was universal, there would be no need for Article 2 (6) since it relates to non-members, who in this case would be non-existent.

Kelsen, however, admits that at the San Francisco Conference, some delegates did propose that membership of the United Nations be made compulsory for all states.[13] This proposal was rejected by the Conference. He concedes too that the 'idea of compulsory membership was certainly not in conformity with the general international law as it existed when the question was being discussed at San Francisco'.[14] But he adds:

Although the principle of compulsory membership was not accepted, Article 2 paragraph 6 . . . does authorize the Organization to 'ensure that States which are not members of the United Nations act in accordance' with the Principles laid down in Article 2 of the Charter so far as may be necessary for the maintenance of international peace and security. Principle 2 prescribes fulfilment of obligations imposed upon the members. Hence, the provision of Article 2 paragraph 6 may be inter-

---

[11] Vienna Convention on the Law of Treaties, Art. 35.

[12] H. Kelsen, 'Sanctions in International Law under the Charter of the United Nations' (1946) 31, *Iowa LR*, 512–13.

[13] (1946) 46, *Columbia LR*, 294.   [14] Ibid.

preted to mean that the Charter also imposes at least the most important obligations of the members upon non-members, and therefore it may be claimed to have the character of general international law . . . If so, the idea of compulsory membership has not entirely been rejected.[15]

This view is strongly criticized by J. L. Kunz, who points out that the Charter itself distinguishes between members and non-members.[16] For instance, the United Nations may reject a state's application for membership of the Organization.[17]

In spite of this, Kunz also suggests that some provisions of the Charter of the United Nations may be binding on all states including non-members of the United Nations. He, however, does not spell out exactly how this could happen. Possibly he intended to refer to provisions of the Charter which codify customary international law. If this is so, it is submitted that Article 2 (6) is not one of those provisions.

In the 1946 edition of their book Goodrich and Hambro were strongly of the opinion that Article 2 (6) does not bind non-member states.[18] But in the 1949 edition of the same book they seem to be in some doubt although they still conclude that it is 'doubtful whether an international instrument like the Charter can impose legal obligations on states which are not parties to it'.[19] Akehurst also argues that Article 2 (6) merely announces the policy which the United Nations will follow in its relations with non-members.[20] This seems to be the correct interpretation of the Charter. Therefore, to talk of the provision as creating obligations for non-members of the United Nations is to miss the point.

The obligation created by this provision binds members only to ensure that on the question of the maintenance of international peace and security, non-members act in accordance with the principles of the Organization. Oppenheim calls this indirect obligation imposed upon non-members.[21] It is submitted that the use of the word

---

[15] Ibid.   [16] Kunz, 124.

[17] e.g. Franco's Spain was refused membership.

[18] Goodrich and Hambro, *The Charter of the United Nations: Commentary and Documents* (Stevens, 1949), 70–1.

[19] Goodrich and Hambro, *The Charter of the United Nations* (Stevens, 1949).

[20] Akehurst, *A Modern Introduction to International Law* (2nd edn.), 163.

[21] Oppenheim, *International Law*, vol. 1 8th edn., 928.

obligation is inappropriate here, be it qualified by 'indirect' or not.

It should be emphasized, however, that the provision none the less is of enormous value in persuading non-member states to comply with decisions of the Security Council, as member states are not likely to take kindly to any actions of a non-member state which are likely to weaken the effectiveness of the Organization. However, this is a far cry from saying such non-members are legally bound. The need for this particular provision was felt very strongly at the Conference at San Francisco as the result of the experiences of the League of Nations from whose membership Germany and Japan withdrew, and subsequently those two powers' acts largely contributed to the outbreak of the Second World War. The drafters of the Charter, therefore, while they could not compel all states to be members of the United Nations, were concerned that those states who opted to remain outside the world body would be made to comply with the Principles of the United Nations as far as the maintenance of international peace and security was concerned.

At the San Francisco Conference the provisions of Article 2 (6) were initially introduced as part of Article 2 (5) of the Charter, but owing to the importance that was attached to those provisions, they were later, by a unanimous decision of the delegates, separated from Article 2 (5) and given their own separate place under Article 2 (6). The conference records, however, do not indicate whether or not the delegates intended Article 2 (6) to create obligations for non-members. It is submitted that, important though this article is, it does not bind non-members of the United Nations. And therefore neither Article 17 of the League Covenant nor Article 2 (6) of the Charter of the United Nations departed from the maxim *pacta tertiis nec nocent nec prosunt*.

Article 2 (6) and the Practice of the United Nations

In practice the major political organs of the United Nations do from time to time pass resolutions which, although some of them do not expressly refer to Article 2 paragraph 6 of the Charter, have a bearing on that provision inasmuch as they are addressed to 'all states'. The number of such resolutions is fairly considerable. Only a few of them will be referred to in this discussion. The first was Resolution 1010 (XV) of the General Assembly on the *Korean* question.[22] The resolution reaffirmed the objectives of the United Nations to bring about by peaceful means the establishment of a unified independent and democratic Korea under a representative form of government, and the full restoration of international peace and security in the area. It further called upon 'all States' and 'authorities' to facilitate this activity on the part of the Commission for the Unification of Korea.[23] However, it is the Security Council resolutions which are significant for this discussion.

On 13 May 1964 the Cambodian representative to the United Nations informed the President of the Security Council of his Government's complaints that the United States and South Vietnamese forces had repeatedly violated the territory of Cambodia. During the discussion of the question in the Council it was argued that although South Vietnam was not a member of the United Nations it was nevertheless not relieved of the responsibility for conducting its affairs in line with the principles of the Charter.[24] The Security Council finally adopted Resolution 189 (1964) by which it *requested* that just and fair compensation be paid to Cambodia, and *invited* those responsible to take all appropriate measures to prevent any violation of the Cambodian frontier and *requested* 'all States and authorities, and in particular the members of the Geneva Conference, to recognize and respect Cambodia's neutrality and territorial integrity'.[25]

The resolution was deliberate in its use of language which clearly indicated that no obligation was intended where it referred to 'all States' or to South Vietnam, a non-member of the United Nations. The words used in this respect are '*invites*'

---

[22] (1964) 1, *Repertory of Practice of the United Nations Suppl.* No. 2, 117.

[23] Nothing further need be said on the General Assembly since its resolutions are not binding on any state with some exceptions which are not relevant to the present context, e.g. under Art. 17 of the Charter.

[24] (1972), *Repertory, Suppl.* No. 3, 176. The principle involved here was the prohibition of use of or threat to force laid down in Art. 2 (4) of the Charter. The fact that this principle is generally considered a rule of customary law might have had something to do with the views expressed during the debate.

[25] Ibid. (emphasis added).

and 'requests'. Where the resolution refers to the Council itself it used the word 'decides', which is normally associated with binding orders of the Security Council. Although such paragraphs are not necessarily binding on the Council, the use of such a word provides a clear distinction in the way the Council addresses non-members on the one hand and members on the other.

If the Security Council addresses itself to member states and wishes its resolution to be binding, it usually chooses terminology appropriate to such a decision. Commonly, it chooses the opening word 'decides' for the paragraph which is intended to be binding in accordance with Article 25. On the other hand, when it does not intend the paragraph to be binding, it usually uses words like 'requests', 'invites', and 'urges', as it often does when addressing non-member states of the United Nations.

Admittedly, the situation is not as simple and neat as proposed above. There are times when paragraphs which are clearly intended to be binding are addressed equally to members and non-members alike. An examination of the resolutions on the Rhodesian situation will clearly reveal this confusing state of affairs. For that reason, the proposition put foward above should therefore not be taken as a rule of thumb to be applied in every case. For instance, in Resolution 216 (1965) on Rhodesia, the Security Council used the word 'decides' in both paragraphs of the resolution notwithstanding that the resolution, as was submitted in Chapter V above, was not binding. Besides, the resolution was addressed to 'all states'.[26] In Resolution 217 (1965) on the same question the Council again did not make any distinction between paragraphs addressed to members and those addressed to 'all States'. It used the words 'calls upon' for all categories of states.

This resolution was also not binding on any states. Consequently, it could be argued that a distinction was therefore not necessary in the circumstances. However, this lack of distinction between members and non-members was again manifested in Resolution 221 (1966), the third resolution on

[26] See Chap. V above.

Rhodesia after the proclamation of UDI. This lack of distinction was significant in respect of this resolution if the argument presented in Chapter VI above is accepted that some of
its paragraphs were mandatory. Paragraph 4 of this resolution
called upon 'all states to ensure the diversion of any of their
vessels reasonably believed to be carrying oil destined for
Southern Rhodesia which may be en route for Beira'.

The distinction between the language used in addressing
members and that used in addressing non-members was made
for the first time in the Rhodesian case in Resolution 232
(1966). One possible explanation for this is that unlike
Resolution 221 (1966) before it, Resolution 232 (1966) was
unambiguously binding on member states. Therefore there
was a clear need to 'order' the members and *'call upon* all
states' to follow a specified pattern of behaviour. In paragraph
2 the Security Council *'Decides* that all States Members' shall
prevent certain activities in relation to Rhodesia in their
respective countries. Paragraphs 3 and 6 invoked Article 25
which makes decisions of the Security Council binding on
member states. Paragraph 5 *'Calls upon* all States not to
render financial or other economic aid to the illegal racist
régime in Rhodesia'. It seems clear that no obligation was
intended by this paragraph notwithstanding the neutrality
of the phrase 'calls upon'.[27] The point is even clearer in
paragraph 7 which states that the Security Council *'Urges*,
having regard to the principles stated in Article 2 of the United
Nations Charter, States not members of the United Nations
to act in accordance with the provisions of paragraph 2 of the
present resolution.'

This pattern was again scrupulously followed by the Security Council in Resolution 253 (1968). This resolution had
twenty-three operative paragraphs and in five of these the
Security Council make it clear that members were obliged
to comply with the measures stipulated in those paragraphs.
It used the obligatory phrases 'decides' and 'shall' to make
this point absolutely certain. Only one paragraph was directed
at non-members and it stated that the Security Council:

---

[27] It should be remembered, however, that the use of the phrase 'calls upon'
does not necessarily mean that the paragraph in which it appears is not binding.
See Chapter V above.

Urges, having regard to the principles stated in Article 2 of the Charter of the United Nations, States not Members of the United Nations to act in accordance with the provisions of the present resolution; . . .

The rest of the paragraphs did not follow any pattern and were addressed to either the United Kingdom or the other members of the United Nations generally.

The proposition offered in the present chapter therefore seems to have been effectively established by the illustrative use of these two resolutions (Resolutions 232 (1966), and 253 (1968)) that while the Security Council may order members to perform or to refrain from certain specified acts, it can only request, urge (possibly call upon), or invite non-members of the United Nations to comply with those specified acts. It has no power to order them to do this.

If the Security Council were to follow this rule religiously in its decisions involving non-members, the question under discussion would be greatly simplified. For instance in its next resolution[28] which contained twenty-four paragraphs the Security Council, *inter alia*:

9. *Decides*, in accordance with Article 41 of the Charter and in further-ing the objective of ending the rebellion, that Member States shall:
    (a) Immediately sever all diplomatic, consular, trade, military and other relations that they may have with the illegal régime in Southern Rhodesia, and terminate any representation that they may maintain in the Territory.

In the paragraph which referred to non-members of the Security Council:

Urges, having regard to the principle stated in Article 2 of the Charter States not Members of the United Nations to act in accordance with the provisions of the present resolution.

The distinction between the two categories of states was clearly preserved; while one category was bound not to recognize, or to break any relations with the Smith regime, the other category was only 'urged' to do so.

This resolution proved to be the highest point of the Security Council's concern with the distinction between members and non-members in its adoption of resolutions on

---

[28] Res. 277 (1970) passed on 18 Mar. 1970.

the Rhodesian independence dispute. In its next resolution, Resolution 288 (1970), a relatively short one (only six operative paragraphs), the Security Council, while still maintaining the use of the word 'urges' when addressing 'all states', also invoked Article 25 in the same paragraph.[29] The same is true of Resolution 324 (1972), passed on 28 February 1972. This resolution in particular never mentioned members as such at all, but merely referred to 'all States' in the three paragraphs which referred to states.[30] In fact in all its resolutions passed since 1970, the Security Council did not distinguish between members and non-members[31] until it passed Resolution 388 (1976) on 6 April 1976 in which it reverted to the distinction under discussion here. This return was reflected again in Resolution 409 (1977), particularly paragraph 1 which referred to 'all member States', and paragraph 2 which referred to 'States not Members of the United Nations'. In Resolution 445 (1979) the Security Council 'requested' all states in paragraph 3, and 'urged' them in paragraph 7 to take or refrain from specified acts.

What is difficult to explain is the trough that existed between 1970 and 1976 in the way the Security Council addressed non-members. Did the members of the Security Council believe that non-members of the United Nations were bound by the decisions of the Security Council? It would appear that this was the case as far as some members were concerned. For example, during the discussion of the Rhodesian situation in December 1966, the United States representative, Mr Goldberg, told the Security Council that the economic measures which were proposed differed from those that had already been implemented because if any member or non-member should substantially fail to carry out the Council's decision this failure would be a violation of the Charter provisions and obligations.[32] The same view was expressed by Mr Matsui of Japan.[33]

[29] This is para. 4 which states that the Security Council *Urges* all States to fully implement all Security Council resolutions pertaining to Southern Rhodesia, in accordance with their obligations under Article 25 of the Charter...

[30] See paras. 2, 4, 5.

[31] See paras. 1 and 2 which referred to members, and para. 3 which referred to non-members.   [32] *UNSCOR*, 1333th mtg., para. 23.

[33] Ibid. para. 4.

After 1971, it is possible that members of the Security Council might have been influenced in their attitude to non-members by the opinion of the International Court of Justice in the *Namibia* case.[34] In that case the Security Council had, by Resolution 276 (1970), declared that South Africa's occupation of Namibia was illegal following the termination of that country's mandate by General Assembly Resolution 2145 (XXI) which was confirmed by Security Council Resolutions 245 (1968), 246 (1968), and 264 (1969). Broadly put, the question was whether Resolution 276 (1970) was universally binding on states. By a majority opinion the Court stated, *inter alia*:

In the view of the Court, the termination of the Mandate and the declaration of the illegality of South Africa's presence in Namibia, are opposable to all States in the sense of barring *erga omnes* the legality of a situation which is maintained in violation of International Law . . .[35]

If this opinion was responsible for the tendency of the members of the Security Council to address non-members during the period between 1970 to 1976 as though they were bound by the decisions of the Security Council, this was a misreading of what the court had said. The statement shows that the members were not bound by the decision of the Security Council as such but were bound only to the extent that the decision of the Council enunciated a rule of general international law.[36] In the Rhodesian case, however, none of the decisions of the Security Council, it would appear, could be said to operate in the same way as did Resolution 276 (1970) on the *Namibia* case because while states are under a duty to refrain from assisting rebels, they are under no obligation under general international law to prevent individuals within their territories from helping either side in a civil war or dispute.[37] It would appear settled therefore that non-members of the United Nations cannot be bound by the resolutions of the Security Council. All the resolutions of the

---

[34] (1971) ICJ Rep. 1.   [35] Ibid. 56.

[36] Ibid. See for instance the separate opinion of Judge de Castro, 207; see also Higgins, 'International Law, Rhodesia and the United Nations' (1967) 23, *World Today*, 76.

[37] Akehurst, *A Modern Introduction to International Law* (2nd edn., 1971), 336-7.

Council on Rhodesia which appeared to bind 'all states' bound only member states while non-members were urged or invited to comply with those resolutions.

This position was clearly illustrated by Switzerland's reaction to the United Nations action in Rhodesia. Following the adoption of the mandatory Resolution 232 (1966) by the Security Council, the Secretary-General of the Organization, in his note dated 13 January 1967, invited Switzerland to comply with the selective mandatory measures of that resolution. In reply, the Swiss Government stated:

The Federal Council has considered the problems which this poses for our country. It has concluded that for reasons of principle, Switzerland, as a neutral State cannot submit to the mandatory sanctions of the United Nations. The Federal Council will, however, see to it that Rhodesian trade is given no opportunity to avoid the United Nations policy through Swiss territory. It is for that reason that it decided, as early as 17 December 1965, independently and without recognizing any legal obligation to do so, to make imports from Rhodesia subject to mandatory authorization and to take the necessary measures to prevent any increase in Swiss imports from the territory.[38]

From this statement, it can be seen that Switzerland's duty did not derive from the Charter of the United Nations, but what duty there was, derived from general international law, and this was for her to observe her neutrality and refrain from positively assisting Rhodesia. It had no duty to act positively to assist the United Nations in its efforts to end the rebellion by, for instance, curbing her private citizens' activities which assisted the Smith regime. Her action in that direction would have purely been one of choice and not of duty.

This is what West Germany did following the adoption of Resolution 217 (1965). The Government unilaterally declared its willingness to comply with the enforcement measures imposed by that resolution. She was, however, not bound by that decision, particularly since that resolution was not mandatory anyway. None the less, the Government of that country took further action on 14 February 1967 after the Security Council had imposed mandatory measures by Resolution 232 (1966), by passing two ordinances to effect

[38] UN Doc. S/7781, Annex II (February 1967), 117.

compliance with those United Nations measures. In a *note verbale* to the Secretary-General, West Germany declared:

Being anxious to give effect to the principle of self-determination of nations, the German Government has repeatedly declared that it neither recognizes . . . Rhodesia as a State nor the minority Government in . . . Rhodesia.

Identifying itself with the decisions of the United Nations, it has taken a number of measures to restrict trade with . . . Rhodesia following resolution 217 (1967) . . . in spite of the fact that the Federal Republic of Germany is not a member of the United Nations and has thereby contributed towards the effectiveness of the sanctions imposed with regard to this territory . . .[39]

Despite the different responses shown by these two countries, none of them was bound to comply with the decisions of the Security Council on Rhodesia as no such decisions could place non-members under any obligation. Therefore, even if a Security Council resolution used the strongest terms and invoked Article 25 of the Charter in reference to 'all states' or even specifically to 'non-members' it should not be supposed that such a resolution imposes any obligations on those states. At best such statements could amount to hardly anything more than an exhortation to non-members to assist the United Nations in its efforts.

[39] Ibid. 93–4. West Germany subsequently joined the United Nations.

VIII

Possible Alternative Basis for the Security Council Action: Articles 24 and 25 of the Charter

WHEN the Security Council adopted Resolution 221 (1966) on 9 April 1966, it became clear that it was acting under Chapter VII of the Charter notwithstanding that the Council did not invoke the Chapter expressly. The Security Council resolutions which were adopted subsequently to Resolution 221 (1966)[1] put beyond any doubt that Chapter VII was the basis of the Security Council's action. The present chapter seeks to determine whether there was any alternative basis on which the Security Council could have acted, such as the general powers of the Security Council under Article 24 of the Charter. If these general powers could have provided an alternative basis for the Security Council action, it will further be necessary to examine whether those general powers could have enabled the Security Council to bind members of the United Nations within the meaning of Article 25 of the Charter.

A. *The Powers of the Security Council under the Charter*

The power of the Security Council are provided for in Article 24 of the United Nations Charter which states as follows:

1. In order to ensure prompt and effective action by the United Nations, its Members confer on the Security Council primary responsibility for the maintenance of international peace and security, and agree that in carrying out its duties under this responsibility the Security Council acts on their behalf.
2. In discharging these duties the Security Council shall act in accordance with the purposes and principles of the United Nations. The

---

[1] See para. 1 of this resolution.

specific powers granted to the Security Council for the discharge of these duties are laid down in Chapters VI, VII, VIII, and XII.

3. . . .

Chapter VI deals with 'pacific settlement of disputes' and situations. Chapter VII, probably the most important Chapter in regard to the maintenance of the peace, relates to 'actions with respect to threats to the peace, breaches of the peace, and acts of aggression'. Chapter VIII is concerned with regional arrangements for maintaining international peace and security, and finally Chapter XII describes the 'international trusteeship system'.

These powers are not exhaustive. For example, Article 26 also contains some powers concerning the maintenance of international peace and security. Furthermore, the use of the word 'specific' in paragraph 2 of Article 24 suggests that there exist other powers which are not specific but which may be implied from the nature of the functions of the Security Council as the organ primarily responsible for the maintenance of international peace and security. At the San Francisco Conference, the delegates resisted a Belgian amendment to the Dumbarton Oaks Proposals which would have limited the obligations of the members under Article 25, to decisions of the Security Council taken under the Chapters specifically mentioned in Article 24 (2).[2] This is also evidence that the Council has wider powers than those to which the amendment attempted to confine it.

The general powers of the Security Council have on a number of occasions been referred to in some Advisory Opinions of the International Court of Justice. For example, in the case of the *Reparation for Injuries Suffered in the Service of the United Nations* the Court stated that:

Under international law, the Organization must be deemed to have those powers which, though not expressly provided in the Charter, are conferred upon it by necessary implication as being essential to the performance of its duties.[3]

The Court also referred to general powers in its Advisory Opinion in the *Namibia* case.[4]

---

[2] (1945) 11, *UNCIO* Doc. 597, 11/1/30; Whiteman, vol. 13, 361–2.
[3] (1949) *I.C.J. Rep.* at 182.   [4] (1971) *I.C.J. Rep.*, 16.

The *Namibia* case followed the adoption of a number of resolutions by the General Assembly and the Security Council on the question of South Africa's continued occupation of Namibia. The General Assembly had on 27 October 1966 passed Resolution 2145 (XXI) terminating the Mandate under which South Africa administered Namibia. It sought the co-operation of the Security Council in accordance with Article 11 (2) of the Charter. In response the Security Council passed a number of resolutions taking note of the Assembly's resolution and calling upon South Africa to withdraw its adminis-tration from Namibia without delay,[5] and by Resolution 269 (1969) the Council invoked Article 25 of the Charter and called upon South Africa to withdraw its administration from Namibia by a specific date. It also passed Resolution 276 (1966) confirming the termination of the South African Mandate over Namibia, and declaring that South Africa's continued presence in Namibia was therefore illegal. Other states were called upon not to recognize South Africa's dealings on behalf of Namibia.

The competence of the Court to give this Advisory Opinion was challenged by South Africa, which argued that the Security Council had no power under the Charter to pass the resolutions referred to above since the question did not come under any of the Chapters on which the powers of the Secur-ity Council were based, namely Chapters VI, VII, VIII, and XII.[6] In its majority Opinion the Court rejected this argument on the ground that the powers of the Security Council are not limited to the 'specific' powers named in paragraph 2 of Article 24 since the reference in that paragraph did 'not exclude the existence of general powers to discharge the responsibilities conferred in paragraph 1'.[7]

The Court reinforced its conclusions by referring to the statement which was made by the Secretary-General in 1947 regarding Article 24 which said that 'the powers of the Council under Article 24 are not restricted to the specific grants of authority contained in Chapters VI, VII, VIII, and XII . . . Members of the United Nations have conferred upon the Security Council powers commensurate with its

---

[5] Res. 264 (1969).   [6] (1971) *I.C.J. Rep.*, 52.   [7] Ibid.

responsibility . . . .'.[8] Going further, the Court pointed out that in its resolutions the Council indicated that it was acting in the exercise of 'what it deemed to be its primary responsibility, the maintenance of peace and security, which, under the Charter, embraces situations which might lead to a breach of the peace'.[9]

One of the judges who dissented from this Opinion was Judge Petrén who argued that Articles 24 and 25 should be interpreted so as to evade the conditions laid down by Chapter VII of the Charter.[10] The strongest dissenting opinion came from Judge Fitzmaurice who said that he did not agree

with the extremely wide interpretation which the opinion of the Court places on [Article 24]. No doubt it does not limit the *occasions* on which the Security Council can act in the preservation of peace and security, provided the threat said to be involved is not a mere figment or pretext. What it does is to limit the type of action the Council can take in the discharge of its peace-keeping responsibilities for the second paragraph of Article 24 states in terms that the *specific* powers granted to the Security Council for these purposes are laid down in the indicated Chapters (VI, VII, VIII, and XII). According to normal canons of interpretation this means that so far as *peace-keeping* is concerned, they are not to be found anywhere else, and are exercisable only as those chapters allow. It is therefore to them that recourse must be had in order to ascertain what the *specific* peace-keeping powers of the Security Council are, *including the power to bind.*[11]

Judge Fitzmaurice in this extract seemed to put forward two views. Firstly, he said that Article 24 does not 'limit the occasions on which the Security Council can act in the preservation of peace and security'. This would appear to be an admission that the powers of the Council are not limited to those contained in the four Chapters listed in Article 24 (2). He said what the Article limits is the types of action which the Council can take. That is to say, it probably restricts the Council's capacity to bind the United Nations

[8] Ibid.; also Schachter, 'The Development of International Law through the Legal Opinions of the Secretary-General', (1948) 25, *BYBIL*, 91.

[9] (1971) *I.C.J. Rep.*, 51–2. See also 89, per Judge Nervo, and 170, per Judge de Castro.   [10] Ibid., 136.

[11] Ibid. 293 (emphasis in the original text). By peace-keeping Judge Fitzmaurice should be taken to mean maintenance of the peace. The term peace-keeping has now assumed a more technical meaning referring to the use of United Nations armed forces to prevent fighting between forces involved in a conflict.

members. Secondly, he said that as far as 'peace-keeping' is concerned the powers of the Council are to be found in the Chapters listed in Article 24 (2) and nowhere else. This second statement seems to contradict the first. At first reading it might appear that he meant that the Council can bind member states only when acting under specific powers and not when acting under general powers which it does have. But when he later said that to ascertain what 'peace-keeping' powers 'including the power to bind' the Council has, recourse must be had to the listed Chapters, he seemed to insist that outside those specific powers, the Council has no powers at all to act in the maintenance of international peace and security. However, if one reads further one finds that the first impression was, after all, his true position.

From this, therefore, it could be concluded that Judge Fitzmaurice admits that the Council may act in the maintenance of the peace even outside the powers contained in Chapters listed in Article 24 (2). What he objects to is the assertion that the Council can bind the members of the United Nations when acting under such general powers.[12] If this conclusion accurately represents Judge Fitzmaurice's position, it would seem that the opposition to the existence of these 'general powers' by the Judges in the *Namibia* case was minimal. Even Judge Petrén, who supported the minority view, seemed to have been more interested in the question of whether or not those general powers could bind members, rather than in the mere existence of such powers.

It would appear from the foregoing that Resolutions 202 (1965), 216 (1965), and 217 (1965),[13] which were passed by the Security Council prior to the determination that the Rhodesian situation constituted a threat to the peace, could have been based on the general powers of the Security Council. However, whether or not the whole United Nations enforcement action in Rhodesia could have been based on these powers as an alternative legal basis to Chapter VII would depend on whether the Security Council could have passed binding resolutions under those powers. This will be examined in the next section of the present chapter.

[12] This question is considered in the next section.
[13] See Chapter V above.

B. *The General Powers of the Security Council and the Operation of Article 25 of the Charter*

Under Article 25 the members of the United Nations agree to accept and carry out the decisions of the Security Council in accordance with the present Charter. The Security Council often invokes this provision to emphasize mandatory resolutions.[14] However, '. . . the text of this Article contains no precise delimitation of the range of question to which it relates'.[15] As already seen in the previous section of the present chapter, doubt was expressed in the International Court of Justice as to whether the Security Council may pass binding resolutions when exercising powers other than those specifically provided under the Chapters listed in Article 24 paragraph 2. It has been suggested, for example, that in the maintenance of international peace and security, the Security Council can bind members under Article 25 only when it is acting under Chapter VII,[16] and that resolutions which it passes when exercising its general powers based on Article 24 of the Charter, could at best be of recommendatory value. Higgins has addressed herself particularly to the question 'what Security Council Resolutions are binding under Article 25 of the Charter?'[17]

In attempting to answer this question Higgins examines the Advisory Opinion of the International Court of Justice in the *Namibia* case in which the Court opined that the members of the United Nations were bound by the resolutions examined in that case, although there was no evidence that the Council had passed them when acting under Chapter VII.[18] As already seen, the combined effect of all the resolutions examined was that South Africa's continued occupation of Namibia after the termination of the Mandate which had

[14] (1971) *Repertory of Practice of the United Nations Organs*, vol. 11, *Supplement* No. 3, 45.

[15] Ibid. *Supplement* No. 2, 295–304; (1971) *I.C.J. Rep.* 165.

[16] Higgins, 'The Advisory Opinion on Namibia: Which U.N. Resolutions are Binding under Article 25 of the Charter?'. (1972) 21, *ICLQ*, 270.   [17] Ibid.

[18] Only two oral statements to the Court appeared to suggest that the relevant resolutions did in fact fall within Chapter VII. These came from the Representative of Pakistan, and Mr Stauropoulos who appeared before the Court on behalf of the Secretary-General.

been granted that country by the League of Nations was illegal.[19]

Member states were therefore bound to recognize this declaration. The Court stated:

It would be an untenable interpretation to maintain that, once such a declaration had been made by the Security Council under Article 24 of the Charter on behalf of all member states, those Members would be free to act in disregard of such illegality or even to recognize violations of law resulting from it.[20]

It added:

It has been contended that Article 25 . . . applies only to enforcement measures adopted under Chapter VII of the Charter. It is not possible to find in the Charter any support for this view, Article 25 is not confined to decisions in regard to enforcement action but applies to 'the decisions of the Security Council' adopted in accordance with the Charter.[21]

The Court also observed that Article 25 was not located in Chapter VII of the Charter but immediately after Article 24 in Chapter V. This suggests that the Court took the view that if Article 25 was meant to refer only to Chapter VII the drafters would have placed it in Chapter VII.

According to the Court, therefore, when the Council passes a resolution which invokes Article 25 such a resolution should be taken as binding unless the contrary be proved. Rejecting the opinion, Judge Fitzmaurice argued that since the question whether or not any given resolution of the Council is binding must be a matter for objective determination in each individual case, the Council cannot merely by invoking Article 25, impart obligatory character to a resolution which would not otherwise possess it according to the terms of the Chapter or Article of the Charter on the basis of which the Council is, or must be deemed to be, acting.[22] Furthermore, he rejected the whole concept that the Security Council can bind members at all except when acting under Chapter VII, or possibly under Chapter VIII too.

This view was subscribed to by the British Government, according to the British Representative at the United Nations

[19] See Resolutions 264 (1969), 269 (1960), and 276 (1970).
[20] (1971) *I.C.J. Rep*, 52–3.   [21] Ibid.   [22] Ibid. 293–4.

during the debate on the Namibia question in 1971.[23] If this is the present position of the British Government on this point, it would appear to represent a marked change from the position that Government held in 1948 as stated by Sir Hartley Shawcross in the *Corfu Channel* case when he submitted that 'one could not find in the Charter itself a shred of support for the view that Article 25 is limited in its application to Chapter VII of the Charter'.[24] If this is the case, the change of heart on the part of Britain could be attributed to what Sir Colin Crowe in the *Namibia* case called 'the clear understanding' of the members 'that the Council could take decisions binding on Member States generally only if there had been a determination under Article 39'.[25] This 'clear understanding', it would appear, was derived from the subsequent practice of the Council.[26]

It is submitted that the better view is that adopted by the majority judges in the *Namibia* case. This may be strengthened by the fact that on many occasions the Council had adopted binding resolutions without specifically indicating the provisions of the Charter under which they were passed.[27] One reason for this may have been the fact that some decisions could not readily be classified under any one or other of the Charter provisions. What seems important is whether or not the Council has power to act. If it does, then the question whether or not a given resolution is binding is a matter to be determined in each individual case according to the intention of the drafters of the resolution as ascertained from the text and *travaux préparatoires* of the resolution as well as all the circumstances surrounding its adoption except on an issue which does not permit the adoption of a binding decision such as under Chapter VI of the Charter.

The power of the Council to bind member states even when it is acting under its general powers in Article 24 was clearly explained by the Secretary-General in his statement to the ninety-first meeting of the Security Council in respect of

[23] Higgins, 'The Advisory Opinion on Namibia: Which UN Resolutions are Binding under Article 25 of the Charter?', (1972), 21 *ICLQ*, 227.
[24] (1949) *I.C.J. Rep.* Preliminary Objections, Pleadings, vol. III, 72, 76–7.
[25] S/PV 1589, 26–7.
[26] Higgins, 'The Advisory Opinion on Namibia', 282.
[27] See Greig, *International Law* (Butterworths, 2nd edn., 1976), 727, 742–3.

Trieste.[28] The statement pointed out that the records of the San Francisco Conference indicated that, as the result of the rejection of the Belgian amendment to restrict the powers of the Council to bind members of the Organization 'the obligation of the Members to carry out the decisions of the Security Council applies equally to decisions under Article 24 and to the decisions made under the grant of specific powers.'[29] What is the legal significance of this statement for the purpose of determining the question under discussion?

There are two factors which make this statement of considerable legal significance. Firstly, according to Article 7 of the Charter, the Secretariat is one of the principal orgâns of the United Nations. The Secretariat comprises the Secretary-General and the staff appointed by him.[30] The Secretary-General, being the 'Chief Administrative Officer of the Organization', is a very important officer of the Organization whose pronouncements carry considerable weight. He has even been referred to, because of this important position he holds, as one of the principal organs of the United Nations.[31]

Secondly, the legal pronouncement of the Secretary-General represents one of the rare occasions when international legal issues have been left to an impartial tribunal.[32] Thus Schachter states that the Secretariat's 'presentation of legal points, while not authoritative, may nevertheless be considered as "technical" and non-political'.[33]

The influence of legal rules pronounced by the Secretary-General rests largely on the fact that their validity is independent of the interests of any particular state or, alternatively, that they coincide with the interest of all states. The former is the characteristic of the pronouncements of the Secretary-General on legal points of great significance because the legal work of the Secretariat is performed by its Legal Department,

---

[28] *UNSCOR* (2nd year), No. 3, 44–5.
[29] (1946–51) *Repertoire of the Practice of the Security Council*, 483.
[30] Arts. 97 and 101 of the Charter.
[31] Alexandrowicz, 'The Secretary-General of the United Nations' (1962) 11, *ICLQ*, 1112.
[32] Schachter, 'The Development of International Law through the Legal Opinions of the Secretary-General', (1948) 25, *BYIL*, 91.
[33] Ibid.

a non-political body which is not seriously subject to control by any particular government.[34]

Although these legal pronouncements of the Secretary-General probably do not bind member states, it would appear that a number of commentators hold the view that his pronouncement on the powers of the Council to bind member states even when it is acting under its general powers was a correct interpretation of Article 24.[35] It is submitted that this position has now been settled by the Advisory Opinion of the International Court of Justice in the *Namibia* case that has already been examined above.[36]

C. *Could the General Powers of the Security Council have Provided an Alternative Basis for the Rhodesian Action to Chapter VII?*

It is now necessary to see how the general powers of the Security Council under Article 24 and the applicability of Article 25 to them as discussed above could have affected the Rhodesian enforcement action. Before this is done a brief summary of how the Rhodesian problem was dealt with in the United Nations may be useful to remind the reader of what has been discussed in order to see the discussion that follows in its correct perspective.

The first United Nations organ to be interested in the Rhodesian independence question was the General Assembly.[37] The early resolutions of this organ concentrated on requesting the United Kingdom to do everything possible to lead Rhodesia to independence on the basis of majority rule.[38] However, the Special Committee on Colonialism soon drew the attention of the Security Council to the problem as it began

---

[34] See the discussion in the Sixth Committee, *UNGAOR*, 44th and 45th mtg. 8-9 Oct., 1947; UN Doc. A/C.6/167/Rev. 1. 14 Oct., 1947.
[35] See e.g. Higgins, 'The Advisory Opinion on Namibia' (1972) 21, *ICLQ*, 270; Cohen, *The United Nations Constitutional Development, Growth and Possibilities* (Harvard UP, 1961); Whiteman, vol. 13, 470; Schachter, 'The Development of International Law', 91; and Castañeda, *Effects of United Nations Resolution* (1969), 90.   [36] (1971) *I.C.J. Rep.* 52-3.
[37] (1962) *YBUN*, 417.
[38] See e.g., Res. 1747 (xvi); 1755 (xvii); 1760 (xvii).

to fear that the situation was becoming 'explosive'. The Security Council discussed it in August 1963.[39] Taking note of this, the General Assembly also expressed deep concern 'at the explosive situation existing in . . . Rhodesia owing to the denial of political rights to the vast majority of the African population and the entrenchment of the minority régime in power . . .'.[40] Following the proclamation of UDI the General Assembly passed Resolution 2024 (xx) recommending to 'the Security Council to consider this situation as a matter of urgency'.[41]

A point worth emphasizing about the work of the General Assembly between 1962 and 1965 is that it was largely concerned with the implementation of the Declaration of the Granting of Independence to Colonial Countries and Peoples, rather than with the maintenance of international peace and security. Even after UDI had been proclaimed the Assembly could only describe the situation as 'explosive' and 'urgent'. This description seems to have been concerned with Rhodesia's internal peace rather than with international peace as such, although it obviously also recognized the relevance of the latter.

However, when the Assembly adopted Resolution 2024 (xx) recommending that the Security Council discuss Rhodesia as a matter of urgency, it had by that time become concerned over the escalation of the danger the Rhodesian situation posed to international peace and security, an area in which the Security Council has primary responsibility. As already seen in Chapter II above, the Security Council had actually discussed the Rhodesian situation but failed to adopt any resolution because of a British veto in 1963. At that time Ghana, Mali, the United Arab Republic, Uganda, Tanganyika, and Morocco were of the opinion that the Rhodesian situation endangered international peace and security. This argument was, however, rejected by the United Kingdom. Similarly, the United States maintained, as did Britain, that the situation in Rhodesia did not warrant any action by the Security Council. As already seen, however, the Council did pass Resolution 202 (1965) on 6 May 1965.[42]

[39] (1962) *YBUN*, 472.   [40] GA Res. 1889 (DVII).
[41] 11 Nov. 1965.   [42] See Chapter II above.

This resolution did not indicate the Charter provision under which it was passed. It merely stated that the Council was 'disturbed at the further worsening of the situation' in Rhodesia. The views of some delegates, however, were more precise on the issue. For example, Mr Daudou Thiam, speaking on behalf of his country, Senegal, and the Organization of African Unity, said that the problem of Rhodesia was undeniably 'a threat to international peace and security and therefore within the competence of the Security Council'.[43] The reference to the phrase 'a threat to international peace and security' was meant to invoke Chapter VII of the Charter, but the attempt was unsuccessful.

When UDI was proclaimed the Security Council passed Resolutions 216 (1965) and 217 (1965) also without invoking Chapter VII. In Chapter II above it was proposed that these resolutions were based on the doctrine of 'international concern'. It could be argued that they could also have been based on the general powers given to the Security Council in Article 24. It should be added, however, that no respresentative made any reference to this provision during the debates. Nevertheless, the absence of any such reference does not necessarily exclude those general powers of the Council. Thus in the *Namibia* case,[44] already discussed, it was seen that the Security Council had not specifically invoked its general powers, yet the International Court of Justice held that the Council had acted under those powers.[45] Even if they were never passed under those general powers, it is, for academic reasons, important to know that the Security Council could have invoked those powers if this was found to be necessary.

Further, if the Security Council had found it necessary, it could, as already seen, have passed binding resolutions as well under the general powers. This, however, should not be taken as indicating that the Security Council could have invoked its general powers under Article 24 in lieu of acting under Chapter VII of the Charter. Although there is nothing constitutionally wrong about that, it is submitted that Article 24 should not be used as a substitute for the specific powers granted to the Security Council, but should be used only in

---

[43] *U.N. Monthly Chronicle*, May 1965, 37.
[44] (1971) *I.C.J. Rep.*, 52.   [45] Ibid.

those cases which do not readily fall within the framework of the more detailed provisions of the Charter.[46] Thus if a given case falls clearly within one or other of the specific powers, only those powers should be invoked. Article 24 should therefore be regarded as a reservoir of authority to be used in the rare cases which need the action of the Security Council and yet cannot be said to come within any of the Chapters named in the second paragraph of Article 24. This interpretation ensures that the use of these powers is not limitless.

In the Rhodesian case, these general powers could not be used to deal with the independence crisis as a whole because the situation that developed after the proclamation of UDI made the problem one that fell clearly within Chapter VII of the Charter. Consequently, it would have been improper to invoke Article 24, in order to impose the enforcement action against the Smith regime.

[46] Schachter, 'The Development of International Law', 101.

IX

The Question of Use of Military Force
Against the Smith Regime

THE usual way of dealing with a rebellion is for the legal
authority to crush it with all the might at its disposal, particularly by using military force. When the Rhodesian Government threatened a unilateral declaration, it seemed logical
that Britain would at least not rule out the use of force to
quell the rebellion. Other states therefore reacted with dismay
when Britain did just that.[1] This seemed to be an open
invitation to the Rhodesian Government to declare Rhodesia
independent. A number of reasons may be put forward to
explain this unexpected behaviour of the British Government.
It has been suggested that the British Government was concerned that British soldiers would have found it difficult to
fire at people of British origin in Rhodesia, and that therefore
the loyalty of some soldiers could not be relied upon. It is
doubtful that this consideration was responsible for the
British repudiation of use of force in Rhodesia, although it is
possible that it was a peripheral factor. Surely if the British
soldiers would have been unwilling to fight the Rhodesian
forces, it stands to reason that the Rhodesian forces would
also find it difficult to fight their kith and kin from Britain.
There are probably two most important reasons for this
strange British reaction to the Rhodesian rebellion. Firstly,
British public opinion was extremely divided, with the majority opposed to use of force.[2] Secondly, the British Government was not likely to carry the support of the Conservative
Party with it if it had decided to use force, and this would
have destroyed the bipartisan policy that had been maintained
up to the time of UDI.

This British position was a source of heated discussion
between Britain and the Afro-Asian countries at the United

[1] *UNSCOR*, 1257th mtg.
[2] See e.g. letters to the editor of *The Times* (London), 27 and 28 Oct. 1965.

Nations. The British Foreign Secretary, Mr Stewart, told the Security Council:

I ought to make clear, as has been made clear before, that we do not believe that the use of military force can solve this problem. I know that there are those who ask for this step. I understand their feelings but I cannot accept their judgement . . . Let us remember . . . that it is one thing to start the use of force, it is another to predict or contain its content.

The British Government, therefore, after the most sober consideration, is resolved that an attempt to impose a constitutional solution by military force in . . . Rhodesia not only would involve misery for millions of innocent people but would thrust into a still more distant future the right and just solution of this problem . . .[3]

This argument was unconvincing, and the other representatives made this clear by citing examples of comparable situations where Britain had lost no time in sending in troops.[4] The British Government, however, rejected the argument that there were parallels between the Rhodesian case and the situations cited.[5]

African nations were convinced that force would have to be used against the rebels. If Britain would not use force someone else would have to do so. Since Britain had ruled this out it seemed likely that forces from some members of the Organization of African Unity would be willing to contribute forces to fight in Rhodesia. Zambia would have had to provide a base for those forces. President Kaunda of Zambia was, however, not willing to allow any forces other than the British ones on Zambian soil.[6] Britain, however, did make a token gesture by sending a battalion of troops and a few RAF aircraft to be deployed on the Zambian side of the border with Rhodesia. Their role was vaguely connected with the guarding of the electricity power house on the southern side of the Kariba Dam jointly owned by Zambia and Rhodesia. This gesture did nothing to mollify the Organization of African Unity (OAU). Some of its most militant members such as Ghana and Guinea wanted African nations to seize the military initiative to bring down the Smith regime, whether Zambia liked it or not. This was, however, not the popular

[3] *UNSCOR*, 1257th mtg., paras. 23–4.
[4] Ibid. paras. 44, 57–8, 69, 124.
[5] Ibid. para. 26.   [6] Good, *UDI*, 96.

view of the generality of the membership of the Organization. It would appear that the stand taken by President Kaunda was well advised. It was quite clear that any intervention by African nations would have posed immense logistical problems. Zambia was right in not taking a chance in a war which Africa could not be sure of winning easily. It should be remembered that Zambia was newly independent, having inherited very few military resources from the Federation of Rhodesia and Nyasaland. Rhodesia, on the other hand, had inherited the federal air force and other military hardware which it could put to use in any war with Africa.

Other troops which could be used in Rhodesia were United Nations forces. Britain was not willing to allow these troops to be involved either. This shows that the decision by Britain not to use force in Rhodesia had very little to do with the feasibility of staging such an exercise. It had very much to do with Britain's will in this matter. Britain simply had no wish to subject her kith and kin to military coercion. Consequently, Britain resisted all pressure to allow the use of the United Nations forces just as much as she resisted pressure to use her own forces in the rebel territory.

The Use of Force by the United Nations

The military powers of the Security Council were generally regarded by the delegates at the San Francisco Conference as the corner-stone of the Council's enforcement measures against aggression.[7] Even so it was made clear at the Conference that they should be used only if peaceful measures had failed or were seen to have no chance of success. 'Peaceful settlement' of international conflict was therefore considered the 'first line of defence', and efforts were to be made to 'make unnecessary, if possible, the use of armed force among the great family of nations'.[8] The spirit of this was adopted unanimously by Committee III of Commission III and embodied in Article 42 of the Charter which provides:

Should the Security Council consider that measures provided for in Article 41 would be inadequate or have proved to be inadequate, it may take such action by air, sea, or land forces as may be necessary to

---

[7] (1945) 11, *UNCIO*, Doc. 1088/111/8, 22.　　　[8] Ibid., 30.

maintain or restore international peace and security. Such action may include demonstrations, blockades and other operations by air, sea, or land forces of members of the United Nations.

The Committee in charge of drafting the provisions concerned with the mechanism of enforcement measures emphasized the importance of the unanimity with which these measures had been adopted. The Committee believed that the unanimity showed the significance which the members attached to the military provisions. It would appear that the Committee held the view that the exercise of the military powers depended on the conclusion of military agreements provided for under Article 43 of the Charter which provides:

All members of the United Nations . . . undertake to make available to the Security Council, on its call and in accordance with a special agreement or agreements, armed forces, assistance, and facilities, including rights of passage, necessary for the purpose of maintaining international peace and security . . . The agreement or agreements shall be negotiated as soon as possible on the initiative of the Security Council. They shall be concluded between the Security Council and members [of the United Nations] . . .

Although the members of the United Nations assumed an obligation to participate in the military operations in accordance with the decisions of the Security Council, that obligation is dependent upon the conclusion of special agreements mentioned in Article 43. Without such agreements no member is bound to participate in any military action taken by the United Nations. At the San Francisco Conference, the delegations of Australia, New Zealand, and India were critical of the Dumbarton Oaks Proposals on this point. They believed that the Proposals allowed excessive latitude to member states with respect to the conclusion of the special agreements. They held the view that the 'obligation imposed upon them was not specific; the consent of the Security Council was presented as a simple formality, to such an extent that one might ask if, in reality, such agreements would be concluded and if they would fulfil their objective'.[9]

However, it was felt that the initiative to conclude the special agreements would come from the Security Council

---

[9] Ibid. 22.

which would constitute one party, and the agreements would be signed between the Security Council and the member concerned. This would ensure, it was felt, both that these agreements were concluded as soon as possible and that the Council as a participant would see that they effectively fulfilled the aims stipulated in the Charter. France was particularly interested in ensuring that the military provisions of the Charter worked because, as M. Dejean pointed out, 'France has twice in a quarter century been the victim of German aggression.'[10] He regarded these provisions as the key 'to the whole of the Dumbarton Oaks plan, because they [determined] whether the new security organization [was] to prove impotent and, therefore, be a failure, or whether it [was] to be provided with the necessary means for carrying out its important task'.[11]

The Rapporteur of Committee III of Commission III spoke very highly of the military provisions which had been adopted.[12] However, as some delegations had feared, no special agreements have up to now been signed as required by Article 43. This is due to disagreements among the permanent members of the Security Council.[13] It was a blow to the efficacy of the United Nations in dealing with aggression. This does not necessarily mean that the United Nations is thus precluded from raising armed forces.[14] This view, it would appear, received support from the International Court of Justice[15] in the *Expenses* case in which the Court was concerned with the United Nations Emergency Force (UNEF) in the Middle East established in 1956, and the United Nations Force in the Congo (ONUC) established in 1960. Neither of these were established under Article 43 special agreements. The Court stated, *inter alia*:

an argument which insists that all measures taken for the maintenance of international peace and security must be financed through agreements concluded under Article 43, would seem to exclude the possibility that the Security Council might act under some other Article of the Charter. The Court cannot accept so limited a view of the powers of the Security

---

[10] Ibid. 25.   [11] Ibid. 26.   [12] Ibid. 24.
[13] Goodrich and Simon, *The United Nations and the Maintenance of International Peace and Security* (Brookings, 1955), 398–405.
[14] *The Expenses* case (1962), ICJ *Pleadings*, 167.   [15] Ibid.

Council under the Charter. It cannot be said that the Charter has left the Security Council impotent in the face of an emergency situation when agreement under Article 43 has not been concluded.[16]

There are three major forms of armed forces which the United Nations may establish: United Nations Observer Forces, Peace-Keeping Forces, and Enforcement Forces. An observer force is a type of military group intended for 'truce and military observation missions' which the United Nations has employed in a number of troubled areas.[17] This form of armed forces has no relevance in the present discussion and will therefore not be pursued further. An enforcement force, on the other hand, has a policy-enforcing function. The force has the responsibility of taking military action to enforce a decision of the United Nations in order to maintain or restore international peace and security. It is essentially and primarily a fighting force such as the one employed in the Korean case in 1950.[18] This is the type which the British Government did not want to see employed in Rhodesia. It is worth noting, however, that in 1966 the United Kingdom did after all allow a limited use of force in the Rhodesian conflict when the Security Council authorized the United Kingdom itself 'to prevent, by the use of force if necessary, the arrival at Beira of vessels reasonably believed to be carrying oil . . . for Rhodesia'.[19] Pursuant to this authorization British frigates intercepted two merchant ships on the high seas, which were bound for Beira, Mozambique.

It has been argued that the Korean operation was not carried out by 'United Nations' forces but by forces of the states which contributed them. It has been pointed out that although the forces had been authorized by the Security Council to fly the United Nations flag, and were awarded United Nations medals by the General Assembly, all the decisions concerning the operations of the forces were taken by the United States, and the Commander took his orders from that country too and not from the United Nations.[20]

[16] Ibid.
[17] Seyersted, 'United Nations Forces: Some Legal Problems', (1961), 37 *BYBIL*, 354.
[18] Higgins, *United Nations Peace-Keeping*, vol. 2, (Oxford, 1970), 160; Seyersted, 356; Bowett, *United Nations Forces*, 29.
[19] Res. 221 (1966).   [20] Akehurst (2nd edn.), 265.

As Akehurst points out, the decisions to dismiss the original Commander, General MacArthur, and to appoint a new Commander were made by the United States.[21]

Other commentators disagree with this argument.[22] Bowett, for example, argues that the evidence supporting his view is that the action was originated by the Security Council resolutions, and that a number of subsequent General Assembly resolutions referred to the action as United Nations action and also referred to United Nations Forces.[23] He maintains that the United States concluded agreements with contributing states only as 'the executive agent of the United Nations Forces in Korea'.[24] There are strong arguments on both sides. It is submitted that the question whether the Korean forces were or were not United Nations forces is of very little legal significance in so far as those forces were authorized by the United Nations. Besides, as already pointed out, in the Rhodesian case, the United Nations authorized the use of force by one member state, Britain, off the Mozambique coast. If the United Nations can authorize a single member to exercise force on its behalf it surely can authorize many states to do likewise. Furthermore, if the United Nations can authorize states to use force on its behalf in the absence of Article 43 agreements, it follows that it can itself use such force in similar circumstances. Obviously, in the absence of special agreements, the United Nations cannot compel member states to contribute contingents to the United Nations for enforcement purposes although it can set up armed forces using troops voluntarily contributed by the members of the Organization and these forces could legitimately be established under Article 42 of the Charter.[25]

The third major form an armed force may take is that of a peace-keeping force whose function is to police an area of conflict to prevent hostilities between warring armies following the signing of a cease-fire agreement. Its aim is to preserve a state of peace in a given area without engaging in actual fighting except in self-defence.[26] This type of armed force

[21] Ibid.   [22] Bowett, 47.
[23] See G.A. Res. 376 (V), 377 (V), 483 (V), 498 (V).
[24] Bowett, 46.   [25] Higgins, vol. 2 176–7.
[26] Frydenberg, *Peace-Keeping* (Oslo, 1964), 280; Seyersted, 354.

was expected to play a role in Rhodesia under the Anglo-American Proposals for Settlement of the Rhodesian dispute. For instance, at the beginning of 1977 there was speculation among political commentators and the mass media that if a Rhodesian constitutional settlement were to be achieved, a Commonwealth peace-keeping force could be established to hold the ring during the transitional period. This idea was, however, dashed when the Commonwealth Heads of Government showed little enthusiasm for it at their London Conference in June 1977.[27] The use of Commonwealth forces, however, remained a possibility throughout that year but when Dr Owen, the British Foreign Secretary, presented a set of settlement proposals to the House of Commons in September that year he included provision not for use of Commonwealth forces but for a United Nations peace-keeping force, whose presence was to be limited to the transitional period before majority rule.[28] Briefly, the arrangements involved the appointment by the Secretary-General of the United Nations, on the authority of the Security Council, of a Special Representative in Rhodesia. The Security Council would establish a United Nations Zimbabwe force whose role would include the supervision of the cease-fire, give support to the civil power, and liaise with the existing Rhodesian armed forces and with the forces of the liberation Armies.[29]

In pursuance of these proposals the Security Council adopted Resolution 415 (1977) on 29 September 1977, requesting the Secretary-General of the United Nations to appoint, in consultation with the Security Council members, a representative to enter into discussion with the British Resident Commissioner designate, and with all the parties, concerning the military and associated arrangements that were considered necessary to effect the transition to majority rule in Rhodesia. Major-General Prem Chand of India was appointed the United Nations Special Representative in Rhodesia. He, together with Field Marshal Lord Carver, the British Resident Commissioner designate to Rhodesia,

[27] *The Times* (London), 8 June 1977.
[28] Press Release, Foreign and Commonwealth Office, 1 Sept. 1977.
[29] Ibid.

visited Southern Africa in October 1977 and held discussions with various parties. The result of those discussions was disappointing. The whole Anglo-American initiative was placed on ice for some time and finally abandoned when Mr Smith concluded his 'internal settlement' in Rhodesia.[30]

The abandonment of the plans for a United Nations peace-keeping force was inevitable since one of the conditions of the deployment of such forces is the consent of the adversaries involved in the conflict. This is necessary because the force is basically a non-combatant one as opposed to an enforcement force which does not require such a consent. For peace-keeping forces to be deployed in Rhodesia it was necessary for both the Smith regime and the liberation forces to give their consent to such a deployment. This, as it turned out, these parties were not ready to give. Even when the Rhodesian problem was finally resolved, no peace-keeping forces were used in Rhodesia. At the Commonwealth Conference in Lusaka, Zambia, in August 1979, the idea of involving the United Nations in Rhodesia during the transition period was touched upon but never seriously canvassed. Britain was against use of United Nations forces in Rhodesia and, in the spirit of goodwill and compromise at the Conference, the other delegations were content with an anodyne phrase to the effect that when a new constitution was reached there would be free and fair elections properly supervised under British Government authority and with Commonwealth observers. This did not appear to rule out United Nations involvement. But as far as Britain was concerned the matter was closed. Thus at the Lancaster House Conference the Patriotic Front insisted on the use of a United Nations peace-keeping force during the transitional period in Rhodesia.[31] Although it received some backing from Mr Shridath Ramphal, the Commonwealth Secretary-General, the British Government argued that that was not part of what was agreed at the Commonwealth Conference. Lord Carrington, the Lancaster House Conference Chairman, insisted on using the existing Rhodesian forces who would be responsible to the British appointed

---

[30] See Chapter I above; *The Times* (London), 4 Mar. 1978, 1.
[31] *African Research Bulletin*, vol. 16, No. 10, 15 Nov. 1979, 5486.

governor.[32] He therefore turned down the counter-proposals of the Patriotic Front on the transitional arrangements which contained provisions for United Nations involvement.

[32] Ibid. 5488.

X

Some Aspects of the Voting Procedure in the Security Council

As a result of the position France had taken on the principle of domestic jurisdiction and the Rhodesian independence crisis, she abstained when the Security Council adopted nearly all the resolutions on Rhodesia. The Soviet Union also often abstained but for different reasons. Thus when the Security Council passed Resolutions 221 (1966), and 232 (1966), both these states again abstained. The Governments of Portugal[1] and South Africa[2] reserved their positions as regards the validity of the two resolutions. These were the first resolutions of real significance on Rhodesia as they purported to bind member states, and Portugal and South Africa were likely to be seriously affected by them if these resolutions were held to be validly adopted, because Portugal was the administrative power in Mozambique, Rhodesia's neighbour, with close trade ties with Rhodesia, and South Africa of course was Rhodesia's big brother in many respects, having, for example, economic and ethnic ties.

The Portuguese reservations were contained in a letter dated 27 April 1966 from that country's Foreign Minister to the Secretary-General of the United Nations, requesting that they be submitted to the Office of Legal Affairs of the United Nations which was further requested to answer the following three questions:

(a) If the abstention of a permanent member of the Security Council is understood not to be equal to a veto, must it then be considered that a resolution under Chapter VII, involving the use of force, can be deemed to be adopted even when all the permanent members have abstained?

(b) If this conclusion is wrong, how many and which of the permanent

---

[1] UN Docs. S/7271, 28 Apr. 1966, and S/7271/Corr. I.

[2] UN Doc. S/7392, July 1966.

members of the Council may abstain without such abstention
causing the rejection of a draft resolution?
(c) If the conclusion is correct, is it to be understood that the non-
permanent members of the Council have the right or the practical
opportunity, to take decisions concerning peace, war and world
security and to formulate and have a policy implemented which
affects the entire community of nations, without the votes of all
or some of the permanent members?

What seemed to be bothering Portugal and South Africa
were the amendments of the Charter which had been adopted
on 17 December 1963 and which came into force on 31
August 1965,[3] as a result of which the membership of the
Security Council was increased from eleven to fifteen by the
addition of four more elective members whose total number
now stands at ten. The minimum number of votes needed to
pass a resolution in the Council was also raised from seven to
nine. It now became possible to obtain the required minimum
votes in the Council without the support of even a single vote
of the permanent members. This had not been possible before
these amendments were effected. The question posed by
Portugal was whether a draft resolution passed in this way
could be considered as validly adopted as long as no permanent member used its veto.

The Portuguese letter further stated:

The Portuguese Government . . . considers that, when action under
Chapter VII is sought for the first time in the fifteen-member Council
and force is resorted to in the face of the abstention of some permanent
members, the entire problem needs urgent examination under the new
conditions prevailing in that important organ of the United Nations.[4]

Similarly, South Africa stated that it had:

given consideration to the legal aspects of this matter particularly as
this is the first occasion since the amendment of Article 27 of the
Charter on which the Security Council purported to give a decision
involving enforcement measures in terms of Chapter VII, and as the
validity of this action has been widely questioned on various grounds
including the fact that two permanent members abstained from voting
on the draft resolution in question.[5]

[3] *UNGAOR*, 18th Sess., Suppl. No. 15, 21–2; G.A. Res. 1991 (XVIII) A.
[4] UN Docs. S/7271, 28 Apr. 1966, and S/7271/Corr. I.
[5] UN Doc. S/7392, July 1966. It is not correct that the action had been widely
questioned. Neither the Soviet Union nor France, both of which abstained,

In reply to these requests the Secretary-General pointed out that it has never been the practice of the office of the Legal Affairs to give advice on sole requests of a member state. He pointed out that only the Security Council was in a position to give an authoritative interpretation of its Resolution 221 (1966). Nevertheless, he observed that a detailed study prepared for his own information did not in its conclusions support any of the reservations advanced by the Portuguese Government.[6]

The voting procedure in the Security Council is contained in Article 27 of the Charter which reads:

1. Each member of the Security Council shall have one vote.
2. Decisions of the Security Council on procedural matters shall be made by an affirmative vote of nine members.
3. Decisions of the Security Council on all other matters shall be made by an affirmative vote of nine members including the concurring votes of the permanent members provided that in decisions under Chapter VI, and under paragraph 3 of Article 52, a party of a dispute shall abstain from voting.

The interpretation of this Article has caused considerable controversy among scholars,[7] and has therefore been widely commented upon. For that reason the discussion will be concentrated only on paragraph 3 which contains the Yalta voting formula. This formula contains the rule of unanimity of the five great powers on votes on all non-procedural questions in the Security Council. It was offered as a compromise proposal by the President of the United States, Mr Roosevelt, and accepted by the leader of the Soviet Union, Stalin, and the Prime Minister of the United Kingdom, Churchill, at the Crimea Conference, and was incorporated in the Dumbarton Oaks proposals which formed the basis for the discussions at the San Francisco Conference in 1945.

The major difficulty is determining the precise meaning of

questioned the resolutions on the grounds of the amendments referred to by Portugal and South Africa. France questioned the whole involvement of the United Nations while the Soviet Union did not think the measures taken were sufficient.

[6] UN Doc. S/7735/Rev. 1, 3.

[7] L. M. Goodrich and E. Hambro, 220; H. Kelsen, *Yale Law Journal* (1946) 59, *Harvard LR*; H. Kelsen, *Law of the United Nations* (1950); L. Gross (1951) 60, *Yale Law Journal* 357; Yuen-li-Liang (1947) 24 *BYBIL*, 357; L. Gross (1968) 62, *AJIL*, 315; and C. A. Stavropoulos (1967) 61, *AJIL*, 737.

the phrase 'concurring votes' in paragraph 3. Some jurists hold the view that it means 'affirmative votes'.[8] They argue, therefore, that there is no ambiguity at all in the meaning of the phrase. Other jurists, however, disagree.[9] The controversy is actually older than the Charter itself because one can see that complete agreement did not exist even among the drafters of the Charter if one studies the *travaux préparatoires* of the San Francisco Conference.[10] Of particular relevance is a question posed by a sub-committee of Committee 111/1 at the Conference which read:

If a motion is moved in the Security Council on a matter, other than a matter of procedure, under the general words in paragraph 3, would the abstention from voting of any one of the permanent members of the Security Council have the same effect as a negative vote by that member in preventing the Security Council from reaching a decision on the matter?[11]

Athough no satisfactory answer was given by the Sponsoring Governments and France at the Conference, the issue of a voluntary abstention by a permanent member on a non-procedural or substantive matter has now been settled by the practice of the Security Council. The relevant practice dates as far back as 1946 when the Soviet delegate abstained from voting on an Australian draft resolution on the Spanish question.[12] That abstention was not treated as a negative vote. Afterwards, a long series followed in which one permanent member or another voluntarily abstained on a non-procedural matter and on each occasion such an abstention was not treated as a veto. R. Higgins in 1967 counted 107 occasions when this occurred.[13] C. A. Stavropoulos in 1966 counted 264 voluntary abstentions.[14] The difference between

[8] L. Gross, 'Voting in the Security Council' (1951) 60, *Yale Law Journal* 210.
[9] M. S. McDougal and R. N. Gardner, 'The Veto and the Charter' (1951) 60, *Yale Law Journal* 261; H. Kelsen, *The Law of the United Nations* (Stevens, 1950), XIV; Yuen-li-Liang, 'The Settlement of Disputes in the Security Council; The Yalta Voting Formula', (1947) 24, *BYBIL*, 357.
[10] (1945) 11 UNCIO, Docs. 417/111/1/19, p. 314; 897/111/1/42, p. 433; 1058/111/1 58, pp. 684–5; 922/111/1/44, pp. 459–60; 1105/111/148(2) p. 534; WD 359/111/155, p. 610; 855/111/1/B/2(a) p. 707; 852/III/1/37(1) p. 611.
[11] UNCIO, Doc. 855/111/1/B/2 (a), 707.
[12] (1946–51) *Repertoire of the Practice of the Security Council*, 173.
[13] R. Higgins, 'International Law, Rhodesia and the United Nations', (1967) 23, *The World Today*, 97. [14] C. A. Stavropoulos, 743.

these two scholars emanates from the difficulty of determining what constitutes a non-procedural matter, and this is another area of controversy. Nevertheless it seems clear that the practice of the Security Council has now established beyond doubt that a voluntary abstention by a permanent member does not amount to a veto. Whether this practice has amended or interpreted the relevant provisions of the Charter remains a moot point.[15]

The Portuguese and the South African Governments also seem to have accepted that as a result of the practice of the Security Council, a voluntary abstention in a non-procedural matter is not a veto. The first, and the third questions put to the Secretary-General by the Portuguese Government suggest that in the light of the changed composition of the Security Council in which it is now possible for non-permanet members alone to obtain the required minimum number of votes to pass a valid resolution, there is now a need to distinguish between resolutions intended to invoke Chapter VII of the Charter, especially those calling for the use of force, and other resolutions, so that the non-permanent members of the Security Council are not afforded 'the practical opportunity to take decisions concerning peace, war and world security, and to formulate and have a policy implemented which affects the entire community of nations, without the votes of all or some of the permanent members'.[16]

This Portuguese sentiment has the support of some jurists. Bowett, for example, argues that there may be room for considering a resolution which is passed with all the permanent members (or even some) abstaining, as constitutionally valid though not binding to the extent that it embodies a decision which purports to be mandatory under Chapter VII.[17] L. Gross also maintains that the amendments of the composition of the Security Council is crucial in that it allows a resolution to be validly adopted even if all permanent members abstain. He holds the view that this appears 'to justify the conclusion

---

[15] See M. B. Akehurst (1974-5), *BYBIL*, 273 and 278, 244. L. Gross, 'Voting in the Security Council', (1968) 62, *AJIL*, 328; D. W. Bowett, *The Law of International Institutions* (1975), 28-9.

[16] UN Docs. S/7271, 28 Apr. 1966, and S/7271/Corr. 1.

[17] D. W. Bowett, *The Law of International Institutions*, 29.

that decisions of the Security Council, particularly under Chapter VII should be regarded as permissive rather than as legally binding'.[18] According to this view, Article 25 of the Charter which states that members of the United Nations are bound by the decisions of the Security Council has also been affected since such decisions would no longer be binding on member states.

The arguments advanced to support this point of view are all political. There is nothing amiss about that, however, since the voting procedure was devised as a political device to give recognition to the predominant role supposed to be played by the most powerful nations in the maintenance of international peace and security. What is doubtful, however, is whether the enlargement of the Security Council with the attendant consequences of the voting procedure has really undermined the dominant political role which the permanent members have always enjoyed in the Security Council.

For a start, it is highly unlikely that a resolution which receives the minimum nine votes in the Security Council would fail to receive the support of even a single permanent member since some non-permanent members are in one way or another associated with one or other of the permanent members. Abstention by all permanent members is likely therefore to be joined by at least some of the non-permanent members and this would defeat the draft resolution in question if it thus receives less than nine votes. In any case, in the unlikely event of at least nine non-permanent members voting for a draft resolution not supported by any of the permanent members, the permanent members can exercise their veto power to prevent that draft resolution being passed. Furthermore, it should be realized that if the permanent members were ever in any doubt about the preservation of their dominant political position after the enlargement of the Security Council, they would not have allowed the amendment of the Charter that brought about changes in the composition of the Security Council.

It would appear from this that the answer to the first and third Portuguese questions put to the Secretary-General of

[18] L. Gross, 'Voting in the Security Council', (1968) 62, *AJIL*, 331-2.

the United Nations should be in the affirmative. In other words a resolution under Chapter VII, involving the use of force, can be deemed to be adopted even when all the permanent members have abstained, and such a resolution would be binding in accordance with Article 25 if it is a decision of the Security Council and a recommendation if it did not fall under Article 25. The Portuguese doubts about the legality of Resolutions 221 (1966) and 232 (1966) on Rhodesia were therefore unfounded. An observer may even doubt whether the reservations put by Portugal and South Africa were honestly held in view of those Governments' policies of non-compliance with the efforts of the United Nations to bring the Rhodesian rebellion to an end. This is particularly so since a number of subsequent resolutions were unanimously passed yet these two Governments still refused to comply with them.[19]

Another issue related to that under discussion is the selection of non-permanent members of the Council. This is governed by Article 23 which provides *inter alia*:

. . . The General Assembly shall elect ten other members of the Security Council, due regard being specially paid, in the first instance, to the contribution of the members of the United Nations to the maintenance of international peace and security and to the other purposes of the Organization, and also to equitable geographical distribution.

L. Gross takes up this issue and points out that in practice the tendency has been to concentrate on the 'equitable geographical distribution' at the expense of the requirement of the 'contribution of the Members . . . to the maintenance of international peace and security and to other purposes of' the United Nations. He criticizes the reinforcement of this practice by the General Assembly Resolution 1991 (XVIII) A. He argues, therefore, that 'no useful purpose will be served . . . in preserving the fiction that the Security Council in its composition is equipped to discharge effectively its primary responsibilities'.[20] For that reason, he maintains, the decision of the enlarged Security Council 'which is not the Security

---

[19] e.g. Resolutions 253 (1968) and 288 (1970) were passed unanimously, and Res. 277 (1970) was supported by all five permanent members of the Security Council.

[20] L. Gross, 'Voting in the Security Council', (1968), 62 *AJIL*, 332.

Council intended by the Charter, should not automatically have the legal significance which Article 25 attributes to the decisions of the Security Council intended by the Charter . . .' Consequently, he concludes:

Resolutions under Chapter VII are legally valid if adopted by nine non-permanent members without the opposing vote of any of the permanent members but they are permissive and not legally binding . . .[21]

The question of the distribution of the seats of non-permanent members has very little, if anything, to do with the voting procedure in the Security Council and does not, therefore, need discussion here. What is worth noting, nevertheless, is that when the question of equitable distribution of seats in the Security Council was debated in the General Assembly in 1963, there appeared to be unanimity among the members on the need for equitable representation in the Security Council.[22] In view of this support of the members for the equitable geographical distribution at the expense of the other criteria in selecting the non-permanent members of the Security Council, there does not appear to be any compelling reason for the argument put forward by Gross.

Moreover, it would appear that Gross falls short of carrying his argument to its logical conclusion; if the Security Council is improperly constituted, 'its' resolutions are not resolutions of the Security Council at all. If this is the case, such resolutions are not merely non-binding but totally void. It seems illogical to argue that they are valid but incapable of being binding; if they are valid, they are also capable of being binding under Article 25 of the Charter depending on the intention of the members and the wording of the resolution concerned.

Any doubt that may have existed about the validity of resolutions of the Security Council either because some permanent member(s) abstained when the resolution was adopted or because the membership of the Security Council is not one intended by the Charter, as Gross maintains, is probably now a matter of history in view of the advisory opinion of the International Court of Justice in the *Namibia* case,[23] where it was stated:

[21] Ibid.   [22] (1964) *YBUN*, 87.
[23] (1971) *I.C.J. Rep.*, 16.

. . . the positions taken by members of the Council, in particular its permanent members, have consistently and uniformly interpreted the practice of voluntary abstention by a permanent member as not constituting a bar to the adoption of resolutions. By abstaining, a permanent member does not signify its objection to the approval of what is being proposed; in order to prevent the adoption of a resolution requiring unanimity of the permanent members, a permanent member has only to cast a negative vote. This procedure followed by the Security Council, which has continued unchanged after the amendment in 1965 of Article 27 of the Charter, has been generally accepted by Members of the United Nations and evidences a general practice of that Organization . . .[24]

This advisory opinion rejected South Africa's argument that Resolution 276 (1970) on Namibia was not valid on account of the abstention of two permanent members of the Council.[25] By a majority decision, the Court advised that member states were obligated to comply with that resolution. The Court's advisory opinion was subsequently reaffirmed by Security Council Resolution 301 (1971).[26]

As S. D. Bailey points out, the International Court of Justice's Opinion on Namibia gives the 'final stamp of approval' to the view that abstention by a permanent member of the Council continues not to amount to a veto notwithstanding the amendment in 1965 of Articles 23 and 27 of the Charter.[27] It is submitted, therefore, that there is no juridical reason for concluding that the enlargement of the Council or the excessive reliance on the criterion of equitable geographical distribution *per se* render Security Council decisions necessarily non-mandatory irrespective of the texts of those resolutions. Whether or not a given resolution of the Council is mandatory is to be assessed from the text first and foremost, and then, if need be, also from the *travaux préparatoires*, of that resolution, and not merely from the fact that some or all of the permanent members of the Security Council abstained when the vote was taken.

In other words, a Security Council resolution which receives at least nine votes in favour may be both valid and binding,

---

[24] Ibid. 22.   [25] Ibid.
[26] *UN Monthly Chronicle*, Nov. 1971, 33.
[27] S. D. Bailey, 'The New Light on Abstentions in the United Nations Security Council', (1974) 50 *International Affairs* 554 at 573.

depending on its wording and/or the *travaux préparatoires*, provided that no permanent member of the Security Council cast a negative vote against it when the voting took place. Therefore the resolutions of the Security Council on Rhodesia which were adopted with one or more of the permanent members of the Council abstaining were not only valid but were also binding if all the relevant evidence so indicated, notwithstanding that they were passed by the enlarged Council whose membership contained non-permanent members selected largely on the basis of the equitable geographical distribution criterion. Consequently, the arguments of Portugal and South Africa had no legal basis whatever.

One other small point which may be mentioned in conclusion is whether the United Kingdom should not have refrained from participating in the voting on the Rhodesia question in compliance with the obligatory abstention required under Article 27 (3). The answer to this question is found in the decision of the International Court of Justice in the *Namibia* case where it was stated that the proviso on obligatory abstention 'requires for its application the prior determination of the Security Council that a dispute exists and that certain members of the Council are involved as parties to such a dispute'.[28] The Rhodesian problem was never treated as a dispute between states, but merely as a 'situation'. Consequently, the proviso did not apply to it.

Having said that, it may be pointed out that there are enormous difficulties in the implementation of this proviso about obligatory abstention. In some cases there are difficulties in distinguishing between a 'dispute' and a 'situation'. Furthermore, parties to a dispute become increasingly difficult to identify because, as Higgins points out, of the ever increasing interdependence of states.[29] In any case, this proviso has on a number of occasions not been complied with even where it was clearly appropriate. Higgins, for instance, cites the case of Ethiopia, which failed to abstain when the Security Council passed resolutions on South West Africa (now Namibia) in the 'dispute' Ethiopia and Liberia had against South Africa, and the case of the Soviet Union which did not abstain when

---

[28] (1971), *ICJ Rep.* 22.   [29] (1970) 64, *AJIL*, 1-2.

the Security Council voted on the problem of the Soviet intervention in Czechoslovakia in 1968.[30] The Rhodesian problem, however, did not suffer from any of these discrepancies, and the participation of the United Kingdom in all the votes which were taken on the Rhodesian question was not a violation of the voting procedure in the Security Council. It is submitted, therefore, that in all aspects of the voting procedure, the adoption of all the resolutions on the Rhodesian independence crisis was proper and there were no legitimate grounds for challenging the validity of any of those resolutions.

[30] Ibid.

XI

Discretionary Powers of the Security Council under Article 39 of the Charter

ARTICLE 39 of the Charter of the United Nations states:

The Security Council shall determine the existence of any threat to the peace, or act of aggression and shall make recommendations or decide what measures shall be taken in accordance with Articles 41 and 42, to maintain or restore international peace and security.

On 9 April 1966, the Security Council, apparently acting under this provision, stated that it was gravely concerned by reports that substantial supplies of oil might reach Rhodesia as the result of the arrival of the oil tanker *Joanna V* at Beira and the approach of another, the *Manuela*, which might lead to the resumption of pumping oil from Beira to Rhodesia. It therefore determined 'that the resulting situation constitute[d] a threat to the peace . . .'. On 16 December 1966 the Security Council expressed deep concern about the inadequacy of the United Nations enforcement measures and those taken by the United Kingdom to bring down the Rhodesian rebellion. Acting 'in accordance with Articles 39 and 41 of the United Nations Charter', it determined 'that the present situation in Southern Rhodesia constitutes a threat to international peace and security . . .'.

The present chapter deals with two major questions on the Security Council's discretion under Article 39. Firstly, was the Security Council correct in determining as and when it did that the Rhodesian situation constituted a threat to the peace? Secondly, has the Security Council unlimited discretion to determine what constitutes a threat to the peace, breach of the peace, and acts of aggression?

*Was the Rhodesian Situation which gave Rise to the
Imposition of Enforcement Action a Threat to
International Peace and Security?*

In trying to answer the question whether the Rhodesian situation which gave rise to the enforcement action constituted a threat to the peace as declared by the Security Council, one is confronted by the imprecision of the terms used in Article 39. The Charter does not define terms such as 'threat to the peace', or 'breach of the peace', or 'acts of aggression'. According to the *travaux préparatoires* of the San Francisco Conference all attempts to insert a paragraph of definition of these terms failed.[1]

Since neither the text of the Charter nor the *travaux préparatoires* seem to contain any explanation of these terms, one may look to the practice of the Security Council. The Council considered the term 'threats to the peace' in the *Spanish* question in 1946 when it set up a sub-committee to investigate and report whether or not the existence of the Franco regime in Spain constituted a threat to the peace.[2] The sub-committee described the existence of Franco's regime as only a potential threat to the peace. In the *Greek Border Incident* case the United States tabled a draft resolution declaring that the support given by Yugoslavia, Bulgaria, and Albania to guerrilla bands operating in Greece constituted 'a threat to the peace within the meaning of Chapter VII' of the Charter. This draft resolution was vetoed by the Soviet Union. What is interesting, however, is that the majority of the members took the view that the situation did constitute a threat to the peace. It would appear that what amounts to a threat to the peace will vary from case to case and whether the Security Council will so declare will always depend on a variety of circumstances, including the number of members who feel that such a declaration is necessary, and the fact that no permanent member of the Council casts a negative vote to prevent such a declaration.

The same is probably true of the meaning of 'breach of the peace'. On 15 July 1948 the Security Council passed a resolution in connection with the *Palestine* question in which

---

[1] *UNSCOR*, 3rd year, 103–4 and 76–7.   [2] *UNSCOR*, 47th mtg., 370.

it warned the parties involved in the conflict that if they
failed to comply with the Council's cease-fire order, that
would 'demonstrate the existence of a breach of the peace
within the meaning of Article 39'.[3] Although this statement
of the Security Council appears to define what acts could
constitute a breach of the peace, this is probably not a definition since breach of the peace will not always take that
form. For example, in the *Korean* case breach of the peace
was declared to have occurred when the North Korean forces
attacked South Korea on 25 June 1950 and the acts involved
there were somewhat different from those found in the
Palestine case.

An attempt to define what acts constitute a breach of the
peace was made by the Australian representative when the
Security Council considered the *Indonesian* question during
its 171st meeting. He suggested that it meant a situation
'where hostilities are occurring, but where it is not alleged
that one particular party is the aggressor or has committed
an act of aggression'.[4] There is no evidence that this attempted
definition was accepted by the other representatives. It would
appear, therefore, that the position remains that the Security
Council must consider each case or situation on its own merits
as it arises.

The last term in Article 39, 'aggression', has caused more
controversy than the two already discussed. This is probably
because it is the most serious violation of international law.
An attempt to define 'aggression' at the San Francisco
Conference was strongly resisted by the major powers on the
ground that states would only distort the definition to exclude some acts which should be included in aggression, since
it was impossible to list all acts which constitute aggression.[5]

Subsequently, the General Assembly and the Security
Council have subjected the issue of the definition of aggression to protracted discussions. It was not until 14 December
1974, that the General Assembly came up with an acceptable
definition of aggression. This was in Resolution 3314 (XXIV)
which provides in part:

[3] *UNSCOR*, 3rd year Suppl., July 1948, 76–7.
[4] *UNSCOR*, 171st mtg., 1623.
[5] Ibid.

Aggression is the use of armed forces by a state against the sovereignty, territorial integrity or political independence of another state or in any other manner inconsistent with the Charter of the United Nations . . .[6]

The resolution goes on to set out in detail factors which may constitute aggression. It points out further that the list is not 'exhaustive and the Security Council may determine that other acts constitute aggression under the provisions of the Charter'.[7] This shows that notwithstanding this definition, the role of the Security Council in determining what constitutes an act of aggression has not been supplanted, and is therefore indispensable.

This therefore suggests that the definition, and the set of fact situations listed by the resolutions, should be viewed more as guidelines than as an inflexible yardstick. The listed fact situations merely provide prima-facie evidence of an act of aggression and the Security Council may, in conformity with the Charter, conclude that a determination that an act of aggression has been committed, merely by the existence of any of the listed fact situations would not be justified in the light·of other relevant circumstances, including the fact that the acts concerned or their consequences are not grave enough. In short, therefore, the definition does not limit the discretion of the Security Council on this issue. This probably also explains why it was possible for the definition to be agreed upon as the members knew that their hands were not tied as to future decisions.

In determining whether in a given situation a threat to the peace existed or breach of the peace or acts of aggression have occurred, the Security Council has to deal with a multiplicity of considerations and influences. An understanding of these factors may enable one to predict the outcome of the debate on any problem. The prediction would thus not be based on the meaning of words alone but also on the fact situation, and the interests and fears of the various groups in the Council. For example, in the *Greek Border Incidents* case already referred to[8] the Soviet veto was almost inevitable

---

[6] Full text in (1975) 69, *AJIL*, 480 ff.

[7] Ibid.; J. Stone, 'Hopes and Loopholes in the 1974 Definition of Aggression', (1977), 71, *AJIL*, 224–6.

[8] See p. 164 above.

because Yugoslavia, Bulgaria, and Albania were Communist allies of the Soviet Union at the time.

Similarly, in the various debates on apartheid in South Africa, and the South African illegal occupation of Namibia, the triple veto of the Western powers is virtually certain any time a draft resolution is tabled aimed at declaring that there existed a threat or breach of the peace or that acts of aggression have occurred.[9] In the *Korean* case, for example, it was possible for the Security Council to declare that a breach of the peace had occurred partly because the United States was ready to take the initiative with its armed forces, and partly, and perhaps more importantly, because the Soviet Union was at the time boycotting the proceedings of the Security Council over the question of Chinese representation at the United Nations and could therefore not use her veto to Communist Korea's advantage.

In considering whether the Rhodesian situation which gave rise to the United Nations enforcement action in fact constituted a threat to the peace both the factual and political considerations should therefore be borne in mind. As far as the factual considerations were concerned, it could be argued that the systematic denial of basic human rights that the Rhodesian Africans suffered prior to and after UDI, constituted a threat to the peace as there was always a danger of a mass uprising of the oppressed people with the consequent likelihood of external intervention that could involve most of the states in the region, and even beyond, in violence.

The proclamation of UDI brought this likelihood even closer since the seizure of power by the Rhodesian white minority regime was rightly to be considered by the international community and, particularly by the Rhodesian Africans, as a further entrenchment of the injustice and repression that had been perpetrated in that country for decades. If the United Nations had done nothing about the situation, the Africans in that country would have been left with no alternative to the use of violence, and they would have received support of all kinds from friendly countries, and breaches of the peace would have been unavoidable. When UDI was

---

[9] *UN Monthly Chronicle*, Nov. 1976, 4.

proclaimed, therefore, all African members of the United Nations took the view that it constituted a threat to the peace. The major Western powers were initially not convinced that there was a need to invoke Chapter VII of the Charter, consequently they argued that the situation in Rhodesia did not constitute a threat to the peace. The only concession they were prepared to make at the time was that the situation constituted a potential threat to the peace.[10] Since the major Western powers had the veto no determination that a threat to the peace existed was possible.

Two reasons for this state of affairs stand out. Firstly Britain was not prepared to lose control of the Rhodesian problem, which she continued to call her sole responsibility. She feared that an invocation of Chapter VII which might lead to the imposition of mandatory action against the Smith regime would take the initiative away from the British Government. Furthermore, it could be argued that Britain was satisfied that the state of emergency that had been declared in Rhodesia five days before UDI and the powerful internal security machinery in that country would keep the Africans under control and prevent an uprising. Even if an uprising had taken place it was clear that the Rhodesian Africans could not have sustained it without external intervention. External intervention was, however, unlikely, given the overwhelming military superiority of Rhodesia in relation to her neighbours. Britain felt, and justifiably so, that the taking of the Rhodesian situation to the United Nations *per se* would have the effect of calming down not only the Rhodesian Africans but their external supporters as well. This was supported by the belief held by some Africans that the Labour Government, unlike the Conservative Government, would stand no nonsense from the Rhodesian white minority.[11]

[10] See Res. 217 (1965) which stated that the existence of the situation resulting from UDI would in time constitute a threat to the peace.

[11] This was an unfortunate belief because, apart from the fact that the Labour Party had been returned to power with only a slender majority, of the two major parties the Conservative Party seems to be the better placed to take really drastic action in colonial situations because it is the party of the establishment. This explains why it was the Conservative Party which made the breakthrough that finally settled the Rhodesian independence crisis. If the Labour Party was in power, the Smith regime always held out in the hope of making a better deal with the Conservative Party when that party came to power later.

It was not until April 1966 that Britain reluctantly conceded that some elements of the Rhodesian problem did in fact constitute a threat to the peace. This was when reports were received that an oil tanker was in Mozambican territorial waters and believed to be carrying oil destined for Rhodesia. This was a breach of the oil embargo against the Smith regime. Britain decided to prevent this by armed force on the high seas. Consequently, she allowed the invocation of Chapter VII although that Chapter was not specifically named in the resolution[12] which was adopted to give Britain power to patrol the high seas off the coast of Mozambique. When the African representatives attempted to widen the scope of this resolution to cover large quantities of oil coming into Rhodesia on land from South Africa, Britain, fearing that this would entail declaring the Rhodesian situation as a whole as constituting a threat to the peace, thereby justifying the imposition of mandatory measures, resisted these pressures. Besides, widening the resolution would have meant confrontation with South Africa, a situation Britain was not prepared to see.

The resolution which was adopted was therefore of only limited scope, declaring that a threat to the peace resulted only from the presence of the oil tanker off the coast of Mozambique, and the reported approach of a second tanker also believed to be carrying oil destined for Rhodesia. However, in December that year (1966) Britain finally conceded that the Rhodesian situation as a whole constituted a threat to the peace.[13] Even so, she succeeded in preventing the Security Council condemning South Africa by name in the resolution for her refusal to comply with the already existing resolutions on Rhodesia.

The foregoing account shows that in determing whether in a given situation there is 'a threat to the peace, breach of the peace, or act of aggression', reference to the factual situation alone is not sufficient: political and other factors must also be considered.

It has been argued that the Rhodesian situation did not constitute a threat to the peace when the Security Council

---

[12] Res. 221 (1966).   [13] Res. 232 (1966).

imposed the enforcement action because the Smith regime had not committed aggression against any other country and that whatever it had done had been done within Rhodesia's borders.[14] C. G. Fenwick, for example, argues that the threat to the peace emanated from the member states of the Organization of African Unity (OAU).[15] Commenting on the stand taken by the OAU members at their Addis Ababa meeting on Rhodesia in November 1966 he maintains:

Here was, indeed, a potential threat to the peace, based upon the principle that the denial of majority rule in one country can justify neighbouring countries in openly intervening to protect a racial group against injustice. But was that situation one that the United Nations could recognize as a threat to the peace? Could the United Nations intervene on its part on the ground that there was danger that certain of its members might violate the law by intervening in Rhodesia on no other ground than the denial of majority rule? If it could, then there might be threats to the peace in a dozen other countries in which one form or another of discrimination, if not racial, might justify intervention . . .

Assuming that the General Assembly and the Security Council were influenced in their separate decisions to apply sanctions because of the danger that neighbouring African states and others might make trouble, was it not the duty of the two bodies, speaking with authority, to issue a restraining order against violent interference by one state in what was still, under law, a domestic situation.[16]

This statement raises a number of legal questions which call for comment. Firstly, the argument that it was the OAU member states and not Rhodesia which threatened the peace, and that therefore the enforcement action should not have been directed at Rhodesia, overlooks one of the essential points in the significance of enforcement actions for the maintenance of international peace and security, i.e. that enforcement action is not supposed to be a sanction aimed at dealing with delictual conduct of a party. It is merely a corrective measure which may not necessarily be directed against an offender; indeed, the offender need not even be identified before the institution of the action. The only exception is where the enforcement action is imposed to deal with acts of aggression, because aggression is a delict. Even here, it is

[14] C. G. Fenwick, 'When is there a Threat to the Peace? — Rhodesia', (1967) 61, *AJIL*, 754.   [15] Ibid.
[16] Ibid.

possible for an action to be enforced not only against the aggressor state but also against the victim if it is seen that the victim is adopting retaliatory measures which are likely to perpetuate the hostilities.

It is submitted, therefore, that whether the Smith regime· or the OAU was to blame for the threat to the peace in the Rhodesian situation was immaterial for the imposition of enforcement measures. Even so, however, it would appear to be an over-simplification of the Rhodesian problem to argue, as does Fenwick, that since the threat of an outbreak of war emanated from outside Rhodesia's borders, the Smith regime is necessarily free from blame. The racial factor in the Rhodesian independence question shows such arguments to be ill conceived. When a very small racial minority seizes power for the purpose of maintaining an oppressive system against an overwhelming majority of the population, this can rightly be considered a provocative act which may create a violent situation that threatens world peace.

Secondly, Fenwick's suggestion that the United Nations, instead of imposing enforcement measures against the Smith regime, should have issued an injunction against the African nations restraining them from making trouble for the Smith regime is not helpful either. Such a move by the United Nations would have been interpreted by the Rhodesian Africans and, ironically, by the Smith regime as well, as an act by the United Nations, condoning the repressive system in Rhodesia. The consequences of this would have been increased violence from both sides.

The third point Fenwick makes is that the Security Council was not justified in intervening in Rhodesia 'on no other ground than the denial of majority rule'. This is again a gross over-simplification of the Security Council's reasons for intervening in Rhodesia. While the denial of majority rule by itself was sufficiently serious to be the concern of the United Nations, the Security Council was entitled to consider the whole systematic denial of basic human rights that UDI was proclaimed to entrench. It was inevitable since all constitutional channels had been closed to them by the banning of their political parties, imprisonment, restriction, and detention of their leaders. The decision of the

Security Council, therefore, as McDougal and Reisman point out:

> recognized that in the contemporary world, international peace and security and the protection of human rights are inescapably inter-dependent and that the impact of flagrant deprivation of the most basic human rights of the great mass of the people of a community cannot possibly stop short within the territorial boundaries in which the physical manifestations first occur.[17]

One is inclined to agree with them again when they argue that the promulgation and application of policies of racism in a context as volatile as that of Rhodesia must give rise to expectation of violence which could influence some states to invoke the controversial principle of humanitarian intervention.[18] They add that:

> people in one territorial community may realistically regard themselves as being affected by activities in another territorial community though no goods or peoples cross any boundaries.[19]

In a situation of this sort it would not be helpful to argue that such intervention would be illegal. The important point is that the existence of a regime such as the one Mr Ian Smith established in Rhodesia was a threat to the peace irrespective of whether the intervening states were acting legally or illegally. The Security Council was therefore justified in intervening in Rhodesia to prevent possible unilateral action by African states against the Smith regime which would have led to devastating results. The propriety of the Council's action in Rhodesia can be illustrated by two decisions of the municipal courts in Britain. In the first one, *Humphries* v. *Connor*,[20] where an action for assault was brought against a police officer, the Irish court held that the policeman was entitled to remove an orange lily from the plaintiff's clothes since this was necessary to prevent a breach of the peace among a crowd in which the emblem aroused animosity. And in *O'Kelly* v. *Harvey*[21] a magistrate was held entitled to

---

[17] M. S. McDougal and M. W. Reisman, 'Rhodesia and the United Nations: The Lawfulness of International Concern' (1968) 62, *AJIL*, 18–19.

[18] Ibid. 10–11.   [19] Ibid.

[20] (1864) 17, *Irish CLR*, 1.

[21] See Wade and Phillips, *Constitutional and Administrative Law* (9th edn., Longmans, 1977), 498.

disperse a lawful meeting since he had reasonable ground to believe the Orangemen opposed to the meeting would use violence and it was necessary to preserve the peace.

It has been further argued that if the United Nations was legally entitled to intervene in Rhodesia, it should also intervene 'in a dozen other countries in which one form or another of discrimination' exists.[22] The argument here is that the fact that discrimination or denial of human rights exists in many other countries is not a valid argument against United Nations intervention in Rhodesia. On the contrary, it is a strong argument in favour of even more intervention by the Organization.[23]

Moreover, as already indicated, the determination that there exists a threat to the peace in a given situation is basically a factual and political act. For that reason, the fact that identical situations exist in two different countries does not necessarily mean that the Security Council will treat them in exactly the same way.[24]

It is submitted, therefore, that the Security Council acted correctly in determining that the Rhodesian situation constituted a threat to the peace. All the criticisms to the contrary appear to have no legal basis. If there are any valid criticisms at all of the Security Council's handling of the Rhodesian case, they are that the determination came too late, and thus delay weakened the impact that the enforcement measures would otherwise have had in ending the Smith rebellion.

Has the Security Council Unlimited Discretion to Determine What Constitutes a Threat to the Peace?

It has been seen that Article 39 of the Charter empowers the Security Council to determine the existence of any threat to the peace, breach of the peace, or act of aggression. This power is related to the powers given by the members of the United Nations to the Security Council under Article 24 to

[22] C. G. Fenwick, 'When is there a Threat to the Peace? – Rhodesia', (1967), 61 *AJIL*, 754.

[23] M. S. McDougal and M. W. Reisman, 'Rhodesia and the United Nations: The Lawfulness of International Concern', (1968), 62 *AJIL*, 16.

[24] R. Higgins, 'International Law, Rhodesia and the United Nations', (1967), 23, *World Today*, 102; see *UN Monthly Chronicle*, Nov. 1976, p. 4 on Namibia.

act on their behalf in the maintenance of international peace and security. The members bind themselves by Article 25 to accept and carry out the decisions of the Security Council in accordance with the Charter.

What is not clear is whether the discretion which the Security Council enjoys under Article 39 is unlimited. At the San Francisco Conference smaller nations were uneasy about what they considered to be too wide a discretion given to an organ dominated by five powerful nations. They felt that this power could be used arbitrarily at their expense. They therefore attempted to introduce amendments to limit the Security Council's discretion but none of the amendments was adopted.[25] The Sponsoring Powers and France assured the smaller nations that there was nothing to fear from the Security Council.[26] Can the failure of those amendments be interpreted as showing that the Security Council's discretion is therefore unlimited?

There are possibly two provisions of the Charter which could be considered as limiting or qualifying the discretionary powers of the Security Council. Both of them are in Article 24. Paragraph 2 of this Article provides that the Council shall act in accordance with the purposes and principles of the United Nations in discharging its duties. And paragraph 3 provides that the Security Council shall submit annual and, when necessary, special reports to the General Assembly. It is doubtful whether these limitations are real. For example, how can anyone say with certainty that the Security Council has not acted in accordance with the purposes and principles of the United Nations? As regards paragraph 3 of Article 24, how frequently have such reports been submitted by the Security Council to the General Assembly, and what steps have been taken to see that the Security Council exercised its powers correctly? It would appear therefore that these limitations are more apparent than real.

Probably the only genuine limitation of the Council is the veto power in Article 27 (3).[27] Any one permanent member can frustrate the Council's efforts to make a specific

---

[25] (1945) 11, *UNCIO* WD 3, Doc. 943 14–16; Barrow, *The UN, Past, Present, and Future* (Free Press, 1972), 21.

[26] (1945) 11, *UNCIO* WD3, 322.   [27] Ibid.

determination under Article 39 of the Charter even if the fourteen other members took the opposite view. What is not clear, however, is whether this should be called a limitation of the Security Council or an abuse of power by the single member concerned whose action would obviously be dictated by selfish interest. If, however, as argued earlier in this chapter, it is accepted that a determination made under Article 39 is governed by considerations of both factual and political factors, it should equally be accepted that political considerations are by and large an effective limiting factor on the Security Council's discretion. Consequently the Security Council is unlikely, for political reasons, to declare a situation which is otherwise calm and peaceful, a threat to the peace. Similarly it may decide not to declare a threat to the peace a situation which on observation appears to constitute such a threat, if it is impossible to follow such a declaration with the requisite enforcement action. In other words if the United Nations is not ready, for political or practical reasons, to apply adequate enforcement measures to deal with a threat to the peace, it serves no purpose to declare that a threat to the peace exists until the Organization is ready to apply those adequate measures.

In the Rhodesian situation, for example, it could be argued that the Security Council postponed determining that the situation constituted a threat to the peace when it adopted Resolution 217 (1965) because the United Kingdom was not at the time prepared to let the United Nations pass mandatory resolutions which could deprive her of the control of the problem.[28] When the United Kingdom finally accepted that the Rhodesian situation constituted a threat to the peace in December 1966 it was not, it is submitted, because the crisis had substantially worsened since 1965, but because the United Kingdom was by that time prepared to apply more severe measures than those applied in 1965, having realized that voluntary measures were ineffective. As a matter of fact, it

---

[28] The United Kingdom feared that should the Council pass mandatory resolutions it would have meant that, even if Britain and the Smith regime reached what in their opinion was a suitable settlement in Rhodesia, Britain could not legally terminate the enforcement unilaterally. This would have restricted Britain's freedom to reach a compromise solution with the rebel leaders in Rhodesia.

could even be argued that the situation in Rhodesia was less of a threat to the peace in December 1966, than it was in November 1965 when UDI was proclaimed, because there was then a more serious danger of a mass uprising by Africans with the attendant danger of external intervention. The answer therefore to the question whether the Security Council has unlimited discretionary power to declare a situation a threat to the peace, breach of the peace, or act of aggression should be that the discretionary power of the Security Council is unlimited in theory. In practice, however, this power is limited by the veto power of the permanent members. Therefore the Security Council's need to get an affirmative vote limits the instances in which it can make a determination under Article 39. This is, however, a procedural limitation and not a substantive one.

XII

Objectives and Purposes of the Enforcement Action

THE details of the enforcement measures discussed in Chapter V above were designed to achieve certain specific objectives and purposes the determination of which may be more difficult than is apparent. At first sight it would appear that the objectives of these enforcement measures were simply to end the Rhodesian rebellion and return Rhodesia to constitutional legality under the United Kingdom. This view was held by a number of British political and legal commentators,[1] as well as by the British Government itself.[2] It is submitted that this is erroneous: the objectives and purposes of the United Nations enforcement action in Rhodesia were much wider.

Before looking at these, however, it might be helpful to clear one issue which could easily lead a reader astray — the use of the word 'sanctions' which was abundantly employed by various commentators in describing the enforcement measures of the United Nations against the Smith regime. According to Austinian terms, a sanction is the evil which will probably be incurred in case a command be disobeyed or in case a duty be broken.[3] As J. L. Kunz states, legal sanctions constitute the reaction of the legal community against a delict.[4] If this is the case, it would appear therefore that sanctions are negative in that they depend for their implementation on the delictual conduct of the target entity.

---

[1] Higgins (1967) 23, *World Today*, 94 at 103.
[2] *UNSCOR*, 1257th mtg., para. 21.
[3] See H. L. A. Hart, *The Concept of Law* (Oxford, 1961), 18–25.
[4] Kunz, 'Sanctions in International Law', (1960) 54, *AJIL*, 324; see also, H. Kelsen, 'Sanctions Under the Charter', (1946) 12, *CJEPS*, 429. Cf. R. St. J. MacDonald who argues that this is an unduly restricted view of sanctions. He maintains: 'If law is merely a principle of order, then sanction in the highest abstraction, is merely a principle of implementing that order. Formally sanctions are those measures that make behaviour conform to the prescriptions that are established to achieve and maintain order . . .'. See 'Economic Sanctions in International Law', (1969), Canadian *YIL*, 65.

In the light of this it is pertinent to ask whether the United Nations enforcement provisions under Chapter VII of the Charter were, legally speaking, designed to be used to impose 'sanctions' as such. Kunz holds the view that they were.[5] He regards it as a 'progressive development that the determination of the delict and the guilty State, the decision of non-military and military sanctions, and the execution of the sanctions were radically centralized in the Security Council . . .'.[6] The Rhodesian independence problem is given in Whiteman's *Digest of International Law* as one case in which sanctions were imposed by the United Nations.

It is true that Chapter VII of the Charter can in certain circumstances be applied in the nature of a penal sanction. Kunz, however, seems to suggest that whenever this Chapter is invoked it operates as a 'sanction' as understood in law. This, however, is not necessarily the case. Under Article 39 the Security Council may determine that there exists a threat to or a breach of the peace without necessarily, as Kunz suggests, indicating that there has been a breach of international law. The Security Council need not even identify the 'guilty party' in so determining. Similarly, contrary to Kunz's suggestion,[7] enforcement measures need not necessarily be directed against states as such. They may be imposed against non-sovereign states, and entities which are not states of any kind.[8] The only obvious times when Chapter VII could operate as a sanction are when it is invoked to deal with an act of aggression, which is clearly a breach of international law,[9] and under Article 94 of the Charter.

From this discussion it seems, therefore, that unless it could be shown that the Rhodesian rebellion involved a violation of international law, those measures could not, legally speaking, be termed 'sanctions'. In Chapter III above it was argued that the Rhodesian rebellion did have some elements of international illegality, such as the systematic suppression of fundamental human rights and of the right of self-determination of the African majority. It is, however, doubtful whether this fact alone could justify calling the

---

[5] See Whiteman's *Digest of International Law*, 332.   [6] Ibid.
[7] Ibid.; see Kelsen, *The Law of the United Nations* (Stevens, 1950), 724.
[8] Akehurst (4th edn., 1982), 182.   [9] Art. 2 (4).

enforcement measures against the Smith regime sanctions. The provisions of the resolutions there were clearly concerned with the maintenance of international peace and security rather than with punitive measures against the Smith regime as such. Furthermore, there is no necessary link between a threat to the peace and a breach of international law.

Chapter VII, it would appear, is primarily meant to fulfil the purpose of the United Nations laid down in Article (1) of the Charter, which is:

To maintain international peace and security, and to that end: to take effective collective measures for the prevention and removal of threats to the peace, and for the suppression of acts of aggression or other breaches of the peace, and to bring about by peaceful means, and in conformity with the principles of justice and international law, adjustment or settlement of international disputes or situations which might lead to a breach of the peace.

In general terms enforcement actions under Chapter VII of the Charter represent a collective action by the international community primarily to affect the values of the target entity[10] in order to force it to comply with a certain defined policy of the United Nations. This collective action has been referred to as 'collective security'.[11] Thus in the Rhodesian situation the members of the Security Council made it plain that their primary concern was that UDI would seriously disturb the peace. Most of them, therefore, referred to it as a matter of world concern.[12] The Security Council itself first determined that the situation resulting from UDI was 'extremely grave' and that its continuance would in time threaten international peace and security.[13] Later the Council had to determine that the situation did constitute a threat to the peace.[14] This suggests that the United Nations was primarily seeking to remove a threat to the peace rather than to enforce international law which might have been violated.

To succeed in removing the threat to the peace in the Rhodesian situation it was necessary to know precisely what aspects of that rebellion threatened international peace and

[10] MacDonald, 79.
[11] R. B. Gray (ed.), *International Security Systems* (Peacock, 1969), 122.
[12] *UNSCOR*, 1257th mtg. para. 21.   [13] Res. 217 (1965).
[14] Res. 221 (1966) para. 1, and esp. 232, para. 1.

security. This ranged from the suppression of human rights and the denial of the African majority's right of self-determination, to the proclamation of UDI itself whose aim was to entrench the existing repressive system, together with the repressive measures taken against those Rhodesians who resisted UDI. For that reason, it would be a gross over-simplification of the objectives of the United Nations to argue that they were meant merely to end the Rhodesian rebellion or to enforce international law as such.

This is particularly true when one considers the fact that UDI was not responsible for introducing the Rhodesian independence problem to the United Nations. It was pointed out in Chapter II above that at the time of UDI the question of Rhodesia had been before the United Nations General Assembly since 1962, and before the Security Council since May 1965 (about seven months before UDI).[15] The issue had been taken before the United Nations following the promulgation of a new Constitution for Rhodesia in 1961. At that time there was no question of any UDI by the white rulers of Rhodesia. The political party in power then was the United Federal Party (UFP) which professed a policy of racial partnership whose declared aim was that as Africans became more educated and their economic position improved, they would steadily be drawn into the decision-making machinery of the country. This policy was seen by the British Government as providing a basis for a constitutional evolution which would eventually lead to African majority rule.

The Rhodesian Africans, however, saw the problem differently. They believed, correctly as it turned out, that the Europeans would not allow majority rule to materialize unless the Africans were given a much stronger say which would ensure that the process of change would not stall. Their distrust of the assurances given by Britain that if they co-operated and gave the 1961 Constitution a chance to work there would be majority rule within a reasonable time was shared by the Afro-Asian states at the United Nations. The campaigns of the Rhodesian Africans against the 1961 Constitution by way of petitions have already been referred to in

---

[15] Res. 202 (1965).

Chapter II above and need not be repeated here. Suffice it so say that these petitions were accepted by the Afro-Asian states who thereupon championed the cause of the Rhodesian Africans in the General Assembly.

The Security Council took an interest in the Rhodesian independence problem in 1963 when in September that year a British veto prevented the adoption of a draft resolution on the question.[16] This was at the time of the dismantling of the Central African Federation of Rhodesia and Nyasaland. Since Rhodesia was the strongest of the three partners in view of the fact that most of the Federal Offices were located there and because of its relatively large white population, African members of the United Nations feared that the Federal Defence forces would be given to Rhodesia which could then use them to impose a constitution that had been rejected by the Rhodesian Africans. They were apprehensive too that Rhodesia might be tempted to use those forces to threaten the security and independence of its former Federal partners. In view of that these states sponsored the draft resolution referred to above which was vetoed by the United Kingdom.[17] The draft resolution called upon Britain not to transfer any powers or attributes of sovereignty, or armed forces and aircraft, on the breakup of the Federation to Rhodesia.[18]

The first Security Council resolution on Rhodesia was passed on 6 May 1965.[19] It recalled all resolutions on Rhodesia which had already been adopted by the General Assembly, and made a number of requests to the British Government in connection with Rhodesia.

This first resolution is illustrative of the proposition offered here, namely that UDI was not responsible for the taking of the Rhodesian problem to the United Nations notwithstanding the popular belief held in some quarters. In other words, even if UDI had not been proclaimed, the Security Council's interest in Rhodesia, which had already been established, would have continued to grow until what this resolution called for was fulfilled.

[16] (1963) *YBUN*, 473; see also Chapter II above.
[17] Ibid. It was sponsored by Ghana, Morocco, and the Philippines.
[18] Ibid.; see also Chapter II.   [19] Res. 202 (1965).

In view of the importance of what it contains, this resolution is quoted here in full.

The Security Council;
  Having examined the situation in Southern Rhodesia,
  Recalling General Assembly resolutions 1514 (xv) . . . 1960, 1747 (xvi) . . . 1962, 1760 (xvii) . . . 1962, 1883 (xvii) . . . 1963 and 1889 (xviii) . . . 1963 and the resolutions of the Special Committee on the situation with regard to the Implementation of the Declaration on the Granting of Independence to Colonial Countries and Peoples, especially its resolution of 22 April, 1965,
  Endorsing the requests which the General Assembly and the Special Committee have many times addressed to the United Kingdom to secure:
  (a) The release of all political prisoners, detainees and restrictees,
  (b) The repeal of all repressive and discriminatory legislation, and in particular the Law and Order (Maintenance) Act and the Land Apportionment Act,
  (c) The removal of all restrictions on political activity and the establishment of full democratic freedom and equality of political rights,
  Noting that the Special Committee has drawn the attention of the Security Council to the grave situation prevailing in Southern Rhodesia and, in particular, to the serious implications of the elections . . . under a constitution which has been rejected by the majority of the people of Southern Rhodesia and the abrogation of which has repeatedly been called for by the General Assembly and the Special Committee since 1962,
  Deeply disturbed at the further worsening of the situation in the territory due to the application of the aforementioned Constitution of 1961 and to recent events, especially the minority Government's threats of unilateral declaration of independence,
  1. *Notes* the United Kingdom Government's statement of 27 October 1964 specifying the conditions under which Southern Rhodesia might attain independence;
  2. *Notes further* and approves the opinion of the majority of the population of Southern Rhodesia that the United Kingdom should convene a constitutional conference;
  3. *Requests* the United Kingdom Government and all States Members of the United Nations not to accept a unilateral declaration of independence for Southern Rhodesia by the minority Government;
  4. *Requests* the United Kingdom to take all necessary action to prevent a unilateral declaration of independence;
  5. *Requests* the United Kingdom Government not to transfer under any circumstances to its colony of Southern Rhodesia, as at present governed, any of the powers or attributes of sovereignty, but to promote the country's attainment of independence by a democratic system of government in accordance with the aspirations of the majority of the population;
  6. *Further requests* the United Kingdom Government to enter into

consultations with all concerned with a view to convening a conference of all political parties in order to adopt new constitutional
provisions acceptable to the majority of the people of Southern
Rhodesia, so that the earliest possible date may be set for independence . . .

It will be seen that two important points stand out from
this resolution: the introduction of a democratic basis of
government in Rhodesia, and the prevention of UDI. As
already seen in Chapter II above, the United Kingdom position
at the time this resolution was passed was that the United
Nations had no jurisdiction to involve itself in the Rhodesian
problem. That is the argument it had previously used to
justify its veto of the draft resolution on Rhodesia in September 1963. On the other hand, the United Kingdom was
concerned about the threats of UDI. This probably explains
Britain's decision not to use its veto to prevent the adoption
of this resolution, although it did not have enough courage
positively to support the draft resolution concerned. It was
not until UDI had been proclaimed that Britain supported
the United Nations jurisdiction on the Rhodesian independence crisis.

Immediately after the unilateral declaration of independence, the United Kingdom imposed a number of economic
enforcement measures against the rebel administration. The
major objective of those measures was undoubtedly to enable
Britain to regain control of the rebel territory so as to facilitate the implementation of a constitutional settlement which
Britain had in mind. This limited British conception triumphed
even at the United Nations so that the first measures which
were imposed by Resolution 217 (1965) were hardly meant
to do anything other than assist Britain to reassert its authority over Rhodesia. To that end Britain succeeded in preventing the Security Council from determining that the Rhodesian
situation constituted at least a threat to international peace
and security, a decision which could have paved the way for
the imposition of mandatory non-military enforcement
measures. Britain feared that such a step would deprive her
of the initiative and control over the developments of the
crisis. Britain was prepared to lose the control of the Rhodesian
situation neither to the Smith regime nor to the United

Nations. The Rhodesian problem had to remain firmly a British responsibility. This position was clearly stated by the British Prime Minister in the House of Commons on 23 November 1965.[20] The Security Council did finally determine that it constituted a threat to the peace.[21] It thereupon imposed enforcement measures, some of which were mandatory. Britain's fears of losing control of the situation were proved baseless. The aim of these and other measures which were added later,[22] it is submitted, was primarily to remove the threat to the peace. This could be achieved by re-establishing British authority in Rhodesia. Britain was expected to use its restored authority to promote the exercise of the right of self-determination among the Rhodesian people. The precise objectives of the United Nations enforcement action in Rhodesia, it would appear, therefore, were not merely to end the rebellion, because that alone could have left unresolved many vital issues which were the root cause of the threat to the peace. The removal of the threat to the peace lay in the introduction of a democratic system of government in Rhodesia in which all citizens had an equal opportunity of participation.[23]

The crucial point was the recognition of the authority of the United Kingdom which would enable that country to introduce the required constitutional changes in Rhodesia. This was accepted by all the members of the United Nations, and was reflected in the Security Council resolutions.[24]

The question to ask is how the enforcement measures were expected to operate. To borrow the British Foreign Secretary's words, how were those measures going 'to cause Southern Rhodesia to return to its allegiance to the British Crown so that Britain can carry out its task of ensuring for all the peoples of Southern Rhodesia an independence and freedom

---

[20] *Weekly Hansard*, No. 673, col. 257.
[21] Res. 221 (1966), 9 Apr. 1966; 232 (1966), 16 Dec. 1966.
[22] See Res. 232 (1966) and 253 (1968), 29 May 1968.
[23] As Halderman points out, the 'Rhodesian case is an example of a situation in which it is widely considered that in order to deal successfully with a threat to peace, the United Nations measures must bring about a permanent change in the relations, internal or external or both, of the State or other entity concerned'. Halderman, 'Some Legal Aspects of Sanctions in the Rhodesian Case', (1968) 17, *ICLQ* 701.   [24] See e.g. Res. 202 (1965) paras. 4 and 5.

that will be genuine . . .'.[25] The answer to this question can be found in the speech of the representative of New Zealand, Mr Corner, who told the Council that, so far as he knew, it was not conceived to be the aim of the economic measures 'to ruin the economy of Rhodesia . . .' He went on:

It has not been unreasonable to assume that the moves already taken by the United Kingdom, backed by the Organization, would have an appreciable effect on the Rhodesian economy and that the pressures building up would have had the desired effect of weakening the unconstitutional régime and encouraging the emergence of those who, either through conviction or for reasons of practical self-interest, do not share Mr Smith's ideas.[26]

Three significant points emerge from this speech. Firstly, the enforcement measures were never intended to ruin the Rhodesian economy; secondly, they were merely intended to weaken the Smith regime; and finally, they would thus encourage the emergence of a more moderate force, obviously among Rhodesia's whites. This is probably the way Britain hoped the problem would be solved. Mr Harold Wilson, who was British Prime Minister at the time, has been reported as saying after the end of the United Nations action, that he never tried to replace Mr Smith in Rhodesia because Britain had no means of doing so. This, however, is not convincing. The truth is probably that Mr Wilson hoped that the enforcement measures would hurt Rhodesia so much that, as Good argues, this would 'galvanize an effective opposition to the rebel régime in Rhodesia and he would be able to work with a reconstituted moderate Government'.[27] Good suggests that after the March 1966 British election, Mr Wilson realized that the non-military measures 'were not going to unseat Smith and produce a swift settlement he had hoped for'. He thus decided to work hard to 'extract a compromise settlement from the rebels whom at first he had vowed to remove'.[28]

The approach Mr Wilson adopted was, to say the least, self-defeating. From the very early stages of the imposition of the enforcement process, he had told the House of Commons that the 'measures must not be vindictive' or 'involve lasting

[25] *UNSCOR*. 1259th mtg., para. 17. [26] Ibid. 1276th mtg. 14.
[27] R. Good, *UDI: The International Politics of the Rhodesia Rebellion*, 293.
[28] Ibid. 293–4.

damage for Rhodesia . . .'.[29] He at the same time said that
the measures should be speedy and effective rather than '. . .
long and drawn out' while 'inflicting agony on Rhodesia'.
This preoccupation with an attempt to avoid measures which
would 'ruin' the Rhodesian economy was largely responsible
for the gradual introduction of the United Nations measures,
which in turn made those measures less effective than they
would have been. It seems self-contradictory to insist on
speedy and effective measures which were non-damaging.
Economic measures are either damaging and effective or
non-damaging and innocuous. They can be speedy if they are
comprehensive and mandatory, and yet this is what the British
Government was reluctant to accept. As a result of this attitude of the British Government, it was inevitable that the
enforcement action would be 'long and drawn out' and
would certainly inflict agony on the Rhodesian people,
especially the Africans for whose benefit the action was
supposedly imposed.

In spite of this apparently obvious weakness, Mr Wilson
assured the members of the Commonwealth of Nations that
there would be a 'quick kill'. Consequently the Commonwealth Heads of Government who met in Lagos, Nigeria, in
1966 produced a Communiqué laying down how Britain
intended to proceed once the rebellion was over. The relevant
part of the Communiqué read:

The conference noted the following decisions of the British Government:
(a) After the illegal régime is ended a legal government will be appointed
    by the Governor and will constitute a broadly based representative
    administration. During this interim period the armed forces and
    police will be responsible to the Governor. Those individuals who
    are detained or restricted [for] political activities will be released
    and normal political activities will be permitted provided that they
    are conducted peacefully and democratically without intimidation
    from any quarter;
(b) The British Government will negotiate with this interim administra-
    tion, a constitutional settlement directed to achieving the objective
    of majority rule . . .;
(c) The constitutional settlement will be submitted for acceptance to
    the people of Rhodesia as a whole by appropriate democratic means;

[29] *Weekly Hansard*, No. 673, col. 249.

(d) The British Parliament and Government must be satisfied that this test of opinion is fair and free and would be acceptable to the general world community.

(e) The British Government will not consent to independence before majority rule unless the people of Rhodesia as a whole are shown to be in favour of it.[30]

Earlier Britain had formulated six principles which had to be satisfied before any constitutional proposals could be considered as a basis for a Rhodesian settlement.[31] The process of bringing Rhodesia to independence was to be based on the six principles laid down by Britain before UDI.[32] According to paragraph (a) of the Communiqué quoted above, the international community had to be satisfied that the test of opinion was fair and free. This is significant in that Britain recognized that the mere ending of the Rhodesian rebellion by itself was not sufficient unless the United Nations accepted the terms on which the rebellion was ended. When the Lancaster House Agreement was signed on 21 December 1979 marking the end of the Rhodesian rebellion and setting up a machinery for transferring political power in Rhodesia genuinely to the African majority, there was no difficulty therefore in the Security Council accepting the arrangement reached among the parties to the Lancaster House Conference and recommending the termination of the United Nations enforcement action.[33]

[30] Cmnd. 4835. [31] Cmnd. 2807; see Chapter I above 11.
[32] See Chapter I, 11.
[33] See Chapter XIII; Res. 460 (1979) or 21 Dec. 1979.

XIII

Termination of the United Nations Enforcement Measures

FOLLOWING the signing of the Lancaster House Agreement on Rhodesia in London on 21 December 1979, the Security Council adopted Resolution 460 (1979) terminating the United Nations enforcement measures in Rhodesia.[1] Referring to that resolution Anthony Parsons, representing the United Kingdom, stated:

Operative paragraph 2 calls upon States to terminate sanctions against Southern Rhodesia. Our view remains, that the obligation to impose those sanctions fell away automatically with the return to legality of the colony.[2]

Britain did not therefore believe that a resolution was necessary to bring that action to an end, although she was glad, 'in a spirit of co-operation, to support a resolution acknowledging that sanctions have fulfilled their purpose'.[3] She did this on the ground that she was conscious that many countries had attached great importance to the adoption of such a resolution by the Security Council.[4]

Britain had in fact unilaterally stopped enforcing the United Nations action as soon as the British-appointed Governor took office in Salisbury before the final Agreement on the transitional arrangements was reached in London. As a result of this, Britain came under heavy criticism from many members of the Security Council who held the view that only the Security Council had power to terminate the United Nations actions.

Mr Lusaka, the representative of Zambia, spoke for all the dissatisfied states when he argued:

The immediate task before the Security Council, and indeed the purpose of this meeting, is to take action in respect of the mandatory sanctions

[1] S/PV 2181, p. 7; Cmnd. 7802.　　[2] Cmnd. 7802.
[3] Ibid.　　[4] Ibid.

imposed by this Council against Southern Rhodesia under Chapter VII of the United Nations Charter.

Then he went on:

Regrettably, we are meeting against the background of actions taken by the United Kingdom and a few other Member States which lifted uni-laterally the mandatory sanctions against Southern Rhodesia. In this regard, I wish to state most emphatically the considered view of my Government that the mandatory sanctions imposed in resolution 253 (1968) by the Security Council against Southern Rhodesia, under Chapter VII of the Charter, can be lifted only by the Security Council itself. Until the Security Council had taken such action, all Member States were morally, politically and legally under [an] obligation to maintain them in accordance with Article 25 of the Charter. No state should be allowed to usurp the authority of the Security Council. This sad precedent should have been avoided before the meeting and decision of the Council today.

By their precipitate, ill-timed and unilateral action, the few Western countries which lifted sanctions unilaterally generated undue controversy and acrimony on the question of sanctions. It was incumbent upon the United Kingdom in particular, as it did when it requested the imposition of the sanctions, to come to this Council and seek their termination. That is a matter both of law and [of] principle. The authority of the Security Council should be scrupulously maintained at all times and its permanent members have a particular duty to uphold its powers . . . .[5].

Mr Lusaka's speech has been quoted here at length because it contains some very forceful arguments, some of which will be reverted to later in this chapter.

Similar criticism came from Mr Clark, the representative of Nigeria.[6] He argued that the imposition of the enforcement measures was not prompted solely by the rebellion, but by the fact that the events leading to the rebellion constituted a threat to international peace and security. Therefore, the end of the rebellion by no means removed that threat, as indeed was shown by the later Rhodesian raids into Botswana, Mozambique, and Zambia. The unilateral lifting of the en-forcement measures by Britain, the United States, and some other Western nations was therefore in violation of Article 25 of the Charter of the United Nations since the Security Council, having imposed the measures, was the only com-petent body to terminate them.[7] Other condemnations of

[5] Ibid. 17.   [6] Ibid. 27.   [7] Ibid.

this unilateral action which may be mentioned in passing came from the representatives of the Soviet Union, Mr Troyanovsky,[8] and Tanzania, Mr Foum.[9]

This controversy was foreseen by some British politicians as soon as the enforcement action was embarked upon. Higgins pointed out in a lecture in 1967, for example, that some members of the British House of Commons had argued that the termination of the United Nations measures could be prevented by a veto of one of the Communist members (most likely the Soviet Union) even if the United Kingdom believed that the time had come to terminate those measures.[10] She pointed out that the argument was that if a veto could be used:

. . . sanctions will henceforth continue, and that to stop them . . . in the eventuality of a settlement regarded as satisfactory by Britain would require a substantive resolution, which could be vetoed . . .

· She criticized this assertion as a misunderstanding of

the way things actually happen at the United Nations. The sanctions are declared to be for the purpose of bringing the rebellion to an end, and it is for the British Government, as the constitutional authority, to decide when that event has occurred. This task cannot be assigned to the United Nations. Should the United Kingdom wish to terminate sanctions, she would declare the rebellion ended and announce that, as the United Nations sanctions had succeeded in their purpose, they were now automatically terminated.[11]

As already seen, this is precisely the position adhered to by Britain. The present chapter seeks to examine the two positions in determining the legal method of terminating a collective action, especially one binding on the participating states. In pursuance of this objective a close analysis will be made of the theoretical aspect of the termination of such an enforcement action, and in this the defunct League of Nations Covenant and the Charter of the United Nations will be used as frames of reference.

[8] Ibid. 57.   [9] Ibid. 83.
[10] (1967) 23, *World Today*, 94 at 103.   [11] Ibid.

A. *A Theoretical Aspect of the Termination of Enforcement Actions*

The Covenant of the League of Nations

The enforcement system of the League of Nations was governed by Article 16 (1) of the Covenant which provided:

Should any Member of the League resort to war in disregard of its covenants under Articles 12, 13, or 15, it shall *ipso facto* be deemed to have committed an act of war against all other Members of the League, which hereby undertake immediately to subject it to the severence of all trade or financial relations, the prohibition of all intercourse between their nationals and the nationals of the Covenant-breaking state, and the prevention of all financial, commercial or personal intercourse between the nationals of the Covenant-breaking State and the nationals of any other State whether a Member of the League or not.

Paragraph 2 of this Article provided that the Council had a duty to recommend to 'the several Governments concerned what effective military, naval or air force the Members of the League were required to contribute to the armed forces to be used to protect the covenants of the League'. Paragraph 3 contained provisions for mutual support for the League Members to minimize the loss and inconvenience resulting from the enforcement measures imposed against the covenant-breaking State. And paragraph 4 contained provisions for the expulsion of a member from the League for the violation of any covenant of the Organization.

The Covenant contained no provisions for the termination of the measures imposed under Article 16. It may be useful to separate the non-military measures in paragraphs 1 and 4 from the military measures contained in paragraph 2. Those contained in paragraph 1 could be implemented by the members of the League unilaterally as soon as the target state resorted to war in disregard of its obligations. It would appear therefore that such unilateral enforcement measures were not taken by a central body of the League.

Paragraph 4 of Article 16 presented a different problem. It provided for the expulsion by a unanimous vote of all the League members present of a member who violated any covenant. By its nature this measure could only be implemented by the Organization itself as opposed to the individual members as was the case with measures contained in paragraph 1. The equivalent of the 'termination' of such a sanction is the readmission of the expelled member. If this is so, it follows that the termination of the sanction is centralized. This could be undertaken under Article 1 (2) of the Covenant which dealt with the admission by a positive two-thirds vote of the members of any fully self-governing State, Dominion, or Colony. This means that the readmission of the member was, like the expulsion of such a member, the responsibility of the Organization itself and not of the individual members of the League of Nations.

Under paragraph 2 of Article 16, the League Covenant provided for military measures. The imposition of these was at the instance of the Council of the League which was under a duty to recommend them to the Governments of the League Members if the need for such measures arose.[12] Members were, however, under no legal obligation to comply with the recommendations of the Council.[13] If the members accepted the recommendations they could contribute in accordance with those recommendations. It is not clear whether such members could only contribute to the armed forces to be used, or if they could employ their forces independently against the covenant-breaking state without contributing to a League of Nations force as such.

It would appear that the absence of obligation on the part of the members to contribute armed forces suggests that members could use their forces independently. If this is so, it could be argued that each member could decide at any time to terminate its participation in the enforcement action. If, however, there was a League force which was established by a Council resolution, it would appear that such a force to which members had contributed contingents could not be dissolved other than by another Council resolution. Even so, however, this did not prejudice the members' right to pull out their own individual units from the League force at any time since they were under no obligation to contribute them in the first place, unless, of course, the members had bound themselves in advance not to withdraw their

[12] 'Essential Facts About the League of Nations' (Geneva 1937, Information Section), 125–6.   [13] Ibid.

contingents until the Council terminated the military action as a whole.

As a general proposition, the enforcement action under the League system could be implemented and terminated by members individually without the intervention of the League itself by way of collective action.[14]

The Charter of the United Nations

Under the Charter of the United Nations the key provision of the enforcement action is Article 39 with which the Security Council must comply before it can impose specific measures which are detailed in Article 41, dealing with non-military action, and Article 42, dealing with military measures. In contradistinction to the provisions of the Covenant of the League of Nations, the provisions of the Charter are not meant primarily to deal with violations of the Charter as such. Therefore while it was possible for individual members of the League to recognize the violations of the provisions of the Covenant which necessitated enforcement action, this is not the case under the Charter, which is primarily concerned with the maintenance of international peace and security.

The decision to impose enforcement measures often follows a considerably lengthy discussion involving many controversial issues some of which may concern vital interests of member states. This as well as the need for more efficiency of the enforcement system made it necessary that this decision be entrusted to a central organ. The members have thus conferred this responsibility upon the Security Council to act on their behalf.[15] This organ decides when and what enforcement measures should be implemented.[16]

Is the termination of these enforcement measures entrusted to the Security Council in the same way as their initiation? If the answer to this question is in the affirmative, it will also be necessary to ask further if that would rule out any right of the members individually to terminate unilaterally their own participation in an enforcement action which in their opinion

---

[14] Goodrich and Simon, *The United Nations and Maintenance of International Peace and Security* (Brookings, 1966), 490; Ruth B. Henig (ed.), *The League of Nations* (1973), 138.

[15] Art. 24.   [16] Art. 39–42.

has achieved its purpose. The answer to both these questions probably depends on the nature of the enforcement action in question. It would appear that measures imposed under a recommendation of the Security Council can be terminated differently from those imposed under an 'order' of the Council.

An analysis of both these forms of enforcement measures involves drawing a distinction between the duration of an enforcement action as envisaged in the resolution implementing it and the continuation of the responsibility of the members to participate in the action. As regards duration of the enforcement action, two possibilities present themselves. Firstly, it could be argued that once an enforcement action is imposed, it remains in force for as long as its purpose has not been accomplished. This presupposes that the purpose of any given action can be ascertained, a task which may prove very difficult, as was observed in the last chapter in respect of the Rhodesian problem. Moreover, it is not so clear who is empowered to determine whether or not the purpose of the action, even if it is known, has been fulfilled. It was seen in the above pages that, because of its special responsibility in the Rhodesian case, Britain held the view that she had the power to determine when the need for the enforcement action had lapsed. Britain believed that the need for the action ceased 'automatically' on the ending of the rebellion.

With respect, it is submitted that if one accepts that the duration of an enforcement action is determined by the accomplishment of its purposes, and this is to be preferred, there should, in keeping with collective action, be a central body which will determine that the declared purpose of the enforcement action has been accomplished. This conclusion has two merits: (a) The central body will determine what is the precise purpose of the action, and whether that purpose has been fulfilled; (b) This will enhance the authority of the United Nations, and strengthen and improve the enforcement system, while at the same time maximizing the effectiveness of the enforcement measures concerned by ensuring that no member will be afforded a pretext to stop prematurely its own participation by arguing that in its view the purpose of the action has been achieved. The most suitable central body to perform this function, it would appear, is the Security Council.

The second possibility is that the duration of an enforcement action may be provided for in the resolution that imposed that action. This may take two forms: the resolution may provide expressly that the enforcement action will no longer be necessary either after a certain event has occurred, or after a certain period has elapsed. Resolutions of this kind are extremely uncommon. Resolution 314 (1972) on Rhodesia came close to a pronouncement of this nature. Its paragraph 1 provided that the Security Council,

Reaffirms its decision that the present sanctions against Southern Rhodesia shall remain fully in force until the aims and objectives set out in resolution 253 (1968) are completely achieved . . .

The purposes of this action, as can be assessed from Resolution 253 (1968), were the removal of the threat to the peace and the achievement of self-determination and independence by the people of Rhodesia.[17] Resolution 314 (1972) quoted above does not, however, say who was to determine that those 'aims and objectives' had 'been completely achieved'. It is submitted that this responsibility fell on the Security Council. It would appear, therefore, that whether one adopts the first possibility or the second one, there will generally be a need for the Security Council to assess the situation before an enforcement action is terminated save in the very rare occasions where the duration of the action is declared to be for a specific definite period which can be determined objectively by each and every member of the United Nations individually.

The next question concerns the withdrawal of individual members from participating in an enforcement action which has not yet been terminated. This is best tackled by distinguishing between recommendatory and mandatory measures of enforcement. Since recommendations of the Security Council do not bind members of the United Nations, legally no member need comply with them. It follows therefore that if a member decides to comply with a recommendatory

17 See Chapter XII above.

action, it remains legally free to stop participating in the action at any time even if the enforcement action has not been terminated. This applies to military as well as non-military measures. If, however, a member decides to partici-pate in a non-mandatory enforcement action and subsequently undertakes not to terminate its participation as long as the enforcement action lasts, such a member is bound by this special agreement, and unilateral withdrawal would be a breach of the obligation undertaken. Such special agreements are provided for under Article 43 of the Charter in relation to military measures. This is the only way a member may be bound not to stop participating in the application of military measures.[18] Therefore, military measures can only, as things presently stand, be imposed by a recommendation.

As a general rule, therefore, members are legally at liberty to pull out of an enforcement action which has been imposed by a recommendation of the Security Council even before that action has been formally terminated. The effect of this is that it is technically possible for all the members of the United Nations to stop participating in such an action. The enforcement action in such circumstances, however, remains in force but unoperational.[19] It is possible for a recommended enforcement action to receive the support of some but not all members, or, more rarely, of all the members at its initiation, but this support may subsequently dwindle to nothing while the action technically remains in force.

Some authorities have argued that this feature of the recommended enforcement action disqualifies it from becom-ing a 'United Nations action'.[20] Halderman, for example, argues that the original intention of the drafters of the Charter was 'that all United Nations measures of tangible pressure would be mandatory . . .'.[21] This might have been the original intention of the Sponsoring Powers who devised the unanimity rule in the Yalta Voting formula, but the Charter as finally drafted certainly does not exclude recommendations from

---

[18] Special agreements are unlikely to be concluded by any state in respect of non-military measures.

[19] Unless the relevant resolution stipulated that when all participants pull out of the action, that action should be deemed to have been terminated.

[20] J. W. Halderman 'Some Legal Aspects of Sanctions in the Rhodesian Case', (1968), 17, *ICLQ*, 685.   [21] Ibid.

initiating enforcement measures. As Halderman correctly points out, even if enforcement measures are imposed on the basis of a 'recommendation' of the Security Council they are as much measures of the United Nations as are madatory measures.[22]

Probably the most important type of enforcement measures for the purpose of this discussion are those of a mandatory enforcement action which is imposed in pursuance of a 'decision' of the Security Council under Article 41 of the Charter. Members of the Organization are bound under Article 25 of the Charter to comply with decisions of the Security Council. Therefore, once the Security Council decides that specified non-military enforcement measures be imposed by the members the element of discretion on their part disappears and every member must comply with that decision. If members have no discretion in whether or not to participate in an enforcement action imposed by a decision of the Security Council, it seems to follow that they equally have no discretion as regards when they should stop participating in that action. Thus the members cannot withdraw from participating until the action is terminated or the mandatory resolution which imposed it is repealed by the Security Council itself.

It would appear, therefore, that once the Security Council had determined that a situation constitutes a threat to the peace, breach of the peace, or act of aggression, and has imposed a mandatory action, no single member of the United Nations is entitled unilaterally to withdraw from the action on the ground that in its opinion a threat to or breach of the peace or acts of aggression no longer existed, or that the purpose of the United Nations action has been achieved. It is submitted that should any member feel that the mandatory action needs to be terminated, it is incumbent upon that member to introduce a draft resolution to that effect in the Security Council to have the action lifted.

The draft resolution, it is submitted, need not be concerned with the termination of the enforcement action as such; it may, for instance, be concerned with the approval of a settlement which may have been reached between the parties to

[22] Ibid.

the conflict with which the United Nations is dealing. This approval could signal the end of the enforcement action and would be treated as a substantive matter in the same way as the initiation of the action in the Council to deal with the conflict.

This necessarily means that the termination of the United Nations enforcement action is subject to the veto power of the permanent members. The resolution concerned, however, need not, and cannot, be mandatory because the Security Council has no power to place a member under an obligation not to take non-military enforcement measures.[23] What is required in the termination of an enforcement action is not an order but a release from an obligation binding the members. This can be achieved by a recommendatory resolution of the Security Council. Admittedly, the resolution terminating the Rhodesian enforcement action was couched in obligatory terms as a 'decision' of the United Nations.[24] This, however, should not derogate from what has been said, especially since the Security Council has often been inconsistent in the use of terms such as 'decides', 'calls upon', and so forth.[25]

Another important issue is that the Council itself has the power to release the members. Thus it would appear that the General Assembly, for instance, cannot release the members from an obligation imposed by the Council, *a fortiori* a member cannot release itself from such an obligation. It may be possible, however, for the Council to delegate this power to the General Assembly or to some other body to exercise on its behalf. If this happens, it could be argued that the resolution which makes this delegation is on a substantive question in so far as it devolves the power of the Council to take a decision on a substantive question. Such a draft resolution, therefore, is subject to a veto power. Such a delegation seems, however, to be unlikely on a matter of this magnitude. It is expected that the Security Council will itself make the decision to terminate the action. As Goodrich and Simon conclude:

---

[23] Although members may be under an obligation already, independently of the Charter. See e.g. GATT, Art. XI, XXI (c).

[24] Res. 460 (1979) of 21 Dec. 1979, para. 2.

[25] See Chapter V above.

If the Council should decide to use measures under Articles 41 and 42 of the Charter, it would subsequently have to decide under what conditions the enforcement measures should be terminated.[26]

The problem that has to be faced in this respect is that of the abuse of the veto power by the permanent members, which could in some cases prevent the termination of an enforcement action which is no longer necessary. This, however, presents no bigger problem than the abuse of the veto power to prevent the imposition of an enforcement action in a case where such action is clearly necessary. If anything, it presents fewer difficulties because an unpopular enforcement action will not be observed by the members and the legal continuance of such an action could be farcical. In any case, it seems logical that if the Security Council is given wide discretionary powers to determine the existence of a threat to, or breach of the peace, or acts of aggression, it should enjoy similar powers when it becomes necessary to determine whether those situations no longer exist. A denial of the latter automatically applies to the former too. These are two sides of the same coin. Besides, to allow members individually to determine when to stop participating in a mandatory action is open to abuse by members. Furthermore, there would be no point in empowering the Security Council to determine the existence of threats to or breaches of the peace, or acts of aggression if members would subsequently decide individually that these situations no longer existed.

B. *The Practical Aspects of the Termination of Enforcement Measures*

This section of the present chapter is a critical examination of the termination of the United Nations enforcement action against the Smith regime on 21 December 1979,[27] fourteen years after it was initiated. Before that is done, it may be useful first to examine briefly how the League of Nations enforcement action against Italy between 1935 and 1936 was terminated, bearing in mind the differences discussed above

---

[26] L. M. Goodrich and Simon, *The United Nations and the Maintenance of International Peace and Security*, 491.   [27] S/PV 2181.

regarding the enforcement systems under the League Covenant and the Charter of the United Nations.

When Italy invaded Ethiopia in 1935, it was declared an
aggressor by the League of Nations. On 8 October, the League
Council decided in accordance with Article 16 of the Covenant to implement economic and financial enforcement
measures against that country.[28] Although these measures
were applied extensively during 1935 and 1936 they did not
prove effective enough to achieve their purpose of ending the
Italian aggression against Ethiopia. The measures were 'relaxed
or brought to an end by the members on their own responsibility, in many cases without waiting for any guidance from
an organ of the League'.[29] This haphazard termination of the
enforcement measures could be attributed to the lack of a
centralized system of enforcement under the League system.

As already seen, the arrangement under the Charter of the
United Nations is different in this respect.[30] As Goodrich and
Simon point out,

Those who wrote the Charter ... thought a more effective system would
be achieved by vesting primary responsibility for initiating, directing
and terminating collective measures in the Security Council.[31]

The termination of the United Nations action against the
Smith regime therefore is significant and could probably
establish a precedent for future cases. In discussing this, it is
necessary to bear in mind what was said in the previous
chapter regarding the purpose and objective of the enforcement action in the Rhodesian case.

In that chapter it was argued that it is a mistake to see the
purpose of the United Nations actions as merely an attempt
to put pressure on the Smith regime to return to its allegiance
to the British Crown. The return to legality of the regime had
to be accompanied by certain political changes which would
make the surrender acceptable not only to the international
community as a whole but to the majority of the Rhodesian
population. Unless such a settlement was achieved the Security

---

[28] V. Margueritte, *The League Fiasco* (Hodge, 1936), 220-1.
[29] Goodrich and Simon, *The United Nations*, 491.
[30] See Chapter XI above.
[31] Goodrich and Simon, *The United Nations*, 491.

Council would have nothing to do with that constitutional legality, and the enforcement action would technically continue with or without the participation of Britain.

This position was recognized by Dr David Owen in 1977 when he was then the British Foreign and Commonwealth Secretary, who stated in respect of the possible termination of the United Nations action, 'it would be folly to lift sanctions until progress to majority rule is, and can be seen by all, to be irreversible . . .'.[32] Although Dr Owen was not expressing a legal requirement but a political one, his statement was significant in the sense that the finding that the threat to the peace has been removed is largely influenced by political considerations.

From the point of view of municipal law Britain could, if she had reached a negotiated settlement with the Smith regime, have terminated its participation in the United Nations action at any time during the fourteen years of that enforcement action. This, however, would not have brought Britain's international obligations under Article 25 of the Charter to an end as regards the enforcement action. For these obligations to come to an end it would have been necessary for Britain or any other member to table a draft resolution in the Security Council to have the enforcement action formally terminated, and, as already argued above, such a draft resolution would be on a substantive matter, and would therefore be subject to a veto power.[33]

It has already been seen that Higgins disagreed with this conclusion.[34] She argued that Britain as the colonial power in Rhodesia could have terminated her own participation in the enforcement action merely by declaration and most Security Council members, and Rhodesia's main trading partners, would follow suit and withdraw their own participation. The onus, according to her, would be upon any state which wished the sanctions to continue to introduce a resolution to this effect. It would be this resolution which would be subject to the negative vote of Britain and her allies.

She added:

[32] *The Times*, 26 May 1977.   [33] See p. 198 above.
[34] Higgins, (1967) 23, *World Today*, 103.

To argue, therefore, that sanctions cannot be lifted without Russian approval seems to . . . miss the point that as a matter of tactics, it is open for the United Kingdom to insist that sanctions lapse when the rebellion ends; and that it is also for the United Kingdom alone to determine that eventually.[35]

It will be seen from what has been said above that the present writer holds a different view from that expressed by Higgins on this point. It is submitted, with respect, that what was wrong with Higgins's proposition was the assumption that the purpose of the United Nations action was solely to end the Rhodesian rebellion. This assumption has already been rejected in the previous chapter and in the present one. What was crucial in that action was not the end of the rebellion as such, but whether or not that end of the rebellion removed the threat to the peace in the eyes, not of the United Kingdom Government, but of the United Nations. For instance, in the *Iranian* question (II), in the Report of the Committee of Experts, the delegations of Austria, Brazil, China, Egypt, Mexico, the Netherlands, the United Kingdom, and the United States made the following observation:

. . . the Security Council may hold that, even after an agreement has been reached between the parties, circumstances may continue to exist which might still leave room for fears regarding the maintenance of the peace, and which justify the questions being retained among the matters entrusted to its care.

The Security Council may, even when the parties announce that they have reached an agreement, find it necessary to remain seized of the matter until the whole or part of the agreement has been executed or even longer . . .[36]

It was technically possible to end the rebellion in Rhodesia without removing the situation that threatened international peace and security. For example, the Smith regime could have accepted settlement proposals offered by the British Government which did not satisfy the aspirations of the African majority in Rhodesia. For example, the agreement on the Douglas-Home-Smith proposals in 1971 was one such possibility.[37]

---

[35] Higgins, (1967) 23, *World Today*, 103.
[36] (1946–51) *Repertoire of the Practice of the Security Council*, 480.
[37] See Chapter I above.

As a corollary to her argument stated above, Higgins asserted that the United Kingdom, as the administering authority in Rhodesia, was the sole judge of when the rebellion had ended and when to terminate the enforcement action. While it is true that Britain was the sole judge of when the rebellion had ended that fact did not make the United Kingdom the sole judge of when the enforcement measures should be terminated. To say that is to argue that the Security Council determined that the Rhodesian situation constituted a threat to international peace and security simply because the United Kingdom said so. This would be wrong because it is well known that the decisions of the Security Council on Rhodesian situation constituted a threat to the peace was the members of the Security Council put much pressure on the United Kingdom not to prevent the invocation of Chapter VII of the Charter.[38] Those members were not mere willing followers of the United Kingdom. The decision that the Rhodesian situation constituted a threat to the peace was the result of an intense co-operative effort of the members of that organ in the exercise of its primary responsibility for the maintenance of international peace and security.

Furthermore, it will be remembered that since 1966 the enforcement measures against Rhodesia had been based on mandatory resolutions of the Security Council, notably Resolution 253 (1968). It is submitted therefore that no single member of the United Nations had power to release itself or, *a fortiori*, other members from their obligations under the Charter. This was a responsibility of the Security Council. Besides, although Britain was the administering power in Rhodesia, it was also a member of the United Nations. As a member of that Organization it was also as bound by the mandatory Security Council resolutions on Rhodesia as any other member. Therefore to argue that the United Kingdom had only to declare that the enforcement measures were no longer necessary and they would lapse automatically seems to be in conflict with the obligations imposed by the United Nations on all the members.

Yet this is precisely the position the United Kingdom took.

---

[38] See e.g. *UNSCOR* 1257th mtg.

Following the Conference of the Commonwealth Heads of Government in Lusaka in August 1979, Britain called a constitutional conference to be held in London in September of that year to be attended by the United Kingdom, the Patriotic Front, and the Salisbury regime. Progress was soon made in the negotiations towards the resolution of the independence conflict. Lord Carrington, the Conference Chairman, adopted an unorthodox method of conducting the negotiations in which he presented one set of proposals and insisted on agreement on that before moving to the next set of proposals.[39] The matter was complicated by the Salisbury delegation's apparent haste in accepting each one of the set of proposals presented while the Patriotic Front wished to negotiate by offering counter-proposals. Once the Salisbury delegation had accepted what was offered, this put enormous pressure on the Patriotic Front to do the same, and made Lord Carrington inflexible in resisting the Patriotic Front's counter-proposals.[40]

One other form of pressure used to advantage by the British Government against the Patriotic Front was the threat of lifting the economic embargo against, and recognition of, the Salisbury administration. This pressure was felt much more strongly in October during the Conservative Party's annual conference as the right wing of the Party called for the end of 'economic sanctions' against Rhodesia. In the end the Party passed a resolution stipulating that the enforcement measures should be lifted 'as soon as is practically possible', to which Lord Carrington promised that '. . . in view of the progress that has been made at Lancaster House the time for lifting sanctions cannot be far off'.[41] Mr Julian Amery, a leading lobbyist of 'White Rhodesia', said in an acclaimed speech that if the economic embargo continued one hour beyond November it would 'make us have blood on our hands'.[42]

The first move towards the end of British participation in the enforcement action came on 7 November 1979 when the

[39] Cmnd. 7802.

[40] *African Research Bulletin*, vol. 16, No. 10, Nov. 1979, 5449 C. If the end justifies the means, this unorthodox approach was probably appropriate in the circumstances. Nevertheless, it injected a considerable degree of mistrust between the Patriotic Front and the British Government.   [41] Ibid.

[42] Ibid.

Government announced that it would not renew some relevant legislation which was about to expire.[43] This included
the Rhodesia Act, 1965, s. 2, which accounted for about
15 per cent of the economic embargo, mainly concerned
with indirect trade between Britain and Rhodesia through
third countries, and civil flights between London and Salisbury. The British Government promised that the remaining
items covered by the enforcement measures would be lifted
as soon as Rhodesia returned to legality with the appointment of a governor by Britain to take over the reins of power
in Rhodesia.[44]

Full agreement on the transitional arrangements was
reached in London on 15 November 1979.[45] Lord Soames
arrived in Salisbury to assume his duties as Governor on
12 December 1979. This formally marked the end of the
fourteen year constitutional conflict between Britain and
her rebel colony. It also marked the end of British participation in the United Nations enforcement action. Although
Britain could not tell the United Nations to end the whole
enforcement action, she had earlier sent formal messages to
that Organization informing the President of the month,
Mr Salim of Tanzania, that all Britain's enforcement measures
were being lifted with immediate effect. Similarly, messages
had also been sent to members of the Commonwealth, and
members of the European Economic Community, and to the
African front-line states.[46] A number of other Western powers
quickly followed suit, much as Higgins had prediced in 1967.[47]
These included New Zealand, the United States, and France.[48]

The following is the statement made by Sir Anthony D.
Parsons, United Kingdom's Representative at the United
Nations, to the President of the Security Council:

I have the honour, on instructions from Her Majesty's Principal Secretary
of State for Foreign and Commonwealth Affairs, to inform your Excellency that the Southern Rhodesia Constitution (Interim Provisions)
Order, 1979, providing for the assumption of full legislative and executive authority over Southern Rhodesia by a British Governor, was made

---

[43] Ibid.   [44] Ibid. No. 11, 31 Dec. 1979, 5325-7.
[45] Ibid.   [46] Ibid.
[47] (1967) 23, *World Today*, 103.
[48] *Keesing's Contemporary Archives*, 30165.

on 3 December 1979. The Governor has assumed his functions in Salisbury today and his authority has been accepted by the commanders of the military and police forces and the leading civil authorities there. Accordingly, the state of rebellion in the territory has been brought to an end.

The action which has been taken to restore Rhodesia to legality is action undertaken in the exercise of the responsibility as administering Power which the Security Council has repeatedly acknowledged as falling uniquely upon the United Kingdom. It will enable the final arrangements for the implementation of a cease-fire to be put into effect. These arrangements are being worked out in the final stage of the Constitutional Conference at Lancaster House, which was preceded by a long period of consultation . . . After three months of negotiation, agreement has been reached on an Independence Constitution providing for genuine majority rule. The Constitution was enacted by Order in Council on 6 December. Agreement has also been reached on the arrangements for the transitional period, including the holding of elections supervised under the United Kingdom's authority, and on the United Kingdom's cease-fire proposals . . . ˙

The situation which was determined by the Security Council in its resolution 232 (1966) of 16 December 1966 to constitute a threat to international peace and security, as re-affirmed by subsequent resolu- tions of the Council, has accordingly been remedied and the purpose of the measures which were decided upon by the Council on the basis of that determination has been achieved. In these circumstances, the obligations of Member States under Article 25 of the Charter in relation to those measures in the view of the Government of the United King- dom, are to be regarded as having been discharged. This being so, the United Kingdom is terminating the measures which were taken by it pursuant to the decisions adopted by the Council in regard to the situation of illegality . . .[49]

As could be expected, this announcement was received with a storm of protest by the African group at the United Nations. In a letter dated 15 December 1979[50] sent by the Permanent Representative of Madagascar to the United Nations they expressed extreme concern over the decision of the United Kingdom Government which they called unaccept- able and illegal. They argued, correctly, it is submitted, that the Security Council Resolution 253 (1968) could be revoked only by a decision of the Security Council, and that any unilateral action in this context was a violation of the respons- ibilities assumed by member states under Article 25 of the Charter. They considered that a colonial situation still existed

[49] S/13796.   [50] S/13693.

in Rhodesia which must be settled by the United Kingdom in the light of the principles laid down by the Charter and re-affirmed by Resolution 1514 (XV). Furthermore, they argued that as matters stood in that country the situation was still a threat to international peace and security in so far as the war still existed since the warring parties had not yet laid down their arms.[51] The African group requested the Security Council to take the necessary measures to preserve its author-ity in that matter.

Another strong protest came from the Representative of the Soviet Union who said that the British action constituted a flagrant violation of the United Nations Charter.[52] He also argued that Security Council Resolution 253 (1968) con-cerning mandatory measures against Rhodesia could only be rescinded by a decision of the Security Council and no uni-lateral action on that matter could be recognized as legal and valid. Other criticisms have already been examined above.[53]

It has already become clear that the present writer agrees with the critics of the United Kingdom's action and the reasons for this stand have also already been made clear. It is doubtful whether Britain itself ever sought to justify its decisions in terms of law. The statement quoted above does not contain any legal justifications. Even where the statement refers to the obligations under Article 25, it is made clear that the statement refers to 'the view of the British Govern-ment'. The explanation of the British action therefore lies somewhere else other than in law. The answer probably lies in the phrase used by Higgins, that is, the statement that *'as a matter of tactics*, it is open for the United Kingdom to insist that the measures lapse when the rebellion ends . . .'[54] Therefore the British action was a matter of tactics and the tactics worked notwithstanding the heavy criticism. It worked, particularly in getting the Patriotic Front to accept the trans-itional arrangements.

It should also be pointed out that the time was itself ripe for a settlement anyway. All that was needed was good faith on the part of the United Kingdom. The African group,

---

[51] Ibid.   [52] S/13702.
[53] See pp. 188–90 above.
[54] Higgins, (1967) 23, *World Today*, 103; emphasis added.

backed by the Soviet Union, kept a considerable level of pressure on the United Kingdom from the time Lord Soames assumed his Governorship to the time of the signing of the full agreement on 21 December 1979 containing all the transitional arrangements. They complained about the presence of South African troops in Rhodesia; about the redeployment of the Rhodesian forces and 'auxiliary' forces; about the Governor's apparent unevenhandedness in favour of Bishop Muzorewa, the last leader under the rebel administration; and about the announcement of the withdrawal of South African troops from Rhodesia which was made jointly by South Africa and the United Kingdom.[55]

The hostility which greeted the unilateral withdrawal by Britain and some other Western Nations from participation in the United Nations enforcement action, and the forceful arguments presented by the states which opposed those withdrawals, coupled with the lack of legal arguments on the part of the states which unilaterally withdrew from the action, demonstrate very clearly that as a matter of law a mandatory enforcement action imposed by the Security Council can only be terminated by the Security Council itself. Besides, this position enhances the authority of the United Nations, particularly the Security Council which is charged with the primary responsibility for the maintenance of international peace and security.

In order to drive the legal point home, the states which opposed the unilateral action of Britain and her allies insisted on the Security Council formally passing a resolution declaring the enforcement action terminated. The resolution provides, in paragraph 2, that the Security Council:

2. *Decides*, having regard to the agreement reached at the Lancaster House conference, to call upon Member States to terminate the measures taken against Southern Rhodesia under Chapter VII of the Charter pursuant to resolutions 232 (1966), 253 (1968) and subsequent related resolutions on the situation in Southern Rhodesia.[56]

[55] Details of the Lancaster House negotiations and the Agreement signed are outside the scope of this work.

[56] Res. 460 (1979), passed on 21 Dec. 1979. The resolution was passed by 13 votes to none with 2 abstentions — the Soviet Union and Czechoslovakia — who argued that it was premature to terminate the enforcement action before independence was attained.

Knowing that things might still go wrong and stall the drive to independence, the members concluded by saying that the Security Council:

9. *Decides* to keep the situation in Southern Rhodesia under review until the Territory attains full independence.

Rhodesia achieved its independence on 18 April 1980 as a Republic.[57]

[57] Southern Rhodesia: The Zimbabwe Constitution Order, 1979.

The Future of United Nations
Non-Military Enforcement System
after the Rhodesian Experience

THE passing of Resolution 460 (1979) by the Security Council saw the formal termination of the United Nations enforcement action against the Smith regime, fourteen years from its initial imposition. While the final conclusion of the Rhodesian independence crisis was certainly a happy one in that it led to peace in Rhodesia and saw a majority rule government installed in Salisbury under an independent Republic of Zimbabwe with a government elected under universal adult suffrage, questions still remain unanswered about the effectiveness of the United Nations non-military enforcement machinery in the maintenance of international peace and security. Could it, for example, be said that this enforcement action was successful against the Smith regime? Is a period of fourteen years of economic war a reasonable length of time for the United Nations to remove a threat to the peace? Has the world community learnt any lessons from this action? Now that the independence crisis is over, no doubt much more information on these questions will come to light.

The present chapter does not seek to discuss in any detail the effectiveness of the enforcement action in the Rhodesian independence question. It proposes to make a general assessment of the action as a whole, looking at the time it took to find a final solution to the crisis, some difficulties it caused for the rebel regime, and the part of the action played in bringing about the resolution of the problem. Although no doubt the United Nations enforcement action was seen by the United Kingdom as the primary, if not the only means of persuading the Rhodesian rebel regime to return to legality under British colonial authority, it is important to note that there are many other factors which operated against the regime at the same time as the United Nations action.[1] What is more, it is not possible to isolate these factors from each other.[2]

A. *Effect of the Enforcement Action on Subsidiary Objectives of the United Nations in Rhodesia*

Four objectives can be identified as falling under the above heading although admittedly it is possible that the list could be expanded. By subsidiary or minor objectives of the enforcement action is meant the short-term purposes which though minor are important for the purpose of gaining time to enable the major objectives to be achieved. The four subsidiary objectives which are considered here were, firstly, the need to prevent revolt by Africans which could lead to great loss of life and property, secondly, the prevention of foreign intervention, thirdly, making life intolerable for the Smith regime so as to force it to negotiate more meaningfully with the United Kingdom, and fourthly, the prevention of the Unilateral Declaration of Independence from winning international recognition.

On his last visit to Rhodesia before UDI was proclaimed, Mr Wilson, the British Prime Minister, was struck by the polarization of the positions held by the whites on the one hand and the blacks on the other.[3] This polarization was caused by what Mr Wilson called hypercharged emotions resulting from fear, distrust, suspicion, and unfounded rumour.[4] Africans suspected that UDI was imminent and were anxious about the future under a ruthless regime in rebellion and the Europeans were concerned about how the Africans would react to UDI when it did come.

When UDI finally came, therefore, Africans were not taken by surprise. In fact, long before UDI in 1965, Africans had been involved in acts of violence throughout the country as they had by that time come to realize that Britain was not prepared to intervene in Rhodesia for their benefit. As a

[1] Doxey, *Economic Sanctions and International Enforcement* (Oxford, 1971), 3.
[2] Ibid.   [3] Good, 51-2.   [4] Ibid.

matter of fact, Africans even suspected that if Britain intervened in Rhodesia at all, it would be to save the white community from African revolt. This suspicion was strengthened by Mr Wilson's proviso when renouncing military intervention, that Britain would not intervene unless there was a total breakdown of law and order. For instance, two weeks before UDI he told the African leaders:

If there are those who are thinking in terms of a thunderbolt hurtling from the sky and destroying their enemy, a thunderbolt in the shape of the Royal Air Force, let me say that the thunderbolt will not be forthcoming, and to continue in this illusion wastes valuable time and misdirects valuable energies.[5]

While this could easily pass as an assurance to white politicians in Rhodesia to have no fears of military intervention should they decide to declare UDI, it also served notice to Africans that if they needed military force they would have to undertake it themselves.

Mr Wilson's repudiation of military force was known well before UDI. While it would probably be an overstatement of the fact to say that Mr Wilson's stand on this matter influenced African leaders in Rhodesia to adopt violent methods, his stand certainly strengthened their rights irrespective of what Britain would or would not do. The Rhodesian Government responded to these African efforts by more and more stringent legislation. Thus at the end of 1964 and early 1965, two amendments were made to the Law and Order (Maintenance) Act to deal with these acts of violence.[6] The first amendment, approved on 7 December 1964 following several incidents involving the throwing of bombs in Salisbury on 30 November to 1 December, made possession of a bomb an offence punishable by death or imprisonment for up to twenty years, and possession of any offensive weapon other than a bomb, by imprisonment for a maximum of twenty years. The second amendment, adopted without a vote on 19 March 1965, extended the maximum period of restriction under the Act from one year to five.[7]

From July 1965 onwards there were numerous trials of Africans charged with undergoing guerrilla warfare and

---

[5] *Weekly Hansard*, 1 Nov. 1965.
[6] (1965–6) *Keesing*, 20874.   [7] Ibid.

sabotage training abroad, in particular in Ghana, but also in China and other Communist countries.[8] The Annual report of the Rhodesian Secretary for Law and Order, Mr A. M. Bruce-Brand, issued on 10 March 1966, referred to a 'very serious threat' of sabotage by 'many saboteurs' who had entered Rhodesia secretly during 1965.[9] On 7 February 1966, twenty-four Africans were tried in the High Court in Salisbury, and were said to be part of a group of fifty-two Africans trained between 24 March and October 1965 in Moscow, Nanking, or Pyongyang in guerrilla warfare and the use of arms and explosives. On 13 April 1966, seven Zimbabwe African National Union (ZANU) members were arrested in the Umtali and Fort Victoria areas carrying rifles, sub-machine-guns, ammunition, and Soviet-made TNT. Exactly a month later, twenty Zimbabwe African People's Union (ZAPU) members were given sentences of ten years' imprisonment each while one was sentenced to five years for entering Rhodesia secretly between April and October 1965 and for being saboteurs and spies trained in China, the Soviet Union, and North Korea for the purpose of overthrowing the Government of Rhodesia.[10]

It was not surprising therefore that whites in Rhodesia were apprehensive and anxious about the future. They had no doubt that when UDI was proclaimed violence would erupt on a much larger scale. Britain too was aware of that and she had to do something to arrest the situation. As she had already renounced the use of force and opted for economic and other non-military measures, Britain had to involve the whole international community. This would serve three purposes. It would demonstrate to Mr Smith and his colleagues that they could not get away with their rebellion easily, while at the same time it assured the international community, especially Africa, that Britain was trying to solve the problem and no other nation should therefore intervene in Rhodesia. Most of all the British action would demonstrate to the Rhodesian Africans that Britain had not completely abandoned them so that they would at best postpone taking up arms against the Rhodesian whites until an equitable solution was found for a Rhodesian settlement.

[8] Ibid. 214221.   [9] Ibid.   [10] Ibid.

However, when UDI finally did come, trouble broke out in Bulawayo among Africans. Rioters ran round townships stoning European-driven cars, and throwing petrol bombs. The Smith regime distributed 300,000 copies of a statement warning Africans that the police and the army were ready to deal with any persons who caused disturbances.[11] On 15 November 1965, the police put down an attempt by some Africans in Bulawayo to prevent others going to work as an act of opposition to UDI. In Salisbury, a bus was burnt and several other buses stoned. A group of fifty Africans emptied three schools of about 2,400 pupils, urging them to go on strike.[12]

In spite of these disturbances, however, the level of African violent revolt was less than many whites and Britain had feared. This may have been due to the draconian measures taken by the Smith regime, a heavy police presence all over the major concentrations of the African population, notably in the large urban areas, particularly Salisbury and Bulawayo. It could be argued too that the United Nations enforcement action had a calming effect on the emotions of the African population in Rhodesia. It is submitted that the United Nations was therefore successful in dealing with this subsidiary objective of preventing widespread African revolt in reply to UDI.

Internationally, there were fears of intervention by African nations in support of the Rhodesian Africans. Many statements had been made by a number of African nations that if Britain was not prepared to use force against her kith and kin, African states would do so themselves. For example, the idea of military intervention in Rhodesia was considered by African states before UDI was proclaimed. As Mr Oscar Kambona, the Tanzanian Minister of Regional Administration, put it to a newly created defence committee of five members of the Organization of African Unity, on 9 November 1965, member states of the OAU had pledged themselves to work unremittingly for the total liquidation of colonialism in Africa by negotiation and to fight to achieve it if necessary.[13] In

[11] *The Times* (London), 13 Nov. 1965, 10.
[12] Ibid., 16 Nov. 1965, 12.
[13] *The Times* (London), 20 Nov. 1965, 17.

similar vein Dr Nkrumah said the time had come for African states to take the initiative in their own defence and that of the people of Rhodesia instead of waiting for Britain to do her duty in her colony.[14]

Similarly, the Presidents of Mali, Senegal, Guinea, and Mauritania, meeting in Nouakshott, called upon every African state to consider itself at war with the illegal regime.[15] Only Dr Banda of Malawi was out of step with the other African leaders, arguing that he did not give what he called African 'parade armies' a chance against even 'ten Rhodesian mercenaries' who could 'whip 5,000 so-called African soldiers'. He insisted that, if pressed, the Rhodesian army 'could conquer the whole of East and Central Africa in one week'.[16]

In spite of these militant statements from African states no African military intervention in Rhodesia materialized. One reason for this was that Zambia was prepared to offer a military base only to British troops to intervene in Rhodesia and not to African, United Nations or any other great power forces as these would risk racial or ideological war.[17] The other reason, it could be argued, was that the intervention by the United Nations with non-military measures, while not considered by Africans as being adequate to meet the rebellion, was sufficient to defuse the situation, making unlikely any unilateral military intervention by any African state. In this respect, therefore, it is submitted that the United Nations enforcement action was successful in this limited objective. Third states' intervention was restricted to front-line states' assistance to liberation forces as authorized by United Nations resolutions.

The third subsidiary objective of the United Nations enforcement action in Rhodesia was to put pressure on Mr Smith to negotiate with the British Government as well as with the black politicians. Britain had been under tremendous pressure at the United Nations since the early 1960s to convene a constitutional conference to be attended by all the interested parties in Rhodesia. Britain was initially unable to do this as the white Rhodesian leaders were not prepared to sit down round the table with African nationalists, whom they insisted

---

[14] Ibid.; see also ibid. 26 Nov. 1965, 12.
[15] Ibid., 13 Nov. 1965, 10.   [16] Good, 21.   [17] Ibid. 96.

did not represent the African population as a whole. Britain argued therefore that there would be no point in convening a constitutional conference, as the ruling whites were only ready to negotiate with her on a government to government basis. However, Britain could not extract sufficient concessions from the whites to make a significant change in the constitutional set up in Rhodesia to form the basis under which that territory could be granted independence. A number of fruitless contacts between the two Governments were made prior to UDI.[18] It was not until 1975 that Mr Smith agreed to attend full-scale talks on the constitutional future of Rhodesia with that territory's African leaders. Firstly, this followed the initiative started by President Kaunda and the South African Prime Minister, Mr Vorster,[19] under the *détente* exercise of Southern Africa. Later on a combination of increased guerrilla warfare and Dr Henry Kissinger's intervention led to an attempt at a constitutional conference in Geneva, which was a fiasco.[20] It is submitted that it is difficult to attribute Mr Smith's change of heart only to the United Nations enforcement action. Nevertheless, it should be considered to have been a factor along with many others, notably, the guerrilla war and American pressure.[21]

Probably the most outstanding achievement of the United Nations action was its policy of non-recognition which, as already seen, held out throughout the crisis.[22]

The success of all the subsidiary objectives was of limited usefulness if the major objectives of removing the threat to international peace and security and the realization of majority rule in Rhodesia were not attained. This was illustrated by the fact that while African violence was quickly put down by the Smith regime soon after the proclamation of UDI, the level of violence gradually started to escalate as years of stalemate in the Rhodesian independence crisis continued. This eventually reached a level of a civil war which finally cost a conservative estimate of 20,000 lives in Rhodesia and many more in Botswana, Mozambique, and Zambia.[23] The next

---

[18] See e.g. Good, 150–160, 170–97.
[19] Martin and Johnson, *The Struggle for Zimbabwe*, 125–57.
[20] *The Times* (London), 25 Sept. 1976, 1.   [21] Ibid.
[22] See Chapter X above.   [23] S/PV 2181, 16, 67, 72.

section of the present chapter examines the major objectives of the United Nations enforcement action to determine how far the non-military enforcement system of the United Nations could be relied upon to deal with similar crises in future.

B. *Removal of the Threat to the Peace*

The major objective of the United Nations enforcement action in Rhodesia was the removal of the threat of international peace and security declared to exist by the Security Council.[24] This objective could be achieved only with the realization of the allied objective of obtaining a satisfactory political settlement in Rhodesia. This in turn depended on the United Kingdom reasserting its physical control in Rhodesia by defeating the rebellion of the Smith regime. The role of the United Nations enforcement action in this respect was to assist the United Kingdom to achieve this goal.

Now that all these objectives have been realized it is interesting to examine briefly how the wide gap that existed between the positions held by the British Government and that held by the Smith regime was closed, thereby creating a conducive climate for the signing of the Lancaster House Agreement on 21 December 1979, an event which was hailed as a historic achievement by virtually all the members who spoke on that day in the Security Council.[25]

The closing of the gap between the two sides could be said to have started in 1975 when Mozambique won its independence from Portugal and joined in the United Nations enforcement action. The impact on the Rhodesian problem of the Portuguese decision to grant Mozambique and her other African colonies independence was very ably summarized by Mr Monteiro of Mozambique when he spoke in the Security Council on 21 December 1979.[26] He pointed out that when the people of Mozambique attained independence, they realized that they could never get peace which they needed to develop their country as long as the Rhodesian problem

---

[24] See Res. 232 (1966) and 253 (1968).   [25] S/PV 2181.
[26] Ibid. 64–7.

remained unresolved. They felt therefore the need to create all conditions to enable the people of Zimbabwe to develop their political and armed struggle within the territory. This called for the 'complete application of sanctions decreed by the international community'. He went on:

Thus, on 3 March 1976, His Excellency the President of the People's Republic of Mozambique, Samora Moises Machel, declared the immediate and complete application of the sanctions decided upon by the Security Council against the racist Ian Smith régime. We are convinced that that decision made it possible to make effective the embargo decided upon by the Security Council.[27]

This action of Mozambique must have demonstrated clearly to the Smith regime that unless it took more drastic steps in self-preservation, its existence was seriously threatened. The regime became brutally aggressive against the neighbouring states of Botswana, Mozambique, and Zambia, particularly the last two. It attacked and destroyed bridges, railways, and telecommunications systems. It also attacked farmers, destroyed harvests, and bombed refugee camps, killing hundreds of people in places like Nyazonia, Doeroi, and Tronga in Mozambique.[28] In the light of this the Security Council passed Resolution 411 (1977) on 30 June 1977 requesting all states to provide immediate and substantial material assistance to enable the Government of Mozambique to strengthen its defence capability in order effectively to safeguard its sovereignty and territorial integrity. States and regional organizations were also requested to provide financial, technical, and material aid to Mozambique to enable it to redress the severe economic loss and destruction of property occasioned by the acts of the Rhodesian rebel administration.

In spite of these measures of the Security Council the Smith regime continued with its operations allegedly in search of guerrillas in Mozambique's productive areas in the Provinces of Manica, Tete, Gaza, and Sofala.[29] Similar punitive actions were carried out by the Smith regime in Zambia where such acts had started even before the independence of Mozambique.[30] In spite of this bellicose stance adopted by the Smith

[27] Ibid. 72.   [28] Ibid. 73.   [29] Ibid.
[30] See *U.N.S.C. Twenty-eight year Supplement* for January–March 1973, Res. 326 (1973) was subsequently adopted; ibid. *Supplement* for January–March

regime it was obvious to informed observers that the regime realized that the wind of change was blowing and Mr Smith wanted to turn it to blow in his favour by negotiating an internal arrangement with some Africans in Zimbabwe in order to avoid an internationally imposed settlement which could deprive the whites of the control of the country for which UDI had originally been declared. Consequently after the collapse of the attempt at the Southern African *détente* initiated by President Kaunda and Prime Minister Vorster,[31] Mr Smith and Mr Nkomo, the leader of the Zimbabwe African People's Union, signed a 'declaration of intention to negotiate a settlement' on 1 December 1975.[32] After about two and half months of meetings between the two leaders no agreement could be reached as Mr Smith was not ready to hand over power to the black majority of the country. He marked the failure of the negotiations by his frequently quoted expression, which probably fills him with shame whenever he hears it, that 'I don't believe in black majority rule ever in Rhodesia — not in a thousand years.'[33]

Mr Smith soon adopted a new strategy of survival by bringing into his Cabinet African Chiefs. What he hoped to achieve by this move is difficult to say since the Chiefs had no following among the Africans who were fighting his regime, nor had they any respect internationally. Britain too had long rejected Mr Smith's argument that Chiefs were the true leaders of the bulk of the African people. In any case this move coincided with the arrival on the Southern African scene of Dr Henry Kissinger, the American Secretary of State who, having probably realized the folly of his country's African policy which was based on the infamous document named NSSM 39, was attempting to salvage something out of the battered American image after the success of the Cubans and Soviets in Angola in their support of the MPLA movement in its bid for power.[34]

The NSSM 39 document had listed five policy options for

1978; Res. 424 (1978) was subsequently adopted. 'No majority rule in 1000 years', Martin and Johnson, 288.

[31] Martin and Johnson, 158.   [32] Ibid, 227.
[33] *Sunday Times* (London), 21 Mar. 1976.
[34] Martin and Johnson, 231.

the United States in assessment of its African policy. None of these options was favourable to Africans.[35] On Rhodesia, as Martin and Johnson indicate, Dr Kissinger specifically advocated the gradual relaxation of the United States participation in the United Nations enforcement measures.[36] Under NSSM 39 Option 2 Dr Kissinger and President Nixon recommended that 'without openly taking a position undermining the United Kingdom and United Nations on Rhodesia, we would be more flexible in our attitude toward the Smith régime'.[37]

When Kissinger arrived in Southern Africa in April 1976 it would appear that he had almost abandoned NSSM 39. He stated that America, in spite of its past mistakes on Africa, now supported peace, racial justice, self-determination, majority rule, equal rights, and human dignity for all the peoples of Southern Africa in the name of moral principle, international law, and world peace.[38] Dr Kissinger set himself the task of convincing Mr Smith of the futility of continuing to resist the inevitable majority rule in Rhodesia. Mr Smith finally caved in, and accepted majority rule in Rhodesia.

In a radio and television broadcast he stated:

It was made abundantly clear to me that, as long as present circumstances prevail in Rhodesia, the country could expect no help or support of any kind from the free world. On the contrary, the pressures on us from the free world would continue to mount.[39]

Negotiations were quickly arranged to take place in Geneva. All the parties turned up at the venue of the constitutional conference but disagreement about various aspects of what Mr Smith had accepted soon brought the conference to a premature end, and Mr Smith returned to Rhodesia to sign an internal settlement agreement two years later with Bishop Muzorewa, Reverend Sithole, and Chief Chirau on 3 March 1978 while Britain and the United States desparately but vainly tried to bring the disputing parties together again.[40]

In spite of all these efforts to end the rebellion, the question of removing a threat to international peace and security

---

[35] Ibid.   [36] Ibid.   [37] Cohen.
[38] Martin and Johnson, 234.
[39] *The Times* (London), 25 Sept. 1976, 1; *Keesing*, 2804. For the details of the terms accepted by Mr Smith see. Chapter I above.
[40] (1978) *Keesing*, 28945-8. These British attempts have already been discussed above. See Chapters I and XII.

remained intractable. In fact each attempt at negotiating towards a settlement ignited new waves of cross-border raids by the Rhodesian forces into the neighbouring countries causing much loss of life and destruction of property. This demonstrated clearly that the removal of the threat to the peace could not be separated from the achievement of a lasting political settlement in Rhodesia. This was brought home firmly when the rebel forces continued to invade targets in Mozambique and Zambia even after agreement on certain aspects of the Rhodesian problem had been reached in London during the Lancaster House Conference. This point was made by Mr Clark, the Nigerian representative to the United Nations, when he criticized Britain for her unilateral decision to terminate her participation in the United Nations action. He stated:

The measures adopted against the rebel colony arose from the fact that the circumstances and events leading to the rebellion constituted a threat to international peace and security. The end of the rebellion has by no means removed that threat as the recent raids against the front line states of Botswana, Mozambique and Zambia show.[41]

Furthermore, the presence of South African troops which were admitted to be in Rhodesia meant that the threat to the peace remained present until well after majority rule was implemented in Rhodesia.

Therefore, to answer the question whether the United Nations action was successful in removing the threat to the peace in Rhodesia, the reply would have to be linked to the question whether the United Nations action was successful in resolving the Rhodesian independence crisis. In answer to both these questions, it would be instructive to look at some statements which were made by the members of the Security Council on 21 December 1979, shortly after the signing of the Lancaster House Agreement in London.

The first person to speak was the Secretary-General of the United Nations who welcomed the formal signing of the Agreement in London. He also spoke highly of the front-line states who had suffered enormous hardship throughout the 14 years of the enforcement action. He noted with satisfaction

[41] S/PV 2181, 27.

that Resolution 460 (1979) terminating the enforcement action had provisions for some assistance to those countries.[42] He thanked the United Kingdom and all the other parties to the London Conference. Sir Anthony Parsons of the United Kingdom also spoke in a similar vein about the suffering of the front-line states during the crisis.[43] Most of the other members also had praise for the front-line states. In addition the African members emphasized the important role played by the black Rhodesians themselves through the guerrilla war.[44] For instance, Mr Lusaka of Zambia said that above all, 'credit must go to the people of Southern Rhodesia as a whole, who, through their national liberation movement, the Patriotic Front, fought heroically for the enjoyment of their inalienable right to self-determination and genuine national independence. It was largely through the efforts of those gallant freedom fighters that suitable conditions were created for the holding of the Lancaster House conference.'[45]

It is clear that the members of the Security Council also took the view that the United Nations enforcement action was invaluable in the resolution of the problem of Rhodesia. It was in this light that most of the members took strong exception to the United Kingdom and some of her allies unilaterally terminating the enforcement measures they had imposed against the Smith regime. They feared that the effect of such acts would be to derogate from the sacrifices that were made by the members of the United Nations who complied with the Organization's decisions. This was particularly true of the sacrifices made by states like Mozambique and Zambia whose traditional trade links with Rhodesia were so close that complying with the enforcement action signified considerable political courage at the time these countries had newly attained their political independence.

The unilateral termination of enforcement measures was particularly significant since it was taken by three of the permanent members of the Security Council, Britain, France, and the United States. It was surprising especially since it was Britain supported by the United States who put much faith

---

[42] S/PV 2181, 7-10.   [43] Ibid. 11-15.
[44] See esp. Mr Monteiro of Mozambique, ibid., 64-75.
[45] Ibid. 16.

in the non-military enforcement measures at the time the African members were sceptical, to say the least.

Understandably African nations were sore about the decisions of these countries because the African states wanted to show that enforcement measures can work if properly applied, for instance against South Africa. For example, Mr Lusaka of Zambia pointed out on 21 December 1979 that if South Africa intervened militarily in Rhodesia, in the event of a Patriotic Front victory, the Security Council could not stand aloof, or take the intervention lightly.[46] These are words of a man who has faith in the efficacy of the United Nations non-military enforcement system, if not by choice then because there is at present nothing better than it.

On the contrary, it could be argued that now that the embarrassing Rhodesian problem is out of the way the Western powers are not too keen to uphold the efficacy of the non-military enforcement action of the United Nations in case there should be demand for it to be used against South Africa to solve the Namibian independence problem or to get rid of apartheid in South Africa itself. It is therefore not surprising that the countries who spoke so persuasively in support of this system of enforcement against the Smith regime are now arguing equally persuasively against the use of the system against South Africa. It is submitted that although it took fourteen years for the last chapter of the Rhodesian independence crisis to be written, the non-military enforcement action of the United Nations was by and large successful in ultimately removing the threat to the peace in Rhodesia. The criticism that may obviously and justifiably be levelled against the system is the length of time it took to achieve its objectives. Even here, however, the problem does not lie in the system but in how it was implemented and enforced, as will be seen below. The fact that there was guerrilla war going on at the same time should not derogate from what has just been said. No doubt the leaders of the freedom fighters would be the first to admit that any action imposed against their enemy was welcome and it helped towards the achievement of the common goal, the removal of an unjust political system

[46] Ibid. 21.

which had forced people to stand up and fight for their rights. It should be remembered too that a large number of the resolutions of the Security Council and the General Assembly recognized the legitimate struggle of the Rhodesian people and authorized member states to give them moral and material support. And in pursuance of these, many states did offer the support requested. Admittedly these countries would probably have given this assistance anyway without the request of the United Nations but the 'authorization' by the United Nations no doubt made such assistance as gifts of military equipment easier to make than would have been the case otherwise.

Effects of the Enforcement Action in Rhodesia

The discussion that follows under this heading is no more than a cursory view of how Rhodesia was affected by the United Nations enforcement action as a detailed analysis of the problem is beyond the scope of this work inasmuch as it really belongs largely to the area of economics. The imposition of the enforcement action against the Smith regime initially appeared to assist economic activity in Rhodesia. This lasted from 1965 for a period of ten years, and reached its watershed in 1975.[47] For instance, during that period agricultural output rose by an estimated 75 per cent, while its value was reported to have more than doubled.[48] This is probably not surprising since as Doxey points out:

To some extent, an economic system can be expected to generate its own defences . . . and this will help to soften the impact of economic sanctions . . .[49]

Moreover, as Doxey again correctly indicates, not all sectors of the economy are necessarily damaged by economic enforcement measures. For example, in Rhodesia the manufacturing industry benefited from the artificial protection afforded by the United Nations action, and this led to some phenomenal expansion. Similarly, the enforced import substitution led to local manufacture of things like crop-spraying

[47] (1977) *Europa Yearbook: A World Survey*, 1370.
[48] Ibid.
[49] Doxey, (1971) *Yearbook of World Affairs*, 156.

and irrigation equipment, medical, veterinary and toilet preparations, ceramics, breakfast cereals, and confectionery.[50] Furthermore there was expansion in the manufacture of clothing and footwear, furniture, paints, and electrical appliances.[51]

Again Doxey points out that in the long run, however, prosperity for those new and expanding enterprises depended on non-Rhodesian markets, and on the rising purchasing power within the Rhodesian market itself.[52] Both of these depended upon the lifting of the United Nations enforcement action. Consequently, after 1975 Rhodesian economic activity began to stagnate and decline as a combination of forces began to operate.

The economy . . . began to feel the effects of international recession . . ., leading to low demand for primary exports, declining export prices, decreased industrial output and strained balance of payment position.

The high cost of the guerrilla campaign was exacerbated in 1976. The closure of the Mozambique border left Rhodesia totally dependent on South Africa for its trade. Extended periods of military service reduced the skilled labour force and white emigration exceeded immigration by 6,000 in 1976. The spread of the guerrilla campaign throughout most of the country hampered communications and reduced the number of tourists by 35 per cent. Defence expenditure accounted for 23 per cent of the record 1976/77 budget, which forecast a deficit of R$21,5 million.[53]

The poor state of the Rhodesian economy was spelt out by Mr Smith himself in January 1978 in his annual New Year radio and television broadcast when he stated that 'sanctions, the civil war and the failure of the international economy had contributed to this position. The coming year would be another one of stress and strains.'[54] This was echoed by a statement made by Rhodesia's biggest commercial bank, the Standard Bank:

More than ever before, time is running out for the economy and in the absence of the break-through to international recognition, it is faced with the spectre of closures and redundancies on a significant scale.[55]

[50] Ibid.
[52] Ibid.
[54] *The Times* (London), 3 Jan. 1978, 5.
[51] Ibid.
[53] (1977) *Europa*, 1370.
[55] Ibid., 11 Apr. 1978, 1.

These difficulties were highlighted again in an article published in *The Economist* where it was stated:

Under forced import substitution, everything from railway rolling stock to pins to wine is now locally made. Scarce foreign-exchange earnings, made scarcer by slack world demand for industrial metals as well as by sanctions, which give middlemen an opening to buy from Rhodesia cheap and sell to it dear, are needed to pay for essential imports and to purchase armaments.[56]

The article pointed out that the country was long past the stage of relatively straightforward labour-intensive import substitution, and was then handicapped by old factories, machines, and mining equipment; South Africa's help was no longer readily available; there was lack of access to foreign loans and investment; there were problems of weak capital formation, problems of an outflow of hot money as white emigrants, who left at a net rate of 900 a month in 1977, found illegal ways of getting their money out of Rhodesia. The guerrilla war cost about R$1.5 million a day; real gross domestic product, according to a Standard Bank estimate, fell by 7 per cent or 8 per cent in 1977. Insulated domestic industry which had been affected by successive devaluations of the Rhodesian dollar (by 6 per cent in October 1977, and 8 per cent in April 1978) badly needed belp. And finally, manufacturing output fell 1.3 per cent in 1975, 6.6 per cent in 1976, and 6.1 per cent in 1977. The article concluded that the situation would change drastically if and when Rhodesia had 'a reasonably stable internationally recognized government'.[57]

It was to win that international recognition and save the Rhodesian economic situation that Mr Smith signed the 'internal settlement' with Bishop Muzorewa, Reverend Sithole, and Chief Chirau.[58] Although the British position regarding the 'internal settlement' was ambivalent,[59] the United Nations rejected it outright.[60] It stated in paragraph 2 of Resolution 423 (1978), that the Security Council:

---

[56] Ibid.   [57] Ibid.
[58] (1978) *Keesing*, p. 28941.
[59] See *The Times* (London), 19 Apr. 1978, 4.
[60] See Res. 423 (1978) of 14 Mar. 1978.

Declares as illegal and unacceptable any internal settlement under the auspices of the illegal régime and calls upon all states not to accord any recognition to such a settlement.

The Problem of International Non-Military Enforcement Action in Rhodesia

According to an analysis prepared in 1965 under the auspices of the Carnegie Endownment on Apartheid and United Nations Collective Measures, the minimum requirements for an effective economic embargo are:

. . . prompt application, all-inclusive support, effective administration and enforcement, mutual aid to the damaged partners, and retention of the measures as long as necessary to secure compliance by the offending state.[61]

When the Smith regime declared UDI, the question was whether there would be the necessary minimum political consensus in the Security Council for the application of Chapter VII of the United Nations Charter. There was fear among the Afro-Asian states that the United Kingdom which had hitherto over the years resisted international jurisdiction in Rhodesia, would refuse to allow any United Nations intervention in that territory. On the contrary, however, when UDI did come Britain itself took the Rhodesian question to the United Nations promptly enough. Even so, however, this most welcome gesture lost its impact because Britain was not ready to allow the invocation of the most effective measures under Chapter VII of the Charter.[62] It was not until after a year that Britain permitted the adoption of mandatory enforcement measures, and these were only selective in their extent.[63] Comprehensive mandatory measures were not passed until nearly two years later on 29 May 1968.[64] As Zacklin points out:

. . . the unfolding of sanctions had been characterized by a painstaking and deliberate escalation from selective optional sanctions through an intermediate stage of selective mandatory sanctions, reaching

---

[61] A. C. Leiss (ed.), *Apartheid and U.N. Collective Measures, an Analysis* (New York: Carnegie Endowment for International Peace, 1965), 99, quoted in Zacklin, *United Nations and Rhodesia* (1974), 62.
[62] See Chapter V above.   [63] Res. 221 (1966) and 232 (1966).
[64] Res. 253 (1968).

comprehensive mandatory sanctions, two and half years after the unilateral declaration of independence . . .[65]

This slow graduation of enforcement measures deprived the measures of their sting and allowed the Rhodesian economy to adapt to them before an additional dose was added. A lesson to be learnt by the international community in this respect is that once the United Nations takes a decision to impose non-military enforcement action, it should impose measures which have a chance of working quickly and effectively so as to prevent the subject of the action adapting its economy to neutralize the effects of those measures. This means that the measures should be both mandatory and comprehensive. The United Kingdom would not allow that as she was concerned mainly with an attempt to persuade the Smith regime by mere arm-twisting methods without really hurting the Rhodesian economy to near destruction.

This method was acceptable also to the main British opposition party which did not want the British Government to surrender the Rhodesian question completely to the United Nations, thereby losing the opportunity of reaching a negotiated settlement with Mr Smith if the right terms could be found.[66]

It is submitted that this policy contributed greatly to the failure of the United Nations enforcement action in Rhodesia to bite quickly and effectively. It led to the piecemeal fashion of applying enforcement measures so as not to cripple the Rhodesian economy too seriously to make it difficult to revive quickly when the independence question was finally settled. The effect of this was that although the Smith regime was induced to maintain negotiations with the British Government, it was nevertheless unwilling to make sufficient concessions to lead to a settlement. The British policy encouraged the Smith regime to hope that the United Nations action could be beaten. This hope in turn militated against the British aim of reaching a satisfactory settlement with the regime. The British policy on Rhodesia, therefore, bore the seeds of

[65] Zacklin, *The UN and Rhodesia*, 45.
[66] *Weekly Hansard*, vol. 727, col. 718; ibid. vol. 720/721, col. 249; see also Chapter XII above.

its own weakness, which was also reflected on the international level.

One other major criticism that may be raised against the way the United Nations action was applied is that it was carried out as part of British domestic policy on Rhodesia. Consequently, although the Afro-Asian members of the Security Council attempted to take an independent line, they were always made to accept the line of action drawn up by the United Kingdom. The Latin American States seemed always eager to adopt a compromise position between that of Britain and her allies, and that of the Afro-Asian states.[67] The result of this was the adoption of relatively mild enforcement measures which, by and large, reflected the British point of view rather than that of the Afro-Asian states.[68] This enabled Britain to continue to negotiate with the Smith regime outside the framework of the United Nations action.

One would have expected Britain to have profited by her experience in the international enforcement action under the League of Nations against Italy in the *Italo-Ethiopian* crisis between 1935 and 1936. In that case, Britain and France, which, prior to the imposition of the League action had been seeking understanding and assurances of support from Mussolini against the growth of Germany under Hitler, were hesitant to sponsor the intensification of the enforcement measures to a point where they might have been effective.[69] Furthermore, these two countries continued to negotiate with Italy outside the framework of the League's action.[70]

What happened in the Italian case in this respect has, to a certain extent, some parallels in the Rhodesian situation. As regards the latter case, the problems of enforcement were compounded by the fact that Rhodesia was legally a British responsibility, a fact which was repeatedly stated in many resolutions of the organs of the United Nations. For this reason, some states regarded the enforcement action as a British action with the assistance of the

---

[67] Res. 217 (1965) was such a compromise.   [68] Ibid.
[69] F. P. Walters, *History of the League of Nations* (Oxford 1960). In particular, they refused to cut off oil supplies to Italy.
[70] Ibid.

United Nations, a view which was held by some British politicians too.[71]

Kapungu raises a number of interesting points regarding the dangers of identifying the United Nations action in Rhodesia with British domestic policy.[72] He points out that although Britain expected and had been assured of international support by most United Nations members in the implementation of that action some scepticism remained in the minds of some rulers about the whole exercise.

He adds that some members could even be considered as deriving a certain amount of satisfaction at seeing Britain failing to solve a seemingly easy problem.[73] He concludes that an 'effective policy of economic sanctions could not emerge in such an atmosphere, which was the result of the recognition by some states that the policy . . . was not a United Nations policy but an aspect of British policy'.[74] He believes that the situation would have been different if the economic action against the Smith regime had been seen as a United Nations action.

It is submitted, with respect, that to argue that the enforcement action in Rhodesia was a British and not a United Nations action, is to miss the point. Admittedly the dichotomy of responsibilities of the British Government on the one hand and those of the United Nations on the other could and did lead to problems. While it is true that the measures that were imposed in the Rhodesian situation represented only those that Britain had introduced or those it had allowed to be introduced, once those measures were ordered by a mandatory resolution of the Security Council they became United Nations measures. No member states of the United Nations including Britain, would be free to ignore them without violating its obligations. Britain was aware of this when she initially resisted the invocation of Chapter VII of the Charter.

The reason why some states and some commentators

---

[71] *The Times* (London), 23 Feb. 1978, p. 6; Higgins, 'International Law, Rhodesia and the UN', (1967), 23, *World Today*, 103.

[72] L. Kapungu, *United Nations and Economic Sanctions in Rhodesia* (Lexington, 1973), 137.

[73] Ibid.   [74] Ibid. 138.

erroneously, it is submitted, identified the enforcement action in Rhodesia as a British action and not a United Nations action was the fact that all the measures which were imposed reflected the British approach to the problem as envisaged in British domestic policy, as already seen. This was caused by the fact that Britain could have vetoed any measures she did not approve. This was not because the action was British, but because Britain was the legal administering power, who also happened to have a veto power. Had the administering power been simply an ordinary member of the United Nations it would have been possible for the United Nations action to take a clearly independent line from that adopted by the administering power. It was unfortunate that Britain encouraged the view that the United Nations action was a British action which Britain could bring to an end whenever it signed a settlement with the Smith regime even if the Security Council was opposed to that settlement. In fact this is the position Britain held until the end of the crisis in Rhodesia, and reflected it by unilaterally pulling out of the enforcement action of the United Nations.

The next question which may be examined at this point is that of universality of the application of the enforcement measures that were imposed by the Security Council. As Zacklin points out, it 'is axiomatic that international sanctions cannot succeed unless rigorous and univerally enforced'.[75] Although nearly every state is now a member of the United Nations, the membership of the Organization is not yet universal. For example, Switzerland is not a member. The reaction of such non-members is therefore important when an enforcement action is imposed by the United Nations since the resolution of the Security Council cannot bind them.

When the Security Council passed Resolution 232 (1966) the Secretary-General sent a note dated 13 January 1967 in which he invited Switzerland to comply with the selective mandatory measures of that resolution. In reply the Swiss Government said that for reasons of principle, Switzerland, as a neutral country, could not submit to the mandatory measures of the United Nations. The statement, however,

---

[75] Zacklin, *The UN and Rhodesia*, 62.

said that Rhodesian trade would not be given any opportunity to avoid the United Nations policy through Swiss territory.[76] West Germany, which at that time had not joined the United Nations, also stated in a *note verbale* to the Secretary-General that it identified itself with the decisions of the Security Council.

Apart from the gap in the membership of the Organization, however, there were some members who overtly adopted policies of non-compliance with Security Council orders.[77] Even among those states which declared themselves ready to abide by their obligations, some sometimes openly violated those obligations. For example, in 1971 the United States ordered chrome from Rhodesia in violation of the binding resolutions of the Security Council.[78]

The other question is that of finding effective machinery for monitoring the implementation of the ordered enforcement measures in order to detect violations. It was not until 1968 that the United Nations established the Security Council Sanctions Committee.[79] However, the machinery under which that Committee worked depended largely on Britain for the provision of information regarding possible violations of the United Nations measures. Furthermore, the Committee had no independent method of verifying the accuracy of the information provided; it had to request the countries in which the violations were alleged to have occurred, to investigate and report back to it. This was a very slow process. Another difficulty was that the Committee lacked powers to stop and search suspected ships on the high seas. This meant that by the time the Committee received information from the British or other governments or of course non-governmental sources, and sent its request to the country-concerned, it was often too late to do anything about the suspected shipment.[80]

In any case the fact that the Committee depended on the governments of the countries where the violation was alleged

---

[76] U.N. Doc. S/7781, Annex II (Feb. 1967), 177; see Chapter VII.
[77] Portugal and South Africa.   [78] Martin and Johnson, 231.
[79] Res. 253 (1968).
[80] Kapungu cites the case of the ship *Goodwill*, to illustrate this point; see Kapungu, 132.

to have taken place hampered the work of the Committee considerably because in some cases, as Mr Sean Gervasi, an independent research consultant based in New York, discovered, 'it is clear that Governments know of the operation' of the networks which breach the enforcement measures, and 'even that they facilitate' their efforts in this breach.[81] This was particularly true in respect of South Africa whose Government refused to respond to any request for information required by the Committee.[82] Even where Governments cooperated with the United Nations effort to end the Rhodesian rebellion, Mr Gervasi points out that breaches took place with the knowledge of Government officials, as happened in respect of the United Kingdom and the case of oil shipment to Rhodesia in violation of the United Nations action.[83] When challenged about this, Governments often sent a reply to the Committee denying any involvement by any of their officials. In some cases they denied involvement even of any of their nationals. Even if one were to give all such Governments the benefit of the doubt, what still remains in doubt is the depth to which their investigations went into the reported cases.

Another weakness of the system of enforcing the United Nations action was the slow pace at which investigation and reporting to the Committee were carried out. The Committee would receive a report on alleged breach and discuss it at a meeting in which it might decide to seek further clarification from the person or group of persons who made the report. Meantime it would send a request to the Government mentioned in the report to investigate the alleged breach and report to the Committee as soon as possible, preferably within a month. In many cases Governments would not reply until a number of reminders had been sent. When reports were received from Governments, they usually indicated that investigations were continuing. A case would thus take a very long time while the breach probably continued.

A classical case was that of the transfer of military aircraft manufactured in a number of western countries under licence

---

[81] 12th Report of the Security Council Committee Established in Pursuance of Resolution 253 (1968) Concerning the Question of Southern Rhodesia, Annex IV, 190.   [82] See e.g. ibid. 187.
[83] Ibid. 191.

given by the United States. This case was the main subject matter of Mr Gervasi's report, involving four types of aircraft, the Augusta-Bell 205, the Cessna-Reims FTB — 337, the Rockwell OV — IOF, and the Britten — Norman Islander.[84] The case dragged on from 30 December 1978, when Mr Gervasi wrote his letter to the Committee, until the Rhodesian independence crisis was finally solved nearly twelve months later. The case was not completed, but the Committee could go no further with it as the problem had been resolved. All they could do was to transmit the information obtained in respect of this case to 'the Security Council Committee on the arms embargo against South Africa for any action that Committee might wish to take on any relevant portions thereof'.[85] It is submitted on the strength of this brief examination that the Committee Established in Pursuance of Resolution 253 (1968) needed more teeth to make its bite effective.

C. *The Impact of this Action on Future Non-Military Enforcement Actions*

The United Nations non-military enforcement action against the Smith regime represents the second experience the world community has had of non-military action to maintain world peace. The first one was that carried out by the League of Nations against Italy to force that country to end its invasion of Ethiopia between 1935 and 1936.[86] That action ended in total failure; as soon as Italy completed its conquest of Ethiopia, there was a significant readiness on the part of the League of Nations to abandon the sanctions that had been imposed.[87] Thus when Italy announced its annexation of Ethiopia on 9 May 1936 the League Council quickly transferred the question to the Assembly to consider whether or not the sanctions should be continued.[88] In July 1936 the Sanctions Committee recommended the lifting of sanctions.

The whole action thus ended in a lamentable failure. Doxey suggests that the collapse of that action 'must be explained

---

[84] Ibid. 164.   [85] Ibid. 195.
[86] Walters, *History of the League of Nations* (1960).   [87] Ibid. 670.
[88] Doxey, *Economic Sanctions*, 52.

largely in terms of the indecisive action and ambivalent policies of the major League powers' and also in terms of the inconsistent goals and limited range of measures applied.[89] She adds that there was no consensus on the merits of non-military collective measures generally, and that furthermore goals were neither clearly stated nor pursued. Finally, she argues, the 'policy of graduated pressure . . . gave Mussolini the opportunity to declare that extention of sanctions would be regarded as hostile acts, while an imposition of an oil embargo would be treated as an act of war'.[90]

The United Nations enforcement action against the Smith regime suffered from most of the difficulties experienced by the League of Nations in the *Italo-Ethiopian* case. As Doxey points out:

. . . it seems that the Rhodesian case exhibits all the difficulties which international enforcement by economic measures may be expected to encounter. It gives little encouragement that conditions might ever be realised in which resort to collective economic coercion by an international body could be successful in achieving political ends.[91]

As regards the Rhodesian problem, fortunately, the enforcement action did not end in disarray. The unilateral termination of enforcement measures by some Western Governments, including the United Kingdom, would have undermined the authority of the United Nations had it been allowed to go by default. The Security Council must be congratulated therefore for bringing order in the termination of that enforcement action so as to end the United Nations involvement in the affairs of Rhodesia, which was soon to become the independent Republic of Zimbabwe. This enhanced the role played by the United Nations in bringing about a satisfactory conclusion of the Rhodesian independence crisis. Any other way of ending that enforcement action than by passing a resolution based on a sober assessment of what the action had achieved over the fourteen years of its existence would have distorted the emphasis of the roles played by various factors and reflect an over-inflated picture of the role played by British diplomacy in ending the Rhodesian independence crisis.

[89] Ibid. 47.　　　[90] Ibid. 58.　　　[91] Ibid. 88.

It is important, therefore, that the end of the enforcement action be pronounced by the United Nations which, it is submitted, was one of the twin causes, along with the guerrilla war, which brought about a successful conclusion of the Rhodesian independence crisis that had defied Britain for many years. This was so particularly because when a difficult problem has finally been resolved, nearly all the parties that had had anything to do with it will nearly always interpret their own role in the best light possible. As Adrian Guelke rightly points out, for instance, the grounds for celebrating Zimbabwean independence have been as varied as they have been numerous.

In Britain the emphasis has been on the success of British diplomacy, the resolution of the conflict thanks to a smooth transition, and the success of constitutionalism and of Western political forms over revolution.[92]

He adds:

In Africa the stress has fallen on the legitimization of armed struggle and on the forging of new frontiers of freedom through the victory of African nationalism. In the United States the outcome has been seen as a belated vindication of the African policy of the Carter administration and a setback for the Soviet Union.[93]

It is submitted that credit for the resolution of the Rhodesian independence crisis should go to the United Nations and the Rhodesian liberation forces specifically. The front-line states should also be singled out for the special role they played as members of the United Nations in that their economies were hardest hit because of their traditional links with the economies of South Africa and Rhodesia. Furthermore, they should be singled out also for the suffering of their peoples at the hands of the Smith regime's military forces. It is submitted therefore that the United Nations non-military enforcement system will play a significant role in future international enforcement action. After all, this seems to be the

---

[92] Guelke, 'Southern Africa and Super-Powers' (1980), *International Affairs*, 648. See e.g. R. Jackson, 'Zimbabwe: a Triumph and Opportunity', in the *Daily Telegraph*, 14 Mar. 1980.

[93] Ibid. See also weekly edition of the *Christian Science Monitor*, 28 Apr. 1980 for the American view.

only major weapon the international community has which can command the widest possible international consensus.

Having said that it should be emphasized that the United Nations action against the Smith regime never worked as well as it should have done. For instance it was widely violated by many states, especially by Rhodesia's traditional trading partners in the Western countries. Because of that, it took an unsatisfactorily long time to bring the Rhodesian problem to a satisfactory end. Without the supplementation of guerrilla war, it is doubtful whether the problem would have been solved by now, or that it would ever have been solved at all. This does not mean, however, that the United Nations system of non-military enforcement can never work without the inclusion of military measures from other quarters. What is suggested here is that the Rhodesian enforcement action suffered from certain peculiarities which are not likely to be present in every other problem, at least not to the same magnitude.

Firstly, Rhodesia's geographical position near a powerful neighbour, South Africa, which refused to participate in the United Nations enforcement action ensured the Smith regime's survival. South Africa had two main reasons for supporting the Smith regime: sympathy for a regime which was somewhat similar to its own, and the determination to ensure that United Nations economic measures should be seen not to work so that the international community would have no illusion about attempting such an action against South Africa itself. Consequently, South Africa was the pivot of virtually all the major activities designed to overcome United Nations measures.

Secondly, the real target of the enforcement action in Rhodesia was the white ruling minority in that country. The origins of those people were Western Europe, particularly Britain. Britain and other West European countries, and the United States were traditional trading partners of Rhodesia. The populations in Western Europe were generally sympathetic to the Smith regime. As Richard Cumming put it, it 'must also be recognized that there is emotional support for the Rhodesian whites though it be vigorously denied'.[94] In

---

[94] Cumming, 'Rhodesian Declaration of Independence' (1973), *New York University Journal of International Law and Politics*, 18.

some of these countries 'Friends of Rhodesia Associations' were formed to help the white Rhodesian cause in all sorts of ways, legal or illegal. For instance, Martin and Johnson indicate that during President Nixon's time 'the Rhodesian Information Office was allowed to remain open, disseminating information, lobbying on Capitol Hill, encouraging American tourism and recruiting Americans for the Rhodesian forces'.[95] They add that in New York the Air Rhodesia office worked closely with American airlines, travel agencies, and credit card companies, promoting tourism to Rhodesia. They indicate that:

The Nixon administration closed its eyes to all these violations which, together, gave the Smith régime a material and psychological lift at a time when the Rhodesian economy was weak and when domestic opposition had been mounting.[96]

Although immigration figures showed that there was a net loss of white people in Rhodesia, thousands were shown to have come to settle in Rhodesia when the country was experiencing many difficulties.

For those major reasons and the others already discussed in the present chapter (namely, the problems of identifying United Nations action in Rhodesia with British domestic policy, the graduated application of the enforcement measures, and the lack of an effective monitoring machinery to prevent or reduce appreciably violations of the measures imposed), the United Nations action in Rhodesia was less effective than it should have been. It does not follow from this that all future cases where the United Nations may contemplate applying enforcement action will also suffer from this combination of factors.

It is true, however, that the Rhodesian experience in this respect shows that there may be some states against which the United Nations cannot successfully impose an enforcement action. This is not surprising since the veto power itself has ensured that no enforcement action can ever be imposed by the United Nations against a permanent member of the Security Council. In the same way, it should be recognized

---

[95] Martin and Johnson, *The Struggle for Zimbabwe* (London and Boston 1981), 232.   [96] Ibid.

that there are certain situations where enforcement action may not work even if the subject of the action is not one of the permanent members, either because certain factors, as in the Rhodesian situation, operate in its favour, or because a permanent member of the Security Council had used its veto.[97]

The fact that the Rhodesian crisis defied the United Nations action for fourteen years and only ended as the result of the development of the guerrilla war should not detract from the usefulness of the United Nations enforcement action in other cases, given the peculiar nature of the Rhodesian situation. Besides, it is 'important to remember that the economic weapon is merely one of a range of measures' that may be used in different situations.[98] It is submitted that, with the Rhodesian experience behind it, the United Nations will now not hesitate to use this form of enforcement if the members can find a consensus.

[97] Doxey, *Economic Sanctions*, 88.

[98] MacDonald, 'Economic Sanctions in the International System', (1969), *Canadian Yearbook of International Law*, 88.

Appendix

The Security Council

Having examined the situation in Southern Rhodesia, Recalling
General Assembly resolutions 1514 (XV) of 14 December 1960, 1747
(XVI) of 28 June 1962, 1960 (XVII) of 31 October 1962, 1883 (XVIII)
of 14 October 1963 and 1889 (XVIII) of 6 November 1963 and the
resolutions of the Special Committee on the Situation with regard to
the Implementation of the Declaration on the Granting of Independence
to Colonial Countries and Peoples, especially its resolution of 22 April
1965,

Endorsing the requests which the General Assembly and the Special
Committee have many times addressed on the United Nations of Great
Britain and Northern Ireland to obtain:

(a) The release of all political prisoners, detainees and restrictees,

(b) The repeal of all repressive and discriminatory legislation, and in
particular the Law and Order (Maintenance) Act and the Land Apportionment Act,

(c) The removal of all restrictions on political activity and the
establishment of full democratic freedom and equality of political
rights,

Noting that the Special Committee has drawn the attention of the
Security Council to the grave situation prevailing in Southern Rhodesia
and, in particular, to the serious implications of the election announced
to take place on 7 May 1965 under a constitution which has been rejected by the majority of the people of Southern Rhodesia and the
abrogation of which has repeatedly been called to by the General
Assembly and the Special Committee since 1962.

Deeply disturbed at the further worsening of the situation in the
Territory due to the application of the aforementioned Constitution
of 1961 and to recent events, especially the minority Government's
threats of a unilateral declaration of independence,

1. *Notes* the United Kingdom Government's statement of 27 October
1964 specifying the conditions under which Southern Rhodesia might
attain independence;

2. *Notes* further and approves the opinion of the majority of the population of Southern Rhodesia that the United Kingdom should convene a
constitutional conference;

3. *Requests* the United Kingdom Government and all States Members

of the United Nations not to accept a unilateral declaration of independence for Southern Rhodesia by the minority Government.

4. *Requests* the United Kingdom to take all necessary action to prevent a unilateral declaration of independence;

5. *Requests* the United Kingdom Government not to transfer under any circumstances to its colony of Southern Rhodesia, as at present governed, any of the powers or attributes of sovereignty, but to promote the country's attainment of independence by a democratic system of government in accordance with the aspirations of the majority of the population;

6. *Further requests* the United Kingdom Government to enter into consultations with all concerned with a view to convening a conference of all political parties in order to adopt new constitutional provisions acceptable to the majority of the people of Southern Rhodesia, so that the earliest possible date may be set for independence;

7. *Decides* to keep the question of Southern Rhodesia on its agenda.

Adopted at the 1202nd meeting by 7 votes to none with 4 abstentions (France, Union of Soviet Socialist Republics, United Kingdom of Great Britain and Northern Ireland, United States of America).

RESOLUTION 216 (1965) OF
12 NOVEMBER 1965

The Security Council

1. *Decides* to condemn the unilateral declaration of independence made by a racist minority in Southern Rhodesia;

2. *Decides* to call upon all States not to recognize this illegal racist minority régime in Southern Rhodesia and to refrain from rendering any assistance to this illegal régime.

Adopted at the 1258th meeting by 10 votes to none, with one abstention (France).

RESOLUTION 217 (1965) OF
20 NOVEMBER 1965

The Security Council

Deeply concerned with the situation in Southern Rhodesia, considering that the illegal authorities in Southern Rhodesia have proclaimed independence and that the Government of the United Kingdom of Great Britain and Northern Ireland, as the administering Power, looks upon this as an act of rebellion,

Noting that the Government of the United Kingdom has taken certain measures to meet the situation and that to be effective these measures should correspond to the gravity of the situation,

1. *Determines* that the situation resulting from the proclamation of independence by the illegal authorities in Southern Rhodesia is extremely grave, that the Government of the United Kingdom of Great Britain and Northern Ireland should put an end to it and that its continuance in time constitutes a threat to international peace and security;

2. *Reaffirms* its resolution 216 (1965) of 12 November 1965 and General Assembly resolution 1514 (XV) of 14 December 1960;

3. *Condemns* the usurpation of power by a racist settler minority in Southern Rhodesia and regards the declaration of independence by it as having no legal validity;

4. *Calls upon* the Government of the United Kingdom to quell this rebellion of the racist minority;

5. *Further calls upon* the Government of the United Kingdom to take all other appropriate measures which would prove effective in eliminating the authority of the usurpers and in bringing the minority régime in Southern Rhodesia to an immediate end;

6. *Calls upon* all States not to recognize this illegal authority and not to entertain any diplomatic or other relations with it;

7. *Calls upon* the Government of the United Kingdom, as the working of the Constitution of 1961 has broken down, to take immediate measures in order to allow the people of Southern Rhodesia to determine their own future consistent with the objectives of General Assembly resolution 1514 (XV);

8. *Calls upon* all States to refrain from any action which would assist and encourage the illegal régime and, in particular, to desist from providing it with arms, equipment and military material, and to do their utmost in order to break all economic relations with Southern Rhodesia, including an embargo on oil and petroleum products;

9. *Calls upon* the Government of the United Kingdom to enforce urgently and with vigour all the measures it has announced, as well as those mentioned in paragraph 8 above;

10. *Calls upon* the Organization of African Unity to do all in its power to assist in the implementation of the present resolution, in conformity with Chapter VIII of the Charter of the United Nations;

11. *Decides* to keep the question under review in order to examine what other measures it may deem it necessary to take.

Adopted at the 1265th meeting by 10 votes to none, with 1 abstention (France).

RESOLUTION 221 (1966)
OF 9 APRIL 1966

The Security Council

Recalling its resolutions 216 (1965) of 12 November 1965 and 217 (1965) of 20 November 1965 and in particular its call to all States to do their utmost to break off economic relations with Southern Rhodesia, including an embargo on oil and petroleum products,

Gravely concerned at reports that substantial supplies of oil may reach Southern Rhodesia as the result of an oil tanker having arrived at Beira and the approach of a further tanker which may lead to the resumption of pumping through the Companhia do Pipeline Mocambique Rodesias pipeline with the acquiescence of the Portuguese authorities,

Considering that such supplies will afford great assistance and encouragement to the illegal regime in Southern Rhodesia, thereby enabling it to remain longer in being,

1. *Determines* that the resulting situation constitutes a threat to the peace;

2. *Calls upon* the Portuguese Government not to permit oil to be pumped through the pipeline from Beira to Southern Rhodesia;

3. *Calls upon* the Portuguese Government not to receive at Beira oil destined for Southern Rhodesia;

4. *Calls upon* all States to ensure the diversion of any of their vessels reasonably believed to be carrying oil destined for Southern Rhodesia which may be en route for Beira;

5. *Calls upon* the Government of the United Kingdom of Great Britain and Northern Ireland to prevent, by the use of force if necessary, the arrival at Beira of vessels reasonably believed to be carrying oil destined for Southern Rhodesia, and empowers the United Kingdom to arrest and detain the tanker known as the *Joanna V* upon her departure from Beira in the event her oil cargo is discharged there.

Adopted at the 1277th meeting by 10 votes to none with 5 abstentions (Bulgaria, France, Mali, Union of Soviet Socialist Republics, Uruguay).

RESOLUTION 232 (1966)
OF 16 DECEMBER 1966

The Security Council,

Reaffirming its resolutions 216 (1965) of 12 November 1965, 217 (1965) of 20 November 1965 and 221 (1966) of 9 April 1966, and in particular its appeal to all States to do their utmost to break off economic relations with Southern Rhodesia,

Deeply concerned that the Council's efforts so far and the measures taken by the administering Power have failed to bring the rebellion in Southern Rhodesia to an end,

Reaffirming that, to the extent not superseded in the present resolution, the measures provided for in resolution 217 (1965), as well as those initiated by Member States in implementation of that resolution, shall continue in effect,

Acting in accordance with Articles 39 and 41 of the United Nations Charter,

1. *Determines* that the present situation in Southern Rhodesia constitutes a threat to international peace and security;

2. *Decides* that all States Members of the United Nations shall prevent:

(a) The import into their territories of asbestos, iron ore, chrome, pig-iron, sugar, tobacco, copper, meat and meat products and hides, skins and leather originating in Southern Rhodesia and exported therefrom after the date of the present resolution;

(b) Any activities by their nationals or in their territories which promote or are calculated to promote the export of these commodities from Southern Rhodesia and any dealings by their nationals or in their territories in any of these commodities originating in Southern Rhodesia and exporting therefrom after the date of the present resolution, including in particular any transfer of funds to Southern Rhodesia for the purposes of such activities or dealings;

(c) Shipment in vessels or aircraft of their registration of any of these commodities originating in Southern Rhodesia and exported therefrom after the date of the present resolution;

(d) Any activities by their nationals or in their territories which promote or are calculated to promote the sale or shipment to Southern Rhodesia of arms, ammunition of all types, military aircraft, military vehicles, and equipment and materials for the manufacture and maintenance of arms and ammunition in Southern Rhodesia;

(e) Any activities by their nationals or in their territories which promote or are calculated to promote the supply to Southern Rhodesia of all other aircraft and motor vehicles and of equipment and materials for the manufacture, assembly, or maintenance of aircraft and motor vehicles in Southern Rhodesia; the shipment in vessels and aircraft of their registration of any such goods destined for Southern Rhodesia; and any activities by their nationals or in their territories which promote or are calculated to promote the manufacture or assembly of aircraft or motor vehicles in Southern Rhodesia;

(f) Participation in their territories or territories under their administration or in land or air transport facilities or by their nationals or vessels of their registration in the supply of oil or oil products to Southern Rhodesia;

notwithstanding any contracts entered into or licences granted before the date of the present resolution;

3. *Reminds* Member States that the failure or refusal by any of them to implement the present resolution shall constitute a violation of Article 25 of the United Nations Charter;

4. *Reaffirms* the inalienable rights of the people of Southern Rhodesia to freedom and independence in accordance with the Declaration on the Granting of Independence to Colonial Countries and Peoples contained in General Assembly resolution 1514 (XV) of 14 December 1960, and recognizes the legitimacy of their struggle to secure the enjoyment of their rights as set forth in the Charter of the United Nations;

5. *Calls upon* all States not to render financial or other economic aid to the illegal racist régime in Southern Rhodesia;

6. *Calls upon* all States Members of the United Nations to carry out this decision of the Security Council in accordance with Article 25 of the United Nations Charter;

7. *Urges*, having regard to the Principles stated in Article 2 of the United Nations Charter, States not Members of the United Nations to act in accordance with the provisions of paragraph 2 of the present resolution;

8. *Calls upon* States Members of the United Nations or members of the specialized agencies to report to the Secretary-General the measures which each has taken in accordance with the provisions of paragraph 2 of the present resolution;

9. *Requests* the Secretary-General to report to the Council on the progress of the implementation of the present resolution, the first report to be submitted not later than 1 March 1967;

10. *Decides* to keep this item on its agenda for further action as appropriate in the light of developments.

Adopted at the 1340th meeting by 11 votes to none, with 4 abstentions (Bulgaria, France, Mali, Union of Soviet Socialist Republics).

RESOLUTION 253 (1968)
OF 29 MAY 1968

The Security Council,

Recalling and reaffirming its resolutions 216 (1965) of 12 November 1965, 217 (1965) of 20 November 1965, 221 (1966) of 9 April 1966, and 232 (1966) of 16 December 1966,

Taking note of resolution 2261 (XXII) adopted by the General Assembly on 3 November 1967,

Noting with great concern that the measures taken so far have failed to bring the rebellion in Southern Rhodesia to an end,

Reaffirming that, to the extent not superseded in this resolution, the measures provided for in resolutions 217 (1965) of 20 November 1965 and 232 (1966) of 16 December 1966 as well as those initiated by Member States in implementation of those resolutions, shall continue in effect,

Gravely concerned that the measures taken by the Security Council have not been complied with by all States and that some States, contrary to resolution 232 (1966) of the Security Council and to their obligations under Article 25 of the Charter of the United Nations, have failed to prevent trade with the illegal régime in Southern Rhodesia,

Condemning the recent inhuman executions carried out by the illegal régime in Southern Rhodesia which have flagrantly affronted the conscience of mankind and have been universally condemned,

Affirming the primary responsibility of the Government of the United Kingdom to enable the people of Southern Rhodesia to achieve self-determination and independence, and in particular their responsibility for dealing with the prevailing situation,

Recognizing the legitimacy of the struggle of the people of Southern Rhodesia to secure the enjoyment of their rights as set forth in the Charter of the United Nations and in conformity with the objectives of General Assembly resolution 1514 (XV) of 14 December 1960,

Reaffirming its determination that the present situation in Southern Rhodesia constitutes a threat to international peace and security,

Acting under Charter VII of the Charter of the United Nations,

1. *Condemns* all measures of political repression, including arrest, detentions, trials and executions which violate fundamental freedoms and rights of the people of Southern Rhodesia, and calls upon the Government of the United Kingdom to take all possible measures to put an end to such actions.

2. *Calls upon* the United Kingdom as the administering Power in the discharge of its responsibility to take urgently all effective measures to bring to an end the rebellion in Southern Rhodesia, and enable the people to secure the enjoyment of their rights as set forth in the Charter of the United Nations and in conformity with the objectives of General Assembly resolution 1514 (XV);

3. *Decides* that, in furtherance of the objective of ending the rebellion, *all States Members* of the United Nations shall prevent:

(a) The import into their territories of all commodities and products originating in Southern Rhodesia and exported therefrom after the date of this resolution (whether or not the commodities or products are for consumption or processing in their territories, whether or not they are imported in bond and whether or not any special legal status with respect to the import of goods is enjoyed by the port or other place where they are imported or stored);

(b) Any activities by their nationals or in their territories which would promote or are calculated to promote the export of any commodities or products from Southern Rhodesia; and any dealings by their nationals or in their territories in any commodities or products originating in Southern Rhodesia and exported therefrom after the date of this resolution, including in particular any transfer of funds to Southern Rhodesia for the purposes of such activities or dealings;

(c) The shipment in vessels or aircraft of their registration or under charter to their nationals, or the carriage (whether or not in bond) by land transport facilities across their territories of any commodities or products originating in Southern Rhodesia and exported therefrom after the date of this resolution;

(d) The sale or supply by their nationals or from their territories of any commodities or products (whether or not originating in their territories, but not including supplies intended strictly for medical purposes, educational equipment and material for use in schools and other educational institutions, publication news material and, in special humanitarian circumstances, food-stuffs) to any person or body for the purposes of any business carried on in or operated from Southern Rhodesia, and any activities by their nationals or in their territories which promote or are calculated to promote such sale or supply;

(e) The shipment in vessels or aircraft of their registration, or under charter to their nationals, or the carriage (whether or not in bond) by hand transport facilities across their territories of any such commodities or products which are consigned to any person or body in Southern Rhodesia, or to any other person or body for the purposes of any business carried on in or operated from Southern Rhodesia;

4. *Decides* that all States Members of the United Nations shall not make available to the illegal régime in Southern Rhodesia or to any commercial, industrial or public utility undertaking, including tourist enterprises, in Southern Rhodesia any funds for investment or any other financial or economic resources and shall prevent their nationals and any persons within their territories from making available to the régime or to any such undertaking any such funds or resources and from remitting any other funds to persons or bodies within Southern Rhodesia, except payments exclusively for pensions or for strictly medical, humanitarian or educational purposes or for the provision of news material and in special humanitarian circumstances, food stuffs;

5. *Decides* that all States Members of the United Nations shall:

(a) Prevent the entry into their territories, save on exceptional humanitarian grounds, of any person travelling on a Southern Rhodesian passport, regardless of its date or issue, or on a purported passport issued by or on behalf of the illegal régime in Southern Rhodesia.

(b) Take all possible measures to prevent the entry into their territories of persons whom they have reason to believe to be ordinarily resident in Southern Rhodesia and whom they have reason to believe to have furthered or encouraged, or to be likely to further or encourage, the unlawful actions of the illegal régime in Southern Rhodesia or any activities which are calculated to evade any measure decided upon in this resolution or resolution 232 (1966) of 16 December 1966;

6. *Decides* that all States Members of the United Nations shall prevent airline companies constituted in their territories and aircraft of their registration or under charter to their nationals from operating to or from Southern Rhodesia and from linking up with any airline company constituted or aircraft registered in Southern Rhodesia;

7. *Decides* that all States Members of the United Nations shall give effect

to the decisions set out in operative paragraphs 3, 4 5 and 6 of this resolution notwithstanding any contract entered into or licence granted before the date of this resolution;

8. *Calls upon* all States Members of the United Nations or of the specialized agencies to take all possible measures to prevent activities by their nationals and persons in their territories promoting, assisting or encouraging emigration to Southern Rhodesia with a view of stopping such emigration;

9. *Requests* all States Members of the United Nations or of the specialized agencies to take all possible further action under Article 41 of the Charter to deal with the situation in Southern Rhodesia, not excluding any of the measures provided in that Article;

10. *Emphasizes* the need for the withdrawal of all consular and trade representation in Southern Rhodesia, in addition to the provisions of operative paragraph 6 of resolution 217 (1965);

11. *Calls upon* all States Members of the United Nations to carry out these decisions of the Security Council in accordance with Article 15 of the Charter of the United Nations and reminds them that failure or refusal by any one of them to do so would constitute a violation of that Article;

12. *Deplores* the attitude of States that have not complied with their obligations under Article 25 of the Charter, and censures in particular those States which have persisted in trading with the illegal regime in defiance of the resolutions of the Security Council, and which have given active assistance to the régime;

13. *Urges* all States Members of the United Nations to render moral and material assistance to the people of Southern Rhodesia in their struggle to achieve their freedom and independence;

14. *Urges*, having regard to the principles stated in Article 2 of the Charter of the United Nations, States not Members of the United Nations to act in accordance with the provisions of the present resolutions;

15. *Requests* States Members of the United Nations, the United Nations Organization, the specialized agencies, and other international organizations in the United Nations system to extend assistance to Zambia as a matter of priority with a view to helping it solve such special economic problems as it may be confronted with arising from the carrying out of these decisions of the Security Council;

16. *Calls upon* all States Members of the United Nations, and in particular those with primary responsibility under the Charter for the maintenance of international peace and security, to assist effectively in the implementation of the measures called for by the present resolution;

17. *Considers* that the United Kingdom as the administering Power should ensure that no settlement is reached without taking into account the views of the people of Southern Rhodesia, and in particular the

political parties favouring majority rule, and that it is acceptable to the people of Southern Rhodesia as a whole;

18. *Calls upon* all States Members of the United Nations or of the specialized agencies to report to the Secretary General by 1 August 1968 on measures taken to implement the present resolution;

19. *Requests* the Secretary-General to report to the Security Council on the progress of the implementation of this resolution, the first report to be made not later than 1 September 1968;

20. *Decides* to establish, in accordance with rule 28 of the provisional rules of procedure of the Security Council, a committee of the Security Council to undertake the following tasks and to report to it with its observations;

(a) To examine such reports on the implementation of the present resolution as are submitted by the Secretary-General;

(b) To seek from any States Members of the United Nations or of the specialized agencies such further information regarding the trade of that State (including information regarding the commodities and products exempted from the prohibition contained in operative paragraph 3 (d) above) or regarding any activities by any nationals of that State or in its territories that may constitute an evasion of the measures decided upon in this resolution as it may consider necessary for the proper discharge of its duty to report to the Security Council;

21. *Requests* the United Kingdom, as the administering Power, to give maximum assistance to the committee, and to provide the committee with any information which it may receive in order that the measures envisaged in this resolution and resolution 232 (1966) may be rendered fully effective;

22. *Calls upon* all States Members of the United Nations, or of the specialized agencies, as well as the specialized agencies themselves, to supply such further information as may be sought by the Committee in pursuance of this resolution;

23. *Decides* to maintain this item on its agenda for further action as appropriate in the light of developments.

Adopted unanimously at the 1428th meeting.

RESOLUTION 277 (1970)
OF 18 MARCH 1970

The Security Council,

Reaffirming its resolutions 216 (1965) of 12 November 1965, 217 (1965) of 20 November 1965, 221 (1966) of 9 April 1966, 232 (1966) of 16 December 1966 and 253 (1968) of 29 May 1968,

Reaffirming that, to the extent not superseded in the present resolution, the measures provided for in resolutions 217 (1965), 232 (1966)

and 253 (1968), as well as those initiated by Member States in implementation of those resolutions, shall continue in effect,

Taking into account the reports of the Committee established in pursuance of Security Council resolution 253 (1968),

Noting with grave concern that:

(a) The measures so far taken have failed to bring the rebellion in Southern Rhodesia to an end,

(b) Some States, contrary to resolutions 232 (1966) and 253 (1968) of the Security Council and to their obligations under Article 25 of the Charter of the United Nations, have failed to prevent trade with the illegal régime of Southern Rhodesia,

(c) The Governments of the Republic of South Africa and Portugal have continued to give assistance to the illegal régime of Southern Rhodesia, thus diminishing the effects of the measures decided upon by the Security Council,

(d) The situation in Southern Rhodesia continues to deteriorate as a result of the introduction by the illegal régime of new measures, including the purported assumption of republican status, aimed at repressing the African people in violation of General Assembly resolution 1514 (XV) of 14 December 1960,

Recognizing the legitimacy of the struggle of the people of Southern Rhodesia to secure the enjoyment of their rights as set forth in the Charter and in conformity with the objectives of General Assembly resolution 1514 (XV),

Reaffirming that the present situation in Southern Rhodesia constitutes a threat to international peace and security,

Acting under Chapter VII of the Charter,

1. *Condemns* the illegal proclamation of republican status of the Territory by the illegal régime in Southern Rhodesia;

2. *Decides* that Member States shall refrain from recognizing this illegal régime or from rendering any assistance to it;

3. *Calls upon* Member States to take appropriate measures, at the national level, to ensure that any act performed by officials and institutions of the illegal régime in Southern Rhodesia shall not be accorded any recognition, official or otherwise, including judicial notice, by the competent organs of their State;

4. *Reaffirms* the primary responsibility of the Government of the United Kingdom of Great Britain and Northern Ireland to enable the people of Zimbabwe to exercise their right to self-determination and independence, in accordance with the Charter of United Nations and in conformity with General Assembly resolution 1514 (XV), and urges that Government to discharge fully its responsibility;

5. *Condemns* all measures of political repression, including arrests, detentions, trials and executions, which violate fundamental freedoms and rights of the people of Southern Rhodesia;

6. *Condemns* the policies of the Governments of South Africa and

Portugal, which continue to maintain political economic, military, and other relations with the illegal régime in Southern Rhodesia in violation of the relevant resolutions of the United Nations;

7. *Demands* the immediate withdrawal of South African Police and armed personnel from the Territory of Southern Rhodesia;

8. *Calls upon* Member States to take more stringent measures in order to prevent any circumvention by their nationals, organizations, companies and other institutions of their nationality, of the decisions taken by the Security Council in resolutions 232 (1966) and (1968), all provisions of which shall fully remain in force;

9. *Decides*, in accordance with Article 41 of the Charter and in furthering the objective of ending the rebellion, that Member States shall:

(a) Immediately sever all diplomatic, consular, trade, military and other relations that they may have with the illegal régime in Southern Rhodesia, and terminate any representation that they may maintain in the Territory;

(b) Immediately interrupt any existing means of transportation to and from Southern Rhodesia;

10. *Requests* the Government of the United Kingdom, as the administering Power, to rescind or withdraw any existing agreements on the basis of which foreign consular, trade and other representation may at present be maintained in or with Southern Rhodesia;

11. *Requests* Member States to take all possible further action under Article 41 of the Charter to deal with the situation in Southern Rhodesia, not excluding any of the measures provided in that Article;

12. *Calls upon* Member States to take appropriate action to suspend any membership or associate membership that the illegal régime of Southern Rhodesia has in the specialized agencies of the United Nations;

13. *Urges* member States of any international or regional organizations to suspend the membership of the illegal régime of Southern Rhodesia from their respective organizations and to refuse any request for membership from that régime.

14. *Urges* Member States to increase moral and material assistance to the people of Southern Rhodesia in their legitimate struggle to achieve freedom and independence;

15. *Requests* the specialized agencies and other international organizations concerned, in consultation with the Organization of African Unity, to give aid and assistance to refugees from Southern Rhodesia and those who are suffering from oppression by the illegal régime of Southern Rhodesia;

16. *Requests* Member States, the United Nations, the specialized agencies and other international organizations in the United Nations system to make an urgent effort to increase their assistance to Zambia as a matter of priority with a view to helping it solve such special economic

problems as it may be confronted with arising from the carrying out of the decisions of the Security Council on this question;

17. *Calls upon* Member States, in particular those with primary responsibility under the Charter for the maintenance of international peace and security, to assist effectively in the implementation of the measures called for by the present resolution;

18. *Urges*, having regard to the principle stated in Article 2 of the Charter, States not Members of the United Nations to act in accordance with the provisions of the present resolution;

19. *Calls upon* Member States to report to the Secretary-General by 1 June 1970 on the measures taken to implement the present resolution;

20. *Requests* the Secretary-General to report to the Security Council on the progress of the implementation of the present resolution, the first report to be submitted no later than 1 July 1970;

21. *Decides* that the Committee of the Security Council established in pursuance of resolution 253 (1968), in accordance with rule 28 of the provisional rules of procedure of the Council, shall be entrusted with the responsibility of:

(a) Examining such reports on the implementation of the present resolution as will be submitted by the Secretary-General;

(b) Seeking from Member States such further information regarding the effective implementation of the provisions laid down in the present resolution as it may consider necessary for the proper discharge of its duty to report to the Security Council;

(c) Studying ways and means by which Member States could carry out more effectively the decisions of the Security Council regarding sanctions against the illegal régime of Southern Rhodesia and making recommendations to the Council;

22. *Requests* the United Kingdom, as the administering Power, to continue to give maximum assistance to the Committee and to provide the Committee with any information it may receive in order that the measures envisaged in the present resolution as well as resolutions 232 (1966) and 253 (1968) may be rendered fully effective;

23. *Calls upon* Member States, as well as the specialized agencies, to supply such information as may be sought by the Committee in pursuance of the present resolution;

24. *Decides* to maintain this item on its agenda for further action as appropriate in the light of developments.

Adopted at the 1535th meeting by 14 votes to none, with one abstention (Spain).

RESOLUTION 288 (1970) OF
17 NOVEMBER 1970

The Security Council,

Having considered the question of Southern Rhodesia,

Reaffirming its resolutions 216 (1965) of 12 November 1965, 217 (1965) of November 1965, 221 (1966) of 9 April 1966, 232 (1966) of 16 December 1966, 253 (1968) of 29th May 1968 and 277 (1970), of 18 March, 1970.

Gravely concerned that certain States have not complied with the provisions of resolutions 232 (1966), 253 (1968) and 277 (1970), contrary to their obligations under Article 25 of the Charter of the United Nations,

Reaffirming the primary responsibility of the Government of the United Kingdom of Great Britain and Northern Ireland to enable the people of Southern Rhodesia to achieve self-determination and independence, and in particular their responsibility of bringing the illegal declaration of independence to an end, taking into account the third report of the Committee established in pursuance of Security Council resolution 243 (1968),

Acting in accordance with previous decisions of the Security Council on Southern Rhodesia, taken under Chapter VII of the Charter.

1. *Reaffirms* its condemnation of the illegal declaration of independence in Southern Rhodesia;

2. *Calls upon* the United Kingdom of Great Britain and Northern Ireland, as the administering Power in the discharge of its responsibility, to take urgent effective measures to bring to an end illegal rebellion in Southern Rhodesia and enable the people to exercise their right to self-determination, in accordance with the Charter of the United Nations and in conformity with the objectives of General Assembly resolution 1514 (XV) of 14 December 1960;

3. *Decides* that the present sanctions against Southern Rhodesia shall remain in force;

4. *Urges* all States to fully implement all Security Council resolutions pertaining to Southern Rhodesia, in accordance with their obligations under Article 25 of the Charter, and deplores the attitude of those States which have persisted in giving moral, political and economic assistance to the illegal régime;

5. *Further urges* all States, in furtherance of the objectives of the Security Council, not to grant any form of recognition to the illegal régime in Southern Rhodesia;

6. *Decides* to remain actively seized of the matter.

Adopted unanimously at the 1557th meeting.

RESOLUTION 314 (1972)
OF 28 FEBRUARY 1972

The Security Council

Having considered the recent developments concerning the question of Southern Rhodesia,

Recalling its resolutions 216 (1965) of 12 November 1965, 217 (1965), of 20 November 1965, 221 (1966) of 9 April 1966, 232 (1966) of 16 December 1966, 253 (1968) of 29 May 1968, 277 (1970) of 18 March 1970 and 288 (1970) of 17 November 1970,

Gravely concerned that certain States have not complied with the provisions of the resolution 253 (1968), contrary to their obligations under Article 25 of the Charter of the United Nations.

Taking into account the fourth report[31] of the Committee established in pursuance of Security Council resolution 253 (1968) and its interim report of 3 December 1971,

Acting in accordance with previous decisions of the Security Council on Southern Rhodesia, taken under Chapter VII of the Charter,

1. *Reaffirms* its decision that the present sanctions against Southern Rhodesia shall remain fully in force until the aims and objectives set out in resolution 253 (1968) are completely achieved;

2. *Urges* all States to implement fully all Security Council resolutions establishing sanctions against Southern Rhodesia, in accordance with their obligations under Article 2, paragraph 6, of the Charter of the United Nations and deplores the attitude of those States which have persisted in giving moral, political, and economic assistance to the illegal régime;

3. *Declares* that any legislation passed, or act taken by any State with a view to permitting, directly or indirectly, the importation from Southern Rhodesia of any commodity falling within the scope of the obligations imposed by resolution 253 (1968), including chrome ore, would undermine sanctions and would be contrary to the obligations of States;

4. *Calls upon* all States to refrain from taking any measures that would in any way permit or facilitate the importation from Southern Rhodesia of commodities falling within the scope of the obligations imposed by resolution 253 (1968), including chrome ore;

5. *Draws the attention* of all States to the need for increasing vigilance in implementing the provisions of resolution 253 (1968) and, accordingly, calls upon them to take more effective measures to ensure full implementation of the sanctions;

6. *Requests* the Committee established in pursuance of Security Council resolution 253 (1968) to meet, as a matter of urgency, to consider ways and means by which the implementation of sanctions may be ensured and to submit to the Council, not later than 15 April 1972, a report containing recommendations in this respect, including any suggestions that the Committee might wish to make concerning its terms of

reference and any other measures designed to ensure the effectiveness of its work;

7. *Requests* the Secretary-General to provide all appropriate assistance to the Committee in the discharge of its task.

Adopted at the 1645th meeting by 13 votes to none, with 2 abstentions (United Kingdom of Great Britain and Northern Ireland, United States of America).

RESOLUTION 318 (1972)
OF 28 JULY 1972

The Security Council,

Recalling its resolution 314 (1972) of 28 February 1972, in which it requested the Committee established in pursuance of Security Council resolution 253 (1968) of 29 May 1968 to consider ways and means by which the implementation of sanctions might be ensured and to submit a report containing recommendations in this respect, including any suggestions that the Committee might wish to make concerning its terms of reference and any other measures designed to ensure the effectiveness of its work,

Having considered the special report of the Committee established in pursuance of Security Council resolution 253 (1968),

Mindful of the need to strengthen the machinery established by the Security Council in order to ensure proper implementation of the relevant resolutions of the Council,

Recalling further that, as stated in previous resolutions of the Security Council the present sanctions against Southern Rhodesia shall remain fully in force until the aims and objectives set out in resolution 253 (1968) are completely achieved,

Gravely concerned that certain States have not complied with the provisions of resolution 253 (1968), contrary to their obligations under Article 25 of the Charter of the United Nations,

1. *Reaffirms* the inalienable right of the people of Southern Rhodesia to self-determination and independence;

2. *Recognizes* the legitimacy of the struggle of the people of Southern Rhodesia to secure the enjoyment of their rights, as set forth in the Charter of the United Nations and in conformity with the objectives of General Assembly resolution 1514 (XV) of 14 December 1960;

3. *Takes note* with appreciation of the special report of the Committee established in pursuance of Security Council resolution 253 (1968);

4. *Approves* the recommendations and suggestions contained in section III of the special report;

5. *Calls upon* all States continuing to have economic and other relations with Southern Rhodesia to end such relations immediately;

6. *Demands* that all Member States scrupulously carry out their obligations to implement fully Security Council resolutions 253 (1968), 277 (1970) of 18 March 1970 and 314 (1972);

7. *Condemns* all acts violating the provisions of Security Council resolutions 253 (1968), 277 (1970) and 314 (1972);

8. *Calls upon* all States to co-operate fully with the Security Council in the effective implementation of sanctions and to give the Council all the necessary assistance that may be required of them towards the fulfilment of this task;

9. *Again draws the attention* of all States to the need for increasing vigilance in all matters relating to sanctions and, accordingly, urges them to review the adequacy of the legislation and the practices followed so far and, if necessary to take more effective measures to ensure full implementation of all provisions of Security Council resolutions 253 (1968), 277 (1970) and 314 (1972);

10. *Requests* the Secretary-General to provide all appropriate assistance to the Security Council Committee established in pursuance of resolution 253 (1968) concerning the question of Southern Rhodesia in the discharge of its responsibilities.

Adopted at the 1655th meeting by 14 votes to none with 1 abstention (United States of America).

RESOLUTION 326 (1973)
OF 2 FEBRUARY 1973

The Security Council,

Taking note of the letter dated 24 January 1973 from the Permanent Representative of Zambia to the United Nations (S/10865), and having heard the statement made by the Permanent Representative of Zambia concerning recent acts of provocation against Zambia by the illegal régime in Salisbury,[12]

Gravely concerned at the situation created by the provocative and aggressive acts committed by the illegal régime in Southern Rhodesia against the security and economy of Zambia,

Reaffirming the inalienable right of the people of Southern Rhodesia (Zimbabwe) to self-determination and independence in accordance with General Assembly resolution 1514 (XV) of 14 December 1960, and the legitimacy of their struggle to secure the enjoyment of such rights, as set forth in the Charter of the United Nations,

Recalling its resolution 232 (1966) of 16 December 1966 in which it determined that the situation in Southern Rhodesia constituted a threat to international peace and security,

Convinced that the recent provocative and aggressive acts perpetrated by the illegal régime against Zambia aggravate the situation,

Deeply concerned that measures approved by the Council have failed to terminate the illegal régime and convinced that sanctions cannot put an end to the illegal régime unless they are comprehensive, mandatory and effectively supervised and unless measures are taken against States which violate them,

Deeply disturbed by the continued illegal presence and by the intensified military intervention of South Africa in Southern Rhodesia, contrary to Security Council resolution 277 (1970) of 18 March 1970, and also by the deployment of South African armed forces on the border with Zambia, which seriously threatens the sovereignty and territorial integrity of Zambia and other neighbouring African States,

Deeply shocked and grieved at the loss of human life and damage to property caused by the aggressive acts of the illegal régime in Southern Rhodesia and its collaborators against Zambia,

Reaffirming the primary responsibility of the Government of the United Kingdom of Great Britain and Northern Ireland over its colony of Southern Rhodesia, in accordance with the relevant United Nations resolutions,

1. *Condemns* all the acts of provocation and harassment, including economic blockade, blackmail and military threats, against Zambia by the illegal régime in collusion with the racist régime of South Africa;

2. *Condemns* all measures of political repression that violate fundamental freedoms and rights of the people of Southern Rhodesia (Zimbabwe), in particular, the recent measures of collective punishment.

4. *Regrets* that measures so far taken have failed to bring the rebellion in Southern Rhodesia (Zimbabwe) to an end;

5. *Condemns* the continued presence of South African military and armed forces in Southern Rhodesia, contrary to Security Council resolution 277 (1970);

6. *Demands* the immediate and total withdrawal of South African military and armed forces from Southern Rhodesia and from the border of that Territory with Zambia;

7. *Calls upon* the Government of the United Kingdom, as the administering Power, to ensure the effective implementation of paragraph 6 of the present resolution;

8. *Requests* the Security Council Committee established in pursuance of resolution 253 (1968) concerning the question of Southern Rhodesia to expedite the preparation of its report undertaken under Security Council resolution 320 (1972) of 29 September 1972, taking into account the recent developments in Southern Rhodesia;

9. *Decides* to dispatch immediately a special mission, consisting of four members of the Security Council, to be appointed by the President of Security Council after consultations with the members, to assess the situation in the area, and requests the mission so constituted to report to the Council not later than 1 March 1973;

10. *Calls upon* the Government of Zambia, the Government of the United Kingdom and the Government of South Africa to provide the special mission with the necessary co-operation and assistance in the discharge of its task;

11. *Decides* to remain actively seized of the matter.

Adopted at the 1691st meeting by 13 votes to none with 2 abstentions (United Kingdom of Great Britain and Northern Ireland, United States of America)

RESOLUTION 327 (1973)
OF 2 FEBRUARY 1973

The Security Council,

Having heard the statement of the Permanent Representative of Zambia to the United Nations,

Recalling its resolutions on the question of Southern Rhodesia, in particular resolution 232 (1966) of 16 December 1966, in which it determined that the situation in Southern Rhodesia constituted a threat to international peace and security.

Recalling further resolutions 253 (1968) of 29 May 1968 and 277 (1970) of 18 March 1970 imposing mandatory sanctions against Southern Rhodesia, particularly the respective provisions therein requesting the international community to extend assistance to Zambia in view of such special economic problems as it may be confronted with arising from the carrying out of the decisions of the Security Council.

Taking into account the decision of the Government of Zambia to sever immediately all remaining trade and communication links with Southern Rhodesia in compliance with the decisions of the Security Council and in strict observance of economic sanctions,

Recognizing that such a decision by the Government of Zambia will entail considerable special economic hardships,

1. *Commends* the Government of Zambia for its decision to sever all remaining economic and trade relations with Southern Rhodesia in compliance with the decisions of the Security Council;

2. *Takes cognizance* of the special economic hardships confronting Zambia as a result of its decision to carry out the decisions of the Security Council;

3. *Decides* to entrust the Special Mission, consisting of four members of the Security Council, referred to in paragraph 9 of resolution 326 (1973), assisted by a team of six United Nation experts, to assess the needs of Zambia, in maintaining alternative systems of road, rail, air and sea communications for the normal flow of traffic;

4. *Further requests* the neighbouring States to accord the Special Mission every co-operation in the discharge of its task;

5. *Requests* the Special Mission to report to the Security Council not later than 1 March 1973.

Adopted at the 1691st meeting by 14 votes to none with 1 abstention (Union of Soviet Socialist Republics)

RESOLUTION 328 (1973) OF
MARCH 1973

The Security Council,

Having considered with appreciation the report of the Security Council Special Mission established under resolution 326 (1973) of 2 February 1973 (S/10896 and Corr. 1 and Add. 1).

Having heard further the statement of the Permanent Representative of Zambia to the United Nations,

Recalling its resolutions 277 (1970) of 18 March 1970 and 326 (1973),

Reaffirming that the situation in Southern Rhodesia constitutes a threat to international peace and security,

Gravely concerned at the persistent refusal of the régime of South Africa to respond to the demands contained in resolutions 277 (1970) and 326 (1973) for the immediate withdrawal of its military and armed forces from Southern Rhodesia and convinced that this constitutes a serious challenge to the authority of the Security Council,

Bearing in mind that the Government of the United Kingdom of Great Britain and Northern Ireland, as the administering Power, has the primary responsibility for putting an end to the illegal racist minority régime and for transferring effective power to the people of Zimbabwe on the basis of the principle of majority rule,

Reaffirming the inalienable right of the people of Zimbabwe to self-determination and independence in accordance with General Assembly resolution 1514 (XV) of 14 December 1960 and the legitimacy of their struggle to secure the enjoyment of their rights as set forth in the Charter of the United Nations.

1. *Endorses* the assessment and conclusions of the Special Mission established under resolution 326 (1973);

2. *Affirms* that the state of tension has been heightened following the recent provocative and aggressive acts committed by the illegal régime in Southern Rhodesia against Zambia;

3. *Declares* that the only effective solution to this grave situation lies in the exercise by the people of Zimbabwe of their right to self-determination and independence in accordance with General Assembly resolution 1514 (XV);

4. *Strongly condemns* the racist régime of South Africa for its persistent refusal to withdraw its military and armed forces from Southern Rhodesia;

5. *Reiterates* its demand for the immediate withdrawal of South African military and armed forces from Southern Rhodesia and from the border of that Territory with Zambia;

6. *Urges* the Security Council Committee established in pursuance of resolution 253 (1968) concerning the question of Southern Rhodesia to expedite the preparation of its report undertaken under Security Council resolution 320 (1972) of 29 September 1972, taking into account all proposals and suggestions for extending the scope and improving the effectiveness of sanctions against Southern Rhodesia (Zimbabwe);

7. *Requests* all Governments to take stringent measures to enforce and ensure full compliance by all individuals and organizations under their jurisdiction with the sanctions policy against Southern Rhodesia and calls upon all Governments to continue to treat the racist minority régime in Southern Rhodesia as wholly illegal;

8. *Urges* the United Kingdom of Great Britain and Northern Ireland, as the administering Power to convene as soon as possible a national constitutional conference where genuine representatives of the people of Zimbabwe would be able to work out a settlement relating to the future of the Territory;

9. *Calls upon* the Government of the United Kingdom to take all effective measures to bring about the conditions necessary to enable the people of Zimbabwe to exercise freely and fully their right to self-determination and independence including:

(a) The unconditional release of all political prisoners, detainees and restrictees;

(b) The repeal of all repressive and discriminatory legislation;

(c) The removal of all restrictions on political activity and the establishment of full democratic freedom and equality of political rights;

10. *Decides* to meet again and consider further actions in the light of future developments.

Adopted at the 1694th meeting by 13 votes to none with 2 abstentions (United Kingdom of Great Britain and Northern Ireland, United States of America)

RESOLUTION 329 (1973) OF
10 MARCH 1973

The Security Council,

Recalling its resolution 253 (1968) of 29 May 1968 requesting assistance to Zambia as a matter of priority,

Recalling further its resolution 277 (1970) of 18 March 1970, as well as resolutions 326 (1973) and 327 (1973) of 2 February 1973 by which it decided to dispatch a special mission to assess the situation in the area and the needs of Zambia,

Having considered the report of the Special Mission (S/10896 and Corr. 1 and Add. 1),

Having heard the statement of the Permanent Representative of Zambia,

Affirming that Zambia's action to divert its trade from the southern route reinforces Security Council decisions on sanctions against the illegal régime in Southern Rhodesia,

1. *Commends* the Government of Zambia for deciding to abandon the use of the southern route for its trade until the rebellion is quelled and majority rule is established in Southern Rhodesia.

2. *Takes note* of the urgent economic needs of Zambia as indicated in the report of the Special Mission and the annexes thereto;

3. *Appeals* to all States for immediate technical, financial and material assistance to Zambia in accordance with resolution 253 (1968) and 277 (1970) and the recommendations of the Special Mission, so that Zambia can maintain its normal flow of traffic and enhance its capacity to implement fully the mandatory sanctions policy;

4. *Requests* the United Nations and the organizations and programmes concerned, in particular the United Nations Conference on Trade and Development, the United Nations Industrial Development Organization and the United Nations Development Programme, as well as the specialized agencies, in particular the International Labour Organisation, the Food and Agriculture Organization of the United Nations, the United Nations Educational, Scientific and Cultural Organization, the World Health Organization, the International Civil Aviation Organization, the Universal Postal Union, the International Telecommunication Union, the World Meteorological Organization and the Inter-Governmental Maritime Consultative Organisation, to assist Zambia in the fields identified in the report of the Special Mission and the annexes thereto;

5. *Requests* the Secretary-General in collaboration with the appropriate organizations of the United Nations system, to organize with immediate effect all forms of financial, technical and material assistance to Zambia to enable it to carry out its policy of economic independence from the racist régime of Southern Rhodesia.

6. *Requests* the Economic and Social Council to consider periodically the question of economic assistance to Zambia as envisaged in the present resolution.

Adopted unanimously at the 1694th meeting

RESOLUTION 388 (1976)
OF 6 APRIL 1976

The Security Council,

Reaffirming its resolutions 216 (1965) of 12 November and 217 (1965) of 20 November 1965, 221 (1966) of 9 April and 232 (1966) of 16 December 1966, 253 (1968) of 29 May 1968 and 277 (1970) of 18 March 1970.

Reaffirming that the measures provided for in those resolutions, as well as the measures initiated by Member States in pursuance thereof, shall continue in effect,

Taking into account the recommendations made by the Security Council Committee established in pursuance of resolution 253 (1968) concerning the question of Southern Rhodesia in its special report of 15 December 1975.

Reaffirming that the present situation in Southern Rhodesia constitutes a threat to international peace and security.

Acting under Chapter VII of the Charter of the United Nations.

1. *Decides* that all Member States shall take appropriate measures to ensure that their nationals and persons in their territories do not insure:

(a) Any commodities or products exported from Southern Rhodesia after the date of the present resolution in contravention of Security Council resolution 253 (1968) which they know or have reasonable cause to believe to have been so exported:

(b) Any commodities or products which they know or have reasonable cause to believe to be destined or intended for importation into Southern Rhodesia after the date of the present resolution in contravention of resolution 253 (1968);

(c) Commodities, products or other property in Southern Rhodesia of any commercial, industrial or public utility undertaking in Southern Rhodesia, in contravention of resolution 253 (1968);

2. *Decides* that all Member States shall take appropriate measures to prevent their nationals and persons in their Territories from granting to any commercial, industrial or public utility undertaking in Southern Rhodesia the right to use any trade name or from entering into any franchising agreement involving the use of any trade name, trade mark or registered design in connexion with the sale or distribution of any products, commodities or services of such an undertaking;

3. *Urges* States not Members of the United Nations, having regard to the principle stated in Article 2 of the Charter of the United Nations, to act in accordance with the provisions of the present resolution.

Adopted unanimously at the 1907th meeting.

RESOLUTION 409 (1977)
OF 27 MAY 1977

The Security Council,

Reaffirming its resolutions 216 (1965) of November and 217 (1965) of 20 November 1965 221 (1966) of 9 April and 232 (1966) of 16 December 1966, 253 (1968) of 29 May 1968, 277 (1970) of 18 March 1970 and 388 (1976) of 6 April 1976,

Reaffirming that the measures provided for in those resolutions, as well as the measures initiated by Member States in pursuance thereof, shall continue in effect,

Taking into account the recommendations made by the Security Council Committee established in pursuance of resolution 253 (1968) concerning the question of Southern Rhodesia in its second special report of 31 December 1976 on the expansion of sanctions against Southern Rhodesia,

Reaffirming that the present situation in Southern Rhodesia constitutes a threat to international peace and security.

Acting under Chapter VII of the Charter of the United Nations,

1. *Decides* that all Members States shall prohibit the use or transfer of any funds in their territories by the illegal régime in Southern Rhodesia, including any office or agent thereof, or by other persons or bodies within Southern Rhodesia, for the purposes of any office or agency of the illegal régime that is established within their territories other than an office or agency so established exclusively for pensions purposes;

2. *Urges,* having regard to the principle stated in Article 2, paragraph 6 of the Charter of the United Nations, States not Members of the United Nations to act in accordance with the provisions of the present resolution;

3. *Decides* to meet not later than 11 November 1977 to consider the application of further measures under Article 41 of the Charter, and meanwhile requests the Security Council Committee established in pursuance of resolution 253 (1968) concerning the question of Southern Rhodesia to examine, in addition to its other functions, the application of further measures under Article 41 and to report to the Council thereon as soon as possible.

Adopted unanimously, without a vote, at the 2011th meeting.

RESOLUTION 415 (1977)
OF 29 SEPTEMBER 1977

The Security Council,

Taking note of the letters dated 1 September and 8 September 1977 from the Permanent Representative of the United Kingdom of Great Britain and Northern Ireland to the President of the Security Council,

Having heard the statement of Mr. Joshua Nkomo, Co-leader of the Patriotic Front of Zimbabwe,

1. *Requests* the Secretary-General to appoint, in consultation with the members of the Security Council, a representative to enter into discussions with the British Resident Commissioner designated and with all the parties concerning the military and associated arrangements that are considered necessary to effect the transition to majority rule in Southern Rhodesia;

2. *Further requests* the Secretary-General to transmit a report on the results of these discussions to the Security-Council as soon as possible;

3. *Calls upon* all parties to co-operate with the representative of the Secretary-General in the conduct of the discussions referred to in paragraph 1 of the present resolution.

Adopted at the 2034th meeting by 13 votes to none, with 1 abstention (Union of Soviet Socialist Republics).

RESOLUTION 411 (1977) OF
30 JUNE 1977

The Security Council,

Taking note of the telegram dated 18 June 1977 from the President of the People's Republic of Mozambique, Mr. Samora Moises Machel, to the Secretary-General, contained in document S/12350 and Add. 1.

Having heard the statement of Mr. Marcelino dos Santos, member of the Permanent Political Committee of FRELIMO and Minister for Development and Economic Planning of Mozambique, concerning the recent acts of aggression against Mozambique committed by the illegal racist minority régime in Southern Rhodesia,

Taking note of the resolution adopted by the Council of Ministers of the Organization of African Unity at its twenty-ninth ordinary session at Libreville, Gabon,

Indignant at the systematic acts of aggression committed by the illegal régime in Southern Rhodesia against the People's Republic of Mozambique and the resulting loss of life and destruction of property,

Gravely concerned at the rapidly deteriorating situation in Southern Rhodesia as a result of the continued existence of the illegal régime,

Reaffirming the inalienable rights of the people of Zimbabwe to self-determination and independence, in accordance with General Assembly resolution 1514 (XV) of 14 December 1960, and the legitimacy of their struggle to secure the enjoyment of such rights as set forth in the Charter of the United Nations,

Recalling its resolution 232 (1966) of 16 December 1966, in which it determined that the situation in Southern Rhodesia constituted a threat to international peace and security,

Cognizant of the fact that the recent acts of aggression perpetrated by the illegal régime against the People's Republic of Mozambique together with that régime's constant acts of aggression and threats against the sovereignty and territorial integrity of the Republic of Botswana and the Republic of Zambia aggravate the existing serious threat of the security and stability of the region,

Recalling its resolutions on sanctions against the illegal régime in Southern Rhodesia in particular resolution 253 (1968) of 29 May 1968,

Conscious of the important contribution made by the Government of the People's Republic of Mozambique through its decision of 3 March 1976 to close its borders with Southern Rhodesia and to apply strictly sanctions against the illegal régime in conformity with United Nations resolutions,

Deeply concerned that the measures approved by the Security Council have so far failed to bring to an end the illegal régime and convinced that sanctions cannot put an end to that régime unless they are comprehensive, mandatory and strictly supervised and unless measures are taken against States which violate them,

Recalling its resolution 386 (1976) of 17 March 1976,

Expressing its particular concern at the continued violation of sanctions by South Africa and its support of the illegal régime in Southern Rhodesia,

Reaffirming the primary responsibility of the United Kingdom of Great Britain and Northern Ireland, as the administering Power, to take all effective measures to bring to an end the illegal régime in Southern Rhodesia, in accordance with the relevant United Nations resolutions,

Reaffirming the relevant provisions of the Maputo Declaration in Support of the Peoples of Zimbabwe and Namibia and in particular those provisions which call for assistance to those front-line States victims of acts of aggression by the racist minority régimes.

Affirming the right of the People's Republic of Mozambique to take all necessary measures, in accordance with the Charter, to safeguard its sovereignty and territorial integrity,

1. *Strongly condemns* the illegal racist minority régime in Southern Rhodesia for its recent acts of aggression against the People's Republic of Mozambique;

2. *Solemnly declares* that these acts of aggression as well as the repeated attacks and threats against the Republic of Zambia and the Republic of Botswana by the illegal régime in Southern Rhodesia constitute a serious aggravation of the situation in the area;

3. *Condemns* South Africa for its continued support of the illegal régime in Southern Rhodesia in contravention of Security Council resolutions on sanctions against the régime at Salisbury;

4. *Reaffirms* that the continued existence of the illegal régime in Southern Rhodesia is a source of insecurity and instability in the region and constitutes a serious threat to international peace and security;

5. *Reaffirms* the right of the people of Zimbabwe to self-determination and independence, in accordance with General Assembly resolution

1514 (XV), and urges all States to intensify assistance to the people of Zimbabwe and their national liberation movement in their struggle to achieve that objective;

6. *Commends* the Government of the People's Republic of Mozambique for its scrupulous observance of sanctions against the illegal régime in Southern Rhodesia and its steadfast support to the people of Zimbabwe in their legitimate struggle, in accordance with the relevant General Assembly and Security Council resolutions;

7. *Demands* that the national sovereignty and territorial integrity of Mozambique be scrupulously respected;

8. *Demands* that all States refrain from providing any support — overt or covert — to the illegal régime in Southern Rhodesia and, in particular, demands that South Africa adhere fully to Security Council resolutions and thus cease from any co-operation or collaboration with the illegal régime at Salisbury in violation of the Council's decisions;

9. *Requests* all States to give immediate and substantial material assistance to enable the Government of the People's Republic of Mozambique to strengthen its defence capability in order to safe-guard effectively its sovereignty and territorial integrity;

10. *Requests* all States, regional organizations and other appropriate intergovernmental organizations to provide financial, technical and material assistance to Mozambique in order to enable it to overcome the severe economic loss and destruction of property brought about by the acts of aggression committed by the illegal régime in Southern Rhodesia and to reinforce Mozambique's capacity to implement United Nations decisions in support of measures against the illegal régime;

11. *Requests* the United Nations and the organizations and programmes concerned, including the Economic and Social Council, the Food and Agriculture Organization of the United Nations, the World Food Programme, the United Nations Children's Fund, the International Fund for Agricultural Development, the United Nations High Commissioner for Refugees, the United Nations Educational, Scientific and Cultural Organization, the United Nations Conference on Trade and Development, the United Nations Development Programme and the World Health Organization, to provide assistance to Mozambique on a priority basis in implementation of the request contained in paragraph 10 of the present resolution;

12. *Calls upon* all States to implement strictly Security Council resolutions on sanctions and requests the Security Council Committee established in pursuance of resolution 253 (1968) concerning the question of Southern Rhodesia to examine as a matter of priority further effective measures to tighten the scope of sanctions in accordance with Article 41 of the Charter of the United Nations and urgently to submit its appropriate recommendations to the Council;

13. *Requests* the Secretary-General to co-ordinate the efforts of the

United Nations system and to organize immediately an effective programme of international assistance to Mozambique in accordance with the provisions of paragraphs 10 and 11 of the present resolution;

14. *Decides* to remain actively seized of the matter.

Adopted unanimously at the 2019th meeting.

RESOLUTION 423 (1978)
OF 14 MARCH 1978

The Security Council,

Recalling its resolutions on the question of Southern Rhodesia and in particular resolution 415 (1977) of 29 September 1977,

Reaffirming that the continued existence of the illegal régime in Southern Rhodesia is a source of insecurity and instability in the region and constitutes a serious threat to international peace and security,

Gravely concerned over the continued military operations by the illegal régime, including its acts of aggression against neighbouring independent States,

Indignant at the continued executions of freedom fighters by the illegal régime,

Considering the need for urgent measures to terminate the illegal régime and establish a government based on majority rule.

1. *Condemns* all attempts and manoeuvres by the illegal régime in Southern Rhodesia aimed at the retention of power by a racist minority and at preventing the achievement of independence by Zimbabwe;

2. *Declares* illegal and unacceptable any internal settlement concluded under the auspices of the illegal régime and calls upon all States not to accord any recognition to such a settlement;

3. *Further declares* that the speedy termination of the illegal régime and the replacement of its military and police forces constitute the first pre-requisite for the restoration of legality in Southern Rhodesia so that arrangements may be made for a peaceful and democratic transition to genuine majority rule and independence in 1978;

4. *Declares* also that such arrangements as envisaged in paragraph 3 of the present resolution include the holding of free and fair elections on the basis of universal adult suffrage under United Nations supervision;

5. *Calls upon* the United Kingdom of Great Britain and Northern Ireland to take all measures necessary to bring to an end the illegal racist minority régime in Southern Rhodesia and to effect the genuine decolonization of the Territory in accordance with General Assembly resolution 1514 (XV) of 14 December 1960 and other United Nations resolutions;

6. *Considers* that, with the assistance of the Secretary-General, the United Kingdom, as the administering Power, should enter into immediate consultations with the parties concerned in order to attain

the objectives of genuine decolonization of the Territory through the implementation of paragraphs 3, 4 and 5 of the present resolution;

7. *Requests* the Secretary-General to report, not later than 15 April 1978, on the results of the implementation of the present resolution.

Adopted at the 2067th meeting by 10 votes to none with 5 abstentions (Canada, France, Germany, Federal Republic of, United Kingdom of Great Britain and Northern Ireland, United States of America).

RESOLUTION 437 (1978)
OF 10 OCTOBER 1978

The Security Council,

Having considered the letter dated 6 October 1978 from the Chairman of the Security Council Committee established in pursuance of resolution 253 (1968) concerning the question of Southern Rhodesia.

Recalling its resolution 253 (1968) of 29 May 1968, by which it made it mandatory for Member States to prevent the entry into their territories of persons ordinarily resident in Southern Rhodesia and connected with the illegal régime there,

Taking note of the statement of the African Group,

Taking note also of the statement of the Government of the United States of America,

1. *Notes* with regret and concern the decision of the Government of the United States of America to allow the entry into the United States of Ian Smith and some members of the illegal régime in Southern Rhodesia.

2. *Considers* that the above-mentioned decision is in contravention of Security Council resolution 253 (1968) and of the obligations under Article 25 of the Charter of the United Nations;

3. *Calls upon* the United States of America to observe scrupulously the provisions of Security Council resolutions concerning sanctions;

4. *Expresses* the hope that the United States of America will continue to exert its influence in order that genuine majority rule may be achieved without further delay in Southern Rhodesia.

Adopted at the 2090th meeting by 11 votes to none with 4 abstentions (Canada, Germany, Federal Republic of, United Kingdom of Great Britain and Northern Ireland, United States of America).

RESOLUTION 424 (1978)
OF 17 MARCH 1978

The Security Council,

Taking note of the letter from the representative of the Republic of Zambia contained in document S/12589,

Having considered the statement of the Minister for Foreign Affairs of the Republic of Zambia.

Gravely concerned at the numerous hostile and unprovoked acts of aggression by the illegal minority régime in Southern Rhodesia violating the sovereignty, air space and territorial integrity of the Republic of Zambia, resulting in the death and injury of innocent people, as well as the destruction of property, and culminating on 6 March 1978 in the armed invasion of Zambia,

Reaffirming the inalienable right of the people of Southern Rhodesia (Zimbabwe) to self-determination and independence in accordance with General Assembly resolution 1514 (XV) of 14 December 1960, and the legitimacy of their struggle to secure the enjoyment of such rights as set forth in the Charter of the United Nations,

Recalling its resolution 423 (1978) of 14 March 1978, in which, inter alia, it declared as illegal and unacceptable any internal settlement concluded under the auspices of the illegal régime and called upon all States not to accord any recognition to such a settlement,

Further recalling its resolutions 326 (1973) of 2 February 1973, 403 (1977) of 14 January, 406 (1977) of 25 May and 411 (1977) of 30 June 1977, in which it condemned the illegal régime in Southern Rhodesia for its acts of aggression against Zambia, Botswana and Mozambique,

Conscious that the liberation of Zimbabwe and Namibia and the elimination of apartheid in South Africa˙are necessary for the attainment of justice and lasting peace in the region and in the furtherance of international peace and security,

Reaffirming that the existence of the minority racist régime in Southern Rhodesia and the continuance of its acts of aggression against Zambia and other neighbouring States constitute a threat to international peace and security.

Conscious of the need to take effective steps for the prevention and removal of threats to international peace and security.

1. *Strongly condemns* the recent armed invasion perpetrated by the illegal racist minority régime in the British colony of Southern Rhodesia against the Republic of Zambia, which constitutes a flagrant violation of the sovereignty and territorial integrity of Zambia;

2. *Commends* the Republic of Zambia and other front-line States for their continued support of the people of Zimbabwe in their just and legitimate struggle for the attainment of freedom and independence and for their scrupulous restraint in the face of provocations by the Rhodesian rebels;

3. *Reaffirms* that the liberation of Namibia and Zimbabwe and the elimination of apartheid in South Africa are necessary for the attainment of justice and lasting peace in the region;

4. *Calls upon* the Government of the United Kingdom of Great Britain and Northern Ireland, as the administering Power, to take prompt effective measures to bring to a speedy end the existence of the illegal

racist minority régime in the rebel colony of Southern Rhodesia, thereby ensuring the speedy attainment of independence under genuine majority rule and thus contributing to the promotion of durable peace and security in the region.

5. *Decides* that, in the event of further acts of violation of the sovereignty and territorial integrity of Zambia by the illegal racist minority régime in Southern Rhodesia, the Security Council will meet again to consider the adoption of more effective measures, in accordance with the appropriate provisions of the Charter of the United Nations, including Chapter VII thereof.

Adopted unanimously at the 2070th meeting.

RESOLUTION 445 (1979)
OF 8 MARCH 1979

The Security Council,

Recalling its resolutions on the question of Southern Rhodesia, and in particular resolutions 253 (1968) of 29 May 1968, 403 (1977) of 14 January and 411 (1977) of 30 June 1977, 423 (1978) of 14 March, 424 (1978) of 17 March and 437 (1978) of 10 October 1978,

Taking note of the statement of the Africa Group contained in document S/13084,

Having heard the statements of the representatives of Angola and Zambia.

Having also heard the statement of the representative of the Patriotic Front of Zimbabwe.

Gravely concerned about the indiscriminate military operations undertaken by the illegal régime and the extension of its premeditated and provocative acts of aggression not only against neighbouring independent countries but also against non-contiguous States, resulting in wanton killings of refugees and civilian populultions,

Indignant at the continued executions by the illegal régime in Southern Rhodesia of persons sentenced under repressive laws.

Reaffirming that the existence of the illegal racist minority régime in Southern Rhodesia and the continuance of its acts of aggression against neighbouring independent States constitute a threat to international peace and security.

Reaffirming the inalienable right of the people of Southern Rhodesia (Zimbabwe) to self-determination and independence in accordance with General Assembly resolution 1514 (XV) of 14 December 1960 and the legitimacy of their struggle to secure the enjoyment of such rights as set forth in the Charter of the United Nations.

Gravely concerned by the moves within certain States to send missions to observe the so-called elections in April 1979 organized by the illegal racist minority régime in Southern Rhodesia, for the purpose of according it some legitimacy and thereby eventually lifting sanctions.

Reaffirming Security Council resolution 423 (1978) particularly its provisions declaring illegal and unacceptable any internal settlement concluded under the auspices of the illegal régime and calling upon all States not to accord any recognition to such a settlement.

Bearing in mind the responsibility of every Member State to adhere scrupulously to Security Council resolutions and decisions, and their responsibility to ensure that institutions and citizens under their jurisdiction will observe the same.

1. *Strongly condemns* the recent armed invasions perpetrated by the illegal racist minority régime in the British colony of Southern Rhodesia against the People's Republic of Angola, the People's Republic of Zambia, which constitute a flagrant violation of the sovereignty and territorial integrity of these countries;

2. *Commends* the People's Republic of Angola, the People's Republic of Mozambique and the Republic of Zambia and other front-line States for their support of the people of Zimbabwe in their just and legitimate struggle for the attainment of freedom and independence and for their scrupulous restraint in the face of serious provocations by the Southern Rhodesian rebels;

3. *Requests* all States to give immediate and substantial material assistance to enable the Governments of the front-line States to strengthen their defence capability in order to safeguard effectively their sovereignty and territorial integrity;

4. *Requests* the administering Power to take all necessary measures to prevent further illegal executions in Southern Rhodesia;

5. *Condemns* all attempts and manoeuvres by the illegal régime, including its so-called elections of April 1979, aimed at retaining and extending a racist minority rule and at preventing the accession of Zimbabwe to independnce and genuine majority rule;

6. *Declares* that any elections held under the auspices of the illegal racist régime and the results thereof will be null and void and that no recognition will be accorded either by the United Nations or any Member State to any representatives or organ established by that process;

7. *Urges* all States to refrain from sending observers to these elections and to take appropriate action to discourage organizations and institutions within their respective areas of jurisdiction from doing so;

8. *Requests* the Security Council Committee established in pursuance of resolution 253 (1968) concerning the question of Southern Rhodesia to meet immediately to consider measures for strengthening and widening the sanctions against Southern Rhodesia and to submit its proposals not later than 23 March 1979;

9. *Decides* to meet, not later than 27 March 1979, to consider the report envisaged in paragraph 8 of the present resolution.

Adopted at the 2122nd meeting by 12 votes to none, with 3 abstentions

(France, United Kingdom of Great Britain and Northern Ireland, United States of America)

RESOLUTION 448 (1979)
OF 30 APRIL 1979

The Security Council,

Recalling its resolutions on the question of Southern Rhodesia, and in particular resolutions 253 (1968), 403 (1977), 411 (1977), 423 (1978), 437 (1978) and 445 (1979) reaffirming the illegality of the Smith régime,

Having heard the statement of the Chairman of the African Group,

Having also heard the statement of the representative of the Patriotic Front of Zimbabwe,

Reaffirming Security Council resolution 445 (1979), particularly its provision declaring any elections held under the auspices of the illegal racist régime and the results thereof null and void and that no recognition will be accorded either by the United Nations or any Member State to any representative or organ established by that process,

Gravely concerned that the illegal racist minority régime in Southern Rhodesia proceeded with the holding of sham elections in the territory in utter defiance of the United Nations,

Convinced that these so-called elections did not constitute a genuine exercise of the right of the people of Zimbabwe to self-determination and national independence and were designed to perpetuate white racist minority rule,

Reaffirming the inalienable right of the people of Southern Rhodesia (Zimbabwe) to self-determination and independence in accordance with General Assembly resolution 1514 (XV) of 14 December 1960 and the legitimacy of their struggle to secure the enjoyment of such rights as set forth in the Charter of the United Nations,

Bearing in mind the responsibility of every Member State to adhere scrupulously to Security Council resolutions and decisions, and their responsibility to ensure that institutions and citizens under their jurisdiction observe the same,

1. *Strongly condemns* all attempts and manoeuvres by the illegal régime including the so-called elections of April 1979 aimed at retaining and extending a racist minority rule and at preventing the accession of Zimbabwe to independence and genuine majority rule;

2. *Reaffirms* the so-called elections, held under the auspices of the illegal racist régime, and the results thereof, as null and void;

3. *Reiterates* its call to all States not to accord recognition to any representative of or organ established by that process and to observe strictly the mandatory sanctions against Southern Rhodesia.

Adopted at the 2143rd meeting by 12 votes to none, with 3 abstentions

(France, United Kingdom of Great Britain and Northern Ireland, United States of America).

RESOLUTION 460 (1979)
OF 21 DECEMBER 1979

The Security Council,

Recalling Security Council resolutions 232 (1966), 253 (1968) and subsequent related resolutions on the situation in Southern Rhodesia,

Reaffirming General Assembly resolution 1514 (XV) of 14 December 1960,

Noting with satisfaction that the Lancaster House Conference in London has produced agreement on the Constitution for a free and independent Zimbabwe providing for genuine majority rule, on arrangements for bringing that Constitution into effect, and on a cease-fire,

Noting also that the Government of the United Kingdom of Great Britain and Northern Ireland, having resumed its responsibility as the administering Power, is committed to decolonize Southern Rhodesia on the basis of free and democratic elections, which will lead Southern Rhodesia to genuine independence acceptable to the international community in accordance with the objectives of General Assembly resolution 1514 (XV),

Deploring the loss of life, the waste and the suffering caused by the 14 years of rebellion in Southern Rhodesia,

Conscious to the need to take effective measures for the prevention and removal of all threats to international peace and security in the region,

1. *Reaffirms* the inalienable right of the people of Zimbabwe to self-determination, freedom and independence, as enshrined in the Charter of the United Nations, and in conformity with the objectives of General Assembly resolution 1514 (XV);

2. *Decides*, having regard to the agreement reached at the Lancaster House Conference, to call upon States Members of the United Nations to terminate the measures taken against Southern Rhodesia under Chapter VII of the Charter pursuant to resolutions 232 (1966), 253 (1968) and subsequent related resolutions on the situation in Southern Rhodesia;

3. *Further decides* to dissolve its Committee established under resolution 253 (1968) in accordance with rule 28 of the provisional rules of procedure of the Security Council;

4. *Commends* States Members of the United Nations, particularly the Front-Line States, for their implementation of the Security Council resolutions on sanctions against Southern Rhodesia in accordance with their obligation under Article 25 of the Charter;

5. *Calls* upon all States Members of the United Nations and the specialized

agencies to provide urgent assistance to Southern Rhodesia and the Front-Line States for reconstruction purposes and to facilitate the repatriation of all refugees or displaced persons to Southern Rhodesia;

6. *Calls* for strict adherence to the agreements reached, and for their full and faithful implementation by the administering Power and all the parties concerned;

7. *Calls* upon the administering Power to ensure that no South African or other external forces, regular or mercenary, will remain in or enter Southern Rhodesia, except those forces provided for under the Lancaster House Agreement;

8. *Requests* the Secretary-General to assist in the implementation of paragraph 5 above, particularly in organizing with immediate effect all forms of financial, technical and material assistance to the States concerned in order to enable them to overcome the economic and social difficulties facing them;

9. *Decides* to keep the situation in Southern Rhodesia under review until the Territory attains full independence.

Adopted at the 2181st meeting by 13 votes to none, with 2 abstentions (Czechoslovakia, Union of Soviet Socialist Republics).

Bibliography

A. BOOKS

Akehurst, M.B., *A Modern Introduction to International Law* (George Allen and Unwin, 2nd, 3rd and 4th edns., 1971 and 1977).

Anzillotti, D., *Cours de Droit International*, vol. i (Paris, 1929).

Bailey, S.D., *The Procedure of the United Nations Security Council* (Oxford, 1975).

Barber, J. *Rhodesia: The Road to Rebellion* (Oxford, 1967).

Barrow, J. (editor), *The United Nations, Past, Present and Future* (Free Press, 1972).

Bentwich, N., and Martin, A., *Commentary on the Charter of the United Nations* (London, 1950).

Bot, B.R. *Non-recognition and Treaty Relations* (Leiden, 1968).

Bowett, D.W., *United Nations Forces* (Stevens, 1964).

—— *The Law of International Institutions* (Stevens, 3rd edn., 1975).

Bowman, L. *Politics in Rhodesia: White Power in an African State* (Harvard, U.P., 1973).

Brierly, J.L., *The Law of Nations* (Oxford, 6th edn., 1963).

Briggs, H.W., *The Law of Nations* (New York, 2nd edn., 1952).

Brownlie, I., *Principles of International Law* (Oxford, 2nd edn., 1973).

—— *International Law and the Use of Force by States* (Oxford, 1963).

—— *Basic Documents in International Law* (Oxford, 2nd edn., 1972).

Castañeda, J., *Legal Effects of United Nations Resolutions* (New York, 1969).

Clark, G., and Sohn, L.B., *World Peace Through Law* (New York, 1960).

Coetzee, J., *The Sovereignty of Rhodesia and the Law of Nations* (Pretoria, 1970).

Cohen, B.V., *The United Nations, Constitutional Development, Growth and Possibilities* (Harvard University Press, 1961).

Colombos, C.J., *The International Law of the Sea* (Longmans, 6th edn., 1967).

Crawford, J. *The Creation of States in International Law* (Oxford, 1979).

Dam, K.W., *The G.A.T.T.: Law and International Economic Organization* (Chicago University Press, 1970).

Doxey, M., *Economic Sanctions and International Enforcement* (Oxford, 1971).

Falk, R.A., *The International Law of Civil War* (Hopkins, 1971).

Fawcett, J.E.S., *The British Commonwealth in International Law* (Stevens, 1963).

—— *The Law of Nations* (Penguin, 2nd edn., 1971).

Foot, P., *Politics of Harold Wilson* (Penguin, 1968).

Friedmann, W.G., *The Changing Structure of International Law* (Stevens, 1964).

Frydenberg, P. (ed.), *Peace-Keeping* (Oslo, 1964).

Good, R.C., *UDI: The International Politics of the Rhodesian Rebellion* (Faber, 1973).

Goodrich, L.M., and Hambro, E., *The Charter of the United Nations: Commentary and Documents* (Stevens, 1949).

Goodrich, L.M., and Simon, A.P., *The United Nations and the Maintenance of International Peace and Security* (Brookings, 1955).

Gray, R.B. (ed.), *International Security Systems* (Peacock, 1969).

Greig, D.W., *International Law* (Butterworth, 1976).

Hackworth, G.H., *Digest of International Law*, vol. iv (1940).

Hall, W.E. *International Law* (8th edn., 1924).

Harris, D.J., *Cases and Materials on International Law* (Sweet and Maxwell, 1973).

Henig, R.B. (ed.), *The League of Nations* (Oliver and Boyd, 1973).

Higgins, R., *The Development of International Law Through the Political Organs of the United Nations* (Oxford, 1963).

— *United Nations Peace-Keeping, 1946–1967* (Oxford, 1970).

James, A., *The Politics of Peace-Keeping* (Chatto and Windus, 1969).

Kapungu, L., *The United Nations and Economic Sanctions in Rhodesia* (Lexington, 1973).

Kelsen, H., *The Law of the United Nations* (Stevens, 1950).

— *Principles of International Law* (Helt; Rinehart and Winston Inc., 1966).

Laqueur, W., *A Dictionary of Politics* (Pan, 1973).

Latham-Brown, D.J., *Public International Law* (Sweet and Maxwell, 1970).

Lauterpacht, H., *Recognition in International Law* (Cambridge, 1947).

Legum, C., *African Handbook*, (Penguin, 1969).

Leiss, A.C. (ed.), *Apartheid and United Nations Collective Measures: An Analysis* (New York, Carnegie Endowment for International Peace, 1965).

Lillich, R.B., *Humanitarian Intervention* (Virginia, 1973).

Lord Lloyd, *Introduction to Jurisprudence* (Stevens, 1972).

Mahmoud, M.A., *The Juridical Manifesto* (The Hague, 1969).

Malone, D., *The Story of the Declaration of Independence* (Oxford, 1975).

Margueritte, W., *The League Fiasco* (Hodge, 1936).

Martin D. and Johnson P., *The Struggle for Zimbabwe* (London and Boston, 1981).

Moore, J.B., *A Digest of International Law* (Washington, 1906).

O'Connell, D., *International Law* (Stevens, 2nd edn., 1970).

Oppenheim, L.F.L., *International Law* (Longmans, 8th edn., 1955).

Palley, C., *The Constitutional History and the Law of Southern Rhodesia* (Oxford, 1966).

Rajan, M.S., *The United Nations and Domestic Jurisdiction* (London, 1958).

Rozakis, C.L., *The Concept of Jus Cogens in the Law of Treaties* (North Halland Publications, 1976).

Russell, R.B., and Muther, J.E., *A History of the United Nations Charter* (Brookings, 1958).

Salmond, J., *Jurisprudence* (London, 11th edn., 1957).

Schwarzenberger, G. *International Law*, vol. 1 (Stevens, 1957).

Schwarzenberger, G., and Brown, E.D., *A Manual of International Law* (Stevens, 6th edn., 1976).

Schwebel, S.M. (ed.), *The Effectiveness of International Decisions* (Oceana, 1971).

Sithole, N. *African Nationalism* (Oxford, 1959).

Sorensen, M. (ed.), *Manual of Public International Law* (MacMillan, 1969).

Starke, J.G., *An Introduction to International Law* (London, 7th edn., 1972).

Stewart, R.B., *Treaty Relations of the British Commonwealth of Nations* (New York, 1939).

Strack, H. *Sanctions: The Case of Rhodesia* (Syracuse U.P., 1978).

Tunkin, G.I., *The Theory of International Law* (Allen and Unwin, 1974).

Wade, E.C.S. and Phillips, G.G., *Constitutional and Administrative Law* (9th edn., 1977).

Walters, F.P., *History of the League of Nations* (Oxford, 1960).

Whiteman, M.M., *Digest of International Law* (Washington, 1968).

Wilcox, F.O., and Marcy, C.M., *Proposals for Changes in the United Nations* (Brookings, 1955).

Wilson, H., *The Labour Government, 1964-1970* (Michael Joseph, 1971).

Windrich, E., *The Rhodesian Problem: A Documentary Record, 1923-1973* (World Studies Series, London, 1975).

Zacklin, R., *United Nations and Rhodesia: a Study in International Law* (Praeger, 1974).

B. PERIODICALS

Akehurst, M.B., 'Enforcement Action by Regional Agencies, With Special Reference to the Organization of American States', (1967) XLII, *British Year Book of International Law*, 175.

—— 'State Responsibility for the Wrongful Acts of Rebels — An Aspect of the Southern Rhodesian Problem', (1968-9) XLIII, *British Year Book of International Law*, 49.

—— 'Custom As a Source of International Law', (1974-5) XLVII, *British Year Book of International Law*, 1.

—— 'The Hierarchy of the Sources of International Law', (1974-5) XLVII, *British Year Book of International Law*, 273.

Alexandrowicz, C.H., 'The Secretary-General of the United Nations' (1962) 11 *International and Comparative Law Quarterly*, 1109.

Andrassy, J., 'Uniting for Peace', (1956) 50, *American Journal of International Law*, 563.

Austin, D., 'Sanctions and Rhodesia', (1966) 22, *World Today*, 106.

Bailey, K., 'Making International Law in the United Nations', (1967), *Proceedings: American Society of International Law*, 233.

Bleicher, S.A., 'The Legal Significance of Re-Citation of General Assembly Resolutions', (1969) 63, *American Journal of International Law*, 444.

Blum, Y.L., 'Sauter pour mieux reculer: The Security Council New Look', (1966) 15, *International and Comparative Law Quarterly*, 863.

Brierly, J.L., 'Matters of Domestic Jurisdiction', (1925) VI, *British Year Book of International Law*, 8.

—— 'The General Act of Geneva, 1928', (1930) XI, *British Year Book of International Law*, 119.

Briggs, H.W., 'Recognition of States: Some Reflections on Doctrine and Practice', (1949) 43, *American Journal of International Law*, 113.

Broderick, M., 'Associated Statehood — A New Form of Decolonization', (1968) 17, *International and Comparative Law Quarterly*, 368.

Brownlie, I., 'Use of Force in Self-Defence', (1961) XXXVII, *British Year Book of International Law*, 183.

Burgenthal, T., 'The United Nations and the Development of Rules Relating to Human Rights', (1965), *Proceedings: American Society of International Law*, 132.

Corbett, P.E., 'Consent of States and the Sources of the Law of Nations', (1925) VI, *British Year Book of International Law*, 20.

Cryer, H.L., 'Legal Aspects of the *Joanna V* and *Manuela* Incidents, April 1966', (1966), *Australian Year Book of International Law*, 85.

Cumming, R.M., 'The Rhodesian Declaration of Independence and the Position of the International Community', (1973), *New York University Journal of International Law and Politics*, 57.

Devine, D.J., 'Status of Rhodesia in International Law', (1967), *Acta Juridica*, 39.

—— 'Status of Rhodesia in International Law', (1973), *Acta Juridica*, 3.

—— 'Status of Rhodesia in International Law', (1974), *Acta Juridica*, 109.

—— 'Requirement of Statehood Re-Examined', (1971) 34, *Modern Law Review*, 410.

Dias, R.W.M., 'International Law — Southern Rhodesia — U.N. — Security Council', (1967), *Cambridge Law Journal*, 1.

Doxey, M., 'The Rhodesian Sanctions Experiment', (1971), *Year Book of World Affairs*, 142.

Dugard, C.J., 'The O.A.U. and Colonialism: An Inquiry Into the Plea of Self-Defence As a Justification for the Use of Force in the Eradication of Colonialism', (1967) 16, *International and Comparative Law Quarterly*, 157.

Einstein, C., 'An Exercise in Shadow Boxing: Madzimbamuto v. Lardner-Burke', (1971), *Sydney Law Review*, 398.

Ekelaar, J.N., 'Rhodesia: Abdication of Constitutionalism', (1969) 32, *Modern Law Review*, 19.

Emerson, R., 'Self-Determination', (1971) 65, *American Journal of International Law*, 459.

Falk, R., 'New Approaches to the Study of International Law', (1967) 61, *American Journal of International Law*, 477.

—— 'On the Quasi-Legislative Competence of the General Assembly', (1966) 60, *American Journal of International Law*, 782.

Fawcett, J.E.S., 'Security Council Resolutions on Rhodesia', (1965–6) XLI, *British Year Book of International Law*, 103.

—— 'Judicial Committee of the Privy Council and International Law', (1967) XLII, *British Year Book of International Law*, 229.

Fenwick, C.G., 'The Scope of Domestic Jurisdiction Questions in International Law', (1925) 19, *American Journal of International Law*, 143.

—— 'The Recognition of New Governments Instituted by Force', (1944) 38, *American Journal of International Law*, 448.

—— 'Intervention: Individual and Collective', (1945) 39, *American Journal of International Law*, 645.

—— 'When Is there a threat to the Peace? – Rhodesia', (1967) 61, *American Journal of International Law*, 753.

Fitzmaurice, G.G., 'The Foundations of Authority of International Law and Problems of Enforcement', (1956) 9, *Modern Law Review*, 1.

—— 'The Law and Procedure of the International Court of Justice, 1951–54: General Principles and Sources of Law', (1953) XXX, *British Year Book of International Law*, 1.

Franck, J.M., and Rodley, N.S., 'After Bangladesh: The Law of Humanitarian Intervention by Military Force', (1973) 67, *American Journal of International Law*, 275.

Galtung, J., 'Effects of Economic Sanctions: Reference to Rhodesia', (1967), 19, *World Politics*, 378.

—— 'On the future of the International System', (1967) *Journal of Peace Research* (Oslo), 305.

Gilmour, D.R., 'The Meaning of Intervene Within Article 2 (7) of the Charter', (1967) 16, *International and Comparative Law Quarterly*, 370.

Goldberg, A.J., 'Law and the United Nations', (1966) 52, *American Bar Association Journal* 813.

Green, L.C., 'Rhodesian Independence – Legal or Illegal?', (1968), *Alberta Law Review*, 37.

Greig, D.W., 'The Advisory Jurisdiction of the I.C.J. and the Settlement of Disputes between States', (1966) 15, *International and Comparative Law Quarterly*, 325.

Gross, L., 'Voting in the Security Council: Abstention From Voting and Absence from Meetings', (1951) 60, *Yale Law Journal*, 209.

—— 'Problems of International Adjudication and Compliance with International Law', (1965) 59, *American Journal of International Law*, 48.

—— 'The United Nations and the Rule of Law', (1965) 19, *International Organizations*, 537.

Gross, L., 'Voting in the Security Council', (1968) 62, *American Journal of International Law*, 315.

Guelke, 'Southern Africa and Super Powers', (1980), *International Affairs*, 648.

Halderman, J.W., 'Legal Basis of United Nations Armed Forces', (1962) 56, *American Journal of International Law*, 971.

—— 'Some Legal Aspects of Sanctions in the Rhodesian Case', (1968) 17, *International and Comparative Law Quarterly*, 672.

Hambro, E., 'International Court of Justice', (1954), *International Affairs*, 31.

Hepple, B.A., O'Higgins, P., and Turpin, C.C., 'Rhodesian Crisis — Criminal Liabilities', (1966) 5, *Criminal Law Review*, 66.

Higgins, R., 'International Law, Rhodesia and the United Nations', (1967) 23, *World Today*, 94.

—— 'The Place of International Law in the Settlement of Disputes by the Security Council', (1970) 64, *American Journal of International Law*, 1.

—— 'The U.N. and Lawmaking: The Political Organs', (1970) 64, *American Journal of International Law, Supplement*, 37.

—— 'The Advisory Opinion on Namibia: Which U.N. Resolutions are Binding Under Article 25 of the Charter?', (1972) 21, *International and Comparative Law Quarterly*, 270.

Hopkins, J., 'International Law — Southern Rhodesia — the Security Council', (1967), *Cambridge Law Journal*, 1.

Hopper, D., 'Lessons of United Nations Peace-Keeping in Cyprus', (1970), *Proceedings: American Society of International Law*, 1.

Howell, J.M., 'Domestic Questions in International Law', (1954), *Proceedings: American Society of International Law*, 90.

—— 'A Matter of International Concern' (1969) 63, *American Journal of International Law*, 771.

Howell, J.M., and Wilson, R.R., 'The Commonwealth and Domestic Jurisdiction', (1961) 55, *American Journal of International Law*, 29.

Hoyt, E.C., 'The Contribution of the I.L.C.', (1965), *Proceedings: American Society of International Law*.

Ijalaye, D.A., 'Was Biafra at any time a State in International Law?', (1971) 65, *American Journal of International Law*, 551.

Jennings, R.Y., 'The Progress of International Law' (1958) XXXIV, *British Year Book of International Law*, 334.

—— 'Recent Developments in the International Law Commission: Its Relations to the Sources of International Law', (1965) 13, *International and Comparative Law Quarterly*, 385.

Johnson, D.H.N., 'The Effect of the General Assembly Resolutions of the U.N.' (1955-6) XXXII, *British Year Book of International Law*, 97.

Jokow, T.J. 'The Effect of the War on the Rural Population of Zimbabwe', *Journal of African Affairs*, Apr. 1980, 133.

Keesing Contemporary Archives.

Kelsen, H., 'Recognition in International Law: Theoretical Observation', (1941) 35, *American Journal of International Law*, 605.
—— 'Sovereign Equality of States', (1944), 53, *Yale Law Journal*, 207.
—— 'Membership of the United Nations', (1946) 46, *Columbia Law Review*, 394.
—— 'Sanctions Under the Charter', (1946) 12, *Canadian Journal of Economic and Political Science*, 429.
—— 'Organization and Procedure of the Security Council', (1946) 59, *Harvard Law Review*, 1089.
—— 'Limitation on the Functions of the United Nations', (1946) 55, *Yale Law Journal*, 997.
—— 'Collective Security and Collective Self-Defence Under the Charter of the United Nations', (1948) 42, *American Journal of International Law*, 783.
Kopelmanas, L., 'Custom as a Means of the Creation of International Law', (1937) XVIII, *British Year Book of International Law*, 127.
Kunz, J.L., 'Revolutionary Creation of Norms of International Law', (1947) 41, *American Journal of International Law*, 119.
—— 'The Inter-American Treaty of Reciprocal Assistance', (1948) 42, *American Journal of International Law*, 111.
—— 'Legal Aspects of the Situation in Korea', (1950) 44, *American Journal of International Law*, 709.
—— 'Critical Remarks on Lauterpacht's Recognition in International Law', (1950) 44, *American Journal of International Law*, 713.
—— 'Bellum Justum and Bellum Legale', (1951) 45, *American Journal of International Law*, 529.
—— 'The United Nations and the Rule of Law', (1952) 46, *American Journal of International Law*, 504.
—— 'Continental Shelf and International Law: Confusion in International Law', (1956) 50, *American Journal of International Law*, 828.
—— 'The Secretary-General and the Role of the United Nations', (1958) 52, *American Journal of International Law*, 300.
—— 'Sanctions in International Law', (1960) 54, *American Journal of International Law*, 324.
Lachs, M., 'Recognition and Modern Methods of International Co-operation', (1959) XXXIV, *British Year Book of International Law*, 252.
Lauterpacht, H., 'Brierly's Contribution to International Law', (1955) 49, *American Journal of International Law*, 16.
Lauterpacht, E. (1964) 1 *British Practice in International Law*.
Leigh, L.H., 'Rhodesia After U.D.I.: Some Aspects of a Peaceful Rebellion', (1966), *Public Law*, 148.
Lissitzyn, O.J. 'International Law in a Divided World', (1963), *International Conciliation*, No. 542.
MacDonald, R. St. J., 'Economic Sanctions in the International System', (1969), *Canadian Year Book of International Law*, 61.

MacGibbon, I.C., 'Customary International Law and Acquiescence', (1957) XXX, *British Year Book of International Law*, 115.

Marshall, H.N., 'Legal Effects and U.D.I.', (1968) 17, *International and Comparative Law Quarterly*, 1022.

McDougal, M.S., and Bebr, G., 'Human Rights in the United Nations', (1964) 58, *American Journal of International Law*, 603.

McDougal, M.S., and Feliciano, F.P., 'Legal Regulation of Resort to International Coercion: Aggression and Self-Defence in Policy Prospective', (1959) 68, *Yale Law Journal*, 1057.

McDougal, M.S., and Gardener, R.N., 'The Veto and the Charter: An Interpretation for Survival', (1951) 60, *Yale Law Journal*, 258.

McDougal, M.S., and Reisman, M.W., 'Rhodesia and the United Nations: The Lawfulness of International Concern', (1968) 62, *American Journal of International Law*, 1.

Meeker, L.C., 'Defensive Quarantine and the Law', (1963) 57, *American Journal of International Law*, 515.

Miller, E.M., 'Legal Aspects of the United Nations Action in the Congo', (1961) 55, *American Journal of International Law*, 1.

Oppenheim, F.E., 'Governments and Authorities in Exile', (1942) 36, *American Journal of International Law*, 568.

'Pollux' (Hambro, E.), 'The Interpretation of the Charter', (1946) XXIII, *British Year Book of International Law*, 54.

Rabinowitz, C., 'United Nations Application of Selective Mandatory Sanctions Against Rhodesia: A Brief Legal and Political Analysis', (1967) 6, *Virginia Journal of International Law*, 161.

Rosenstock, R., 'The Declaration of Principles of International Law Concerning Friendly Relations: A Survey', (1971) 65, *American Journal of International Law*, 713.

Rovine, A., 'Contemporary Practice of U.S. Relating to International Law', (1975) 69, *American Journal of International Law*, 141.

Salter, L.M., 'Embargoes, Quarantines and Sanctions: Is the U.N. Nagging Rhodesia and South Africa?', (1973) 7, *International Lawyer*, 177.

Schachter, O., 'The Development of International Law through the Legal Opinions of the Secretary-General', (1948) 25, *British Year Book of International Law*, 91.

—— 'The Enforcement of Judicial and Arbitral Decisions Against States', (1960) 54, *American Journal of International Law*, 1.

—— 'The Relation of Law, Politics and Action in the United Nations', (1963) 109, *Hague Academy Recueil des Cours*, 171.

Schwarzenberger, S., 'Problems of U.N. Forces', (1959) 12, *Current Legal Problems*, 247.

—— 'Myths and Realities of Treaty Interpretation', (1969), *Current Legal Problems*, 205.

Schwelb, E., 'Some Aspects of International Jus Cogens', (1967) 61, *American Journal of International Law*, 946.

Seyersted, I., 'United Nations Forces: Some Legal Problems', (1961) XXXVII, *British Year Book of International Law*, 351.

Sha Hasin Hasan, 'Discovery by Intervention', (1959) 53, *American Journal of International Law*, 595.

Sloan, B., 'The Binding Force of a "Recommendation" of the General Assembly of the U.N.', (1948) XXV, *British Year Book of International Law*, 1.

Stavropoulos, C.A., 'The Practice of Voluntary Abstention by Permanent Members of the Security Council Under Article 27 (3) of the Charter of the United Nations' (1967) 61, *American Journal of International Law*, 737.

Stephen, M. 'Natural Justice At the United Nations: The Rhodesian Case', (1973) 67, *American Journal of International Law*, 479.

Stone, J., 'Hopes and Loopholes in the 1974 Definiton of Aggression', (1977) 71, *American Journal of International Law*, 224.

Thomas, A.J., 'Non-Intervention and Public Order in the Americas', (1959), *Proceedings: American Society of International Law*, 72.

Timberg, S., 'Corporate Fiction: Logical, Social and International Implication', (1946) 46, *Columbia Law Review*, 533.

Trindade, A.A., 'The Domestic Jurisdiction of States in the Practice of the United Nations and Regional Organization', (1976) 25, *International and Comparative Law Quarterly*, 715.

Tunkin, G.I., 'Remarks on the Jurisdical Nature of Customary Norms', (1961) 49, *California Law Review*, 419.

Turack, D.C., 'Passports Issued by Some Non-State Entities', (1968–6) XLIII *British Year Book of International Law*.

Vallat, F.A., 'The Competence of the United Nations General Assembly of the U.N.', (1959) 97, *Hague Academy Recueil Des Cours*, 203.

Wilcox, O., 'The Rule of Unanimity in the Security Council', (1946), *Proceedings: American Society of International Law*, 55.

Wright, Q., 'Is Discussion Intervention?', (1956) 50, *American Journal of International Law*, 102.

Yuen-li-Liang, 'The Settlement of Disputes in the Security Council: Yalta formula', (1947) XXIV, *British Year Book of International Law*, 330.

—— 'Abstention and Absence of a Permanent Member in Relation to the Voting in the Security Council and Absence from Meetings', (1950) 44, *American Journal of International Law*, 694.

Zacklin, R., 'Challenge of Rhodesia'; (1969), *International Conciliation*, No. 575.

Zwanenberg, A. van, 'Interference with ships on the High Seas', (1961) 10, *International and Comparative Law Quarterly*, 785.

British Government Publication

Rhodesia: Proposals for a Settlement (HMS Stationery Office, 1981), *The Boyd Report.*

Index